Creative Ideas for Childre. ⌐ worship

Creative Ideas for Children's Worship

Based on the Sunday Gospels, Year C

Sarah Lenton

Theological consultant:
Andrew Davison

CANTERBURY
PRESS
Norwich

© Text and cartoons Sarah Lenton 2012

First published in 2012 by the Canterbury Press Norwich
Editorial office
3rd Floor, Invicta House,
108–114 Golden Lane
London EC1Y 0TG

Canterbury Press is an imprint of Hymns Ancient and Modern Ltd
(a registered charity)
13A Hellesdon Park Road, Norwich,
Norfolk, NR6 5DR, UK

www.canterburypress.co.uk

British Library Cataloguing in Publication data

A catalogue record for this book is available
from the British Library

978 1 84825 241 7

Typeset by Regent Typesetting, London
Printed and bound in Great Britain by
CPI Group (UK) Ltd, Croydon, CR0 4YY

Contents

THE SESSIONS

Where two descriptions are given, the first is the name in the Church of England and the second is the name in the Roman Catholic Church. Very occasionally the readings are different for the two Churches. In that case two different scripts are provided and marked accordingly. Some scripts can come either before Lent or after Easter depending on whether Easter is late or early: it is always best to check against the actual Gospel reading being used in Church.

The Roman Catholic Church does not single out a Sunday two weeks before Lent for special observance. In the Church of England use this script rather than one with a 'proper' number for this particular date.

If Easter is late you will use some scripts from Script 32 onwards in the period leading up to Lent.

Some of the following scripts will be used before Lent if Easter is late

This book is dedicated to
the two parish priests who made it possible,
Bishop Pat Lynch SSCC
and
Fr Kevin Morris, St Michael and All Angels, Bedford Park

Acknowledgements

This book is the result of twenty years of ecumenical work in the London parishes of Our Lady of Lourdes, Acton (Catholic), and St Michael and All Angels, Bedford Park (Anglican). Both churches were unstintingly generous in their provision of space, time and resources, and to everyone involved, priests, congregations and children, I offer heartfelt thanks.

The children's church in Acton owes its existence to the enlightened leadership of Bishop Pat Lynch (then the parish priest) and his lay administrator Ellie McKeown.

Ellie, working on the 'vocation by compulsion' principle, roped in a large and varied group to look after the children, and in the fullness of time her net caught me. The immediate cause of my recruitment was Nicholas Rodger, one of the founder members of the group, who brought his fine scholarship – and scarcely less remarkable dramatic skills – to an already talented team. Among them I am particularly grateful to Sr Miriam McNulty, Janusz Jankowski, Peter Robertson, Margaret Fry, Joan Hughes, Paddy Green and Susan Cunningham. To Deacon Tito Pereira, whose devotion to the gospel was the dynamo that powered our team meetings, and whose ideas I have shamelessly plundered, I owe more than a mere acknowledgement can express.

In Bedford Park, Fr Kevin Morris has been equally generous in his encouragement and support. The press gang is as active at St Michael's as it is at Our Lady's, and among our 'volunteers' I am extremely grateful to Wendy Callister, Bernadette Halford, Nicola Chater, Pamela Bickley and Christina Whiteway, all of whom have led the team with a commitment that went way beyond the call of duty.

To my family, who have endured twenty years of disrupted Sunday mornings, my brothers Christopher and Andrew, whose features I default to whenever I draw the Apostles, and my sister Jane for giving the dialogue some sort of street credibility, I offer as always my love and thanks.

Fr Andrew Davison's meticulous reading of the text, as theological consultant, has ensured the scripts are faithful to the teaching of the Church (any errors that have crept in since his scrutiny are my own). I am deeply grateful to him and to Christine Smith and Mary Matthews of the Canterbury Press, paragons of encouragement and patience, David Beresford, James Holmes and Rosemary Green for doing the photo shoots, Anne Tennant, a friend in need when the unedited scripts threatened to overwhelm me, Alan Trigle for providing the French and German for Script 29, Rosie Stevenson for sharing her Mozambique experience with us, Dilys Jones for helping with the Index, and, last of all, Margaret Stonborough, who insisted that I responded to Nicholas's call in the first place, and has found it involved her in more prop making and keyboard bashing than she can ever have anticipated.

Introduction

Children

Children are part of the Church. Everyone knows that, and most churches do their best to make them feel at home. Even so, there are times, particularly at the beginning of the Eucharist, when it seems kind to offer the kids an alternative to a full set of Bible readings and the sermon.

Enter Children's Church! Or Sunday School, Children's Liturgy, Children's Club, it doesn't matter what you call it.

The idea is that the children are shepherded out of church to a hall – or somewhere suitably out of earshot – where they hear the Gospel and worship Almighty God in their own way, and at their own pace. They reappear at Communion time to rejoin their families at the altar, ready with a presentation to share their discoveries with the rest of the congregation.

Such a group presupposes adult leaders, and if you're one of them – and don't have time to think up children's activities week after week – this book is for you.

Scripts for Children's Church

Our purpose is to provide material that will help children acquire a familiarity with the life of Christ and the events of the church year, in a way that is vivid and memorable. Better still, they'll enjoy it. The material does not require a great deal of preparation, nor a degree in theology – in fact you and the children will probably learn the faith together.

This book provides a session for every Sunday of the liturgical Year C,* in the form of an easy-to-use script. Each one is headed up by the theme of the day, a list of

---

* The readings for the Eucharist are arranged in three cycles, A, B and C, and run from the beginning of the liturgical year (Advent Sunday) to its end (Christ the King).

the toys, props and pictures you'll need, the prayers that open and close each session, the Gospel reading and (most importantly) your 'lines': the sort of things you'll say to the kids, their (probable) response, and the games and activities that will reinforce the Gospel message. Given a modicum of preparation (see below), all you'll have to do on Sunday is set up the hall, print off the script, and the children's session should practically run itself.

Pictures

The book is full of pictures and each session comes with its own set of images: these can be found on the CD-Rom attached to the back cover.

Art Resources

The great pictures in our galleries and churches were made to tell the Christian story. Buying books and postcards when you visit a gallery or cathedral (at home and abroad) will pay dividends when you want to engage the kids in the standard Bible stories.

Particularly good are the pictures of Duccio, Velasquez, Piero della Francesca, Giotto, Memling, any of the Van Eycks and Bellini. Stained glass (Victorian as well as Medieval) often tells the stories in an accessible, cartoon-like, way, and the porches and gateways of most cathedrals have a large number of stone saints, angels, and scenes from the Bible.

Many galleries allow you to upload the images from their collections on to your computer and, as long as you use their websites, follow their guidelines – and don't make illegal downloads – you can access their pictures and gather the kids round your screen to look at them.

The National Gallery in London has a very good website which allows you to access any picture in their collection – and zoom in on the details.

Children's Church and the Eucharist

The main act of worship on a Sunday is the Eucharist. The service is composed of two sections: the Liturgy of the Word, and the Liturgy of the Sacrament. The Liturgy of the Word is, naturally, centred on the Bible: it reaches its climax with the Gospel reading and is concluded by the sermon that follows. The Liturgy of the Sacrament is centred round the altar as bread and wine are consecrated and we receive the Body and Blood of Christ.

These sessions provide a child-friendly Liturgy of the Word that parallels the adult version going on in church, and allows the children to return to church in plenty of time for the Liturgy of the Sacrament. As a result they follow the structure of the Eucharist closely.

The normal pattern in parishes where I have worked is: the children are sent out by the priest, with their own Gospel Book, at the beginning of the service. They reassemble in the church hall and join in a simplified version of the prayers of penitence and the Opening Prayer. Then they turn their attention to the Gospel – which is where the fun begins.

The Gospel passages are so rich that we've found the most effective way to teach them is to concentrate on one leading idea. Pentecost, for example, could be about the Holy Spirit coming in tongues of fire, or as a mighty rushing wind but, for Year C, we've gone for His gift of language.

The children may not realize immediately that building a large cardboard tower, and knocking it down, has anything to do with this useful gift but as everything in the Pentecost script (game, story and meditation) is about language, they'll have got the idea by the end of the session.

Growing in the Christian Faith

A major advantage of these scripts is that the children hear exactly the same Gospel as the rest of the church, so their contribution at the end of the service will tie in with something the adults have already encountered. Added to which, living with these scripts, Sunday by Sunday, means that children and leaders experience a whole Christian year together and discover that church is more interesting (and a great deal more energetic) than they'd realized.

Setting up a Children's Church Team

Recruitment

Recruitment to a Children's Church team is usually done via a press gang. All the same, an assurance that the load will be spread evenly over the year usually calms people down – that, and a guarantee that all a leader has to do is follow a script: everything else will be provided.

Leaders

The liturgies in this book assume that a 'leader' is someone who feels OK about getting up in front of children and presenting a script, but there's plenty of scope for more nervous types who may prefer to help from the side. It's good to have a variety of 'voices' presenting the session, so two leaders are the basic minimum to make it effective, four leaders mean you can give people Sundays off, and twelve leaders are practically ideal.

Double Acts

Many of the sessions in Year C set up a dialogue between Leader 1 and Leader 2. Swap these roles from session to session, otherwise you'll find Leader 2 becoming the comedian of the team, with Leader 1 as his/her 'stooge'.

Team Meetings

You will find it helpful to meet at least once a term. There will be rotas and practical matters to discuss of course, but the core of these meetings should be a read through of the sessions coming up. Each script comes with its Gospel reading, notes on understanding the passage, and suggestions for activities and devotions. Talking this through will help you get on top of the material and indicate what toys and props you'll need to gather. This is also the moment to modify the scripts to suit local circumstances.

Child Protection/Safeguarding

Churches have clear rules about child protection, find out what they are and follow them. If you have any uncertainties about the national requirements, consult the websites of the Catholic Diocese of Westminster (Safeguarding Advisory Service) – www.rcdow.org.uk – or, for the Anglican version – www.london.anglican.org (Child Protection) – or consult the published guidelines, *Protecting All God's Children* (Church House Publishing). The national website – www.direct.gov.uk – also advises on keeping children safe. All three sites give ample information. It is now mandatory for all volunteers to have a CRB check; it is also important to note that (at least) two adults must always be present with the children in your care. Larger parishes may have a children's advocate who will help advise you and sort out the paperwork. It's good practice to keep a register of all the sessions – it helps you find out who the kids are.

The School Year

Children's Church usually only operates in school terms, as there can be a sharp decline in numbers in the holidays. However, we've provided a session for every Sunday in the year – just in case the church is heaving with children after all.

Young Children

As a rule of thumb liturgy works best with children who have started school and are used to basic school rules, like sitting quietly on the floor, putting up their hands before they speak and playing games in an organized way. You don't have time to instil this into a riotous toddler. If parents want to bring small children along, ask them to remain to look after them. Sending little ones in under the care of a sibling doesn't usually work.

Teenagers

You'll find that some of the older children don't want to move on, partly because they like you and partly because they feel children's liturgy is more fun than adult church. Obviously you'll know your own kids and how to deal with this. Teenagers can be very helpful as auxiliary helpers, as long as they are *never* allowed to stand along the back wall! See below . . .

Cool Dudes

Cool dudes who hang around at the back are the death of liturgy. From about the age of eleven onwards, kids have a tendency to drift to the back wall, lean up against it, and watch the proceedings with their mates. With all the sympathy in the world for teenage angst, you can't let this happen. If you do, you'll get a hall divided between enthusiastic little kids, cool dudes, and a middle group who want to

copy the big ones. You have to sort this. Liturgy is about participation; big kids are fine if they want to join in, otherwise – back to the service in church.

Discipline

Children's Church is not school. Nobody has to come but, as kids have to be *somewhere* in the church complex, they're either with you – and behaving – or back in church. The irritating thing about sending children back to church is you have to accompany them there, or call their parents out to collect them. Fortunately the resulting interview between parent and child usually ensures it never happens again.

Some subversive types might think it great fun to shout out silly answers but you can usually block this by applying a 'hands up' only rule. Gameboys and iPods are a total bore. We killed an outbreak of texting once by saying, 'Hands up who's got a mobile?' Up shot the hands. 'OK, bring them down the front and leave them on the table.' (Of course this only works once.)

Parents

Some parents process out with their children to settle them, or look after the little ones. 'Spare' parents should be encouraged to return to the main service.

Helpers

They can be parents, big kids, Confirmation candidates, or nervous adults thinking about committing to Children's Church at a future date: they are unbelievably useful. Be realistic about what they can actually do.

Runners

You need to know when to bring the children back into church and it's useful to have some well-disposed people in church ready to nip round and tell you when the Offertory (or whatever your agreed cue is) is about to start. Teenagers can be very helpful here – especially if they're able to tell you the news via a mobile.

Clergy

As the children's and adults' liturgies should form an organic whole, make sure your priest knows what's going on, particularly when it comes to the presentation. Some priests prefer to be the one who asks the children what they've been doing, others are happy to let the team get on with it. Either way, check there's time for a presentation at the end – if there isn't, don't rehearse it. There's nothing worse than a pew full of disappointed kids.

Setting Up

The most basic requirement is a separate room. Obviously you have to take what is given, but it is surprising how quickly you can adapt any space to your needs.

Rooms/Halls

If you are given a room, clear away as much furniture as you can and make an empty space at one end. If you're given the church hall, mark off one bit as the holy area – the place from which you'll be leading prayers and reading the Gospel. Limits are important in church halls as the mere sight of acres of floorboards makes children want to rush around.

Furniture

Try to appropriate a cupboard or filing cabinet to store your props. You'll need a lectern or a little table on which to place the Gospel Book (see below under *Gospel*). Another table at the front is also very useful: you can drape it in the liturgical colour of the day, and use it to focus attention on the icon, candle, toy, or whatever you are going to use in the liturgy.

Chairs, oddly enough, are not a great idea. They inhibit the children from acting together, and they usually can't resist the temptation to swing their legs and kick the chair in front. Cut the chairs down to a couple for the leaders and visiting grown-ups.

The Floor

Nothing really beats getting the kids to sit on the floor. On mats, if your church has them, but the floorboards if need be. Children are used to sitting on the floor for assembly at school. In small spaces it means you can accommodate more children and bring them nearer the front to see what's going on. If you're up to it, sitting on the floor yourself among the children works very well – especially if you're telling them a story.

Props

Every liturgy comes with a list of the props you'll need; the most frequent are listed below. It looks formidable, but most churches have a fair amount of equipment and a few visits to the toy shop should supply the rest.

Ordinary Equipment

- Either a flip-chart, an easel, or a whiteboard, or a place you can stick up sheets of blank A1 paper.
- Blu Tack or something similar.
- Large coloured marker pens for the leaders (get bullet point nibs, rather than chisel, they are easier to draw with) or white board markers.
- Matches – but use tapers to actually light the candles; they look nicer and are easier to handle.
- Candle snuffers.
- The use of a photocopier or computer printer.

Useful Extras

- Any costumes: all-purpose Shepherd, King or Angel. Burglars are handy as DIY villains – a mask and any stripy top will do.
- Crowns, even paper ones from a cracker, are invaluable.
- Any helmets: Policeman, Roman Soldier, Knight.
- Flower canes, all sizes.
- Large dice – made by covering square (or near square) cardboard boxes in stout white paper and marking gigantic dots on the sides. Some party shops sell blow-up dice, which are superb for group games.
- Some large, nice-looking rocks, picked up on the beach, at least one large shiny one.
- Toy animals – particularly sheep.
- Crook or old-fashioned wooden walking stick.

- At least one football.
- Toy shop props: plastic swords, crowns, doctor's sets, handcuffs and those useful plastic scythes and pitchforks you can get at Hallowe'en.
- Torches.
- Treasure – plastic pearls, any tacky jewellery, preferably in a 'Jewel Box'.
- Gold-covered chocolate money or a bag of pirate 'doubloons' from a toy shop.
- If you find a confectioner selling chocolate fish at Easter, buy a few – they'll come in handy later on.

Art Extras

- Colouring pens and pencils in working order.
- Ordinary white paper.
- Child-friendly scissors.
- Adult scissors.
- Gold and silver paper.
- Thin card.
- Glue.
- Masking tape.

Holy Props

- A Gospel book: use one of the recognized translations of the complete Bible rather than a 'children's Bible'. The latter may not have the complete Gospel and much of it will be paraphrased. We recommend the New Revised Standard Version of the Bible (the NRSV), the New Jerusalem Bible (study edition) or, for good simple language, the Christian Community Bible (Catholic pastoral edition).
- The use of a lectionary – that's the list of readings for the church year. Your priest should have one.
- A crucifix.
- Pieces of cloth to hang over the table in the liturgical colours – green, red, purple, pink, white (and gold if you come across some lamé). Synthetic material doesn't crease as badly as the good stuff.
- Candles in portable candlesticks.

- Small handbells.
- A stout candle that can stand securely on its own.
- And, if your church uses them:
  - A holy water stoup and sprinkler ('aspergillum').
  - A spare thurible, charcoal and incense (though check the latter won't set the fire alarm off).

Holy Extras

- Icons, posters or postcards of holy pictures, small statues of the saints (plastic is fine!). Try to have at least one image of the patron saint of your church. The National Gallery has an excellent range of posters and postcards on holy subjects by some of the greatest painters in the world. Their website is www.nationalgallery.org.uk. Alternatively you can use images from Wikimedia Commons (commons.wikimedia.org), the Web Gallery of Art for slide presentation, or simply displayed on your laptop screen, absolutely free: the Web Gallery of Art website is www.wga.hu/.
- CDs with kids' hymns, Taizé chants and quiet mood music are very useful.
- Sweet-smelling oils – you can get cheap flasks of myrrh and frankincense at cathedral gift shops but aromatherapy oils from chemists are good substitutes.
- Any holy toys, like a Noah's Ark or a crib set.
- Artefacts from the Jewish faith are also very helpful especially for Scripts 10 and 13. An educational supplier, TTS, sells a starter pack with a Torah scroll, Seder plate for the Passover and a Menorah candlestand at a very reasonable price. Their website is www.tts-shopping.com.

Images in Church

Look round your church. Even the plainest building can yield a surprising number of pictures. They can be anywhere: in the windows, carved on the memorials, embroidered on the vestments and painted on the banners. Everything is worth noticing – flames, lambs, keys, clusters of grapes – as well as the more obvious pictures and statues of saints.

DIY Props

'Our Father' cards are a good standby for those moments when you've got five minutes to fill in. You make them by putting the Lord's Prayer, phrase by phrase, on various sheets of A4 paper, laminating them – and shuffling.

The idea is that the children go for a land speed record in reassembling the prayer and then, when they've quietened down, pray it. It works for any prayer or creed you wish the children to learn. (You may want to make some 'Hail Mary' cards for Script 4.)

High Tech Helps

- All forms of projection: scoop up any offers of unwanted projectors (provided they work). See if you can borrow the church's overhead projector, slide projector, or (in very lucky parishes) a digital projector. The latter only works with a laptop.
- A portable music player.
- Keyboard.
- Extension leads.
- Gaffer tape or masking tape to stick over leads and ensure the kids don't trip up.
- A roving mike, for the presentation back in church, is a great asset.

How to Use this Book

Once you've got your team, a hall and some children – you'll need a liturgy.

Simply find out what Sunday Gospel you should be preparing for, and look it up in the contents list. The Sundays are listed in chronological order, so once you've found your first, all should be plain sailing.

However, church being what it is, there are a couple of complications. Given the variable date of Easter, we have to allow for some extra Sundays before Easter (in case it's late) or some extra Sundays after Easter (in case it's early). There is also a tiny amount of variation between the Catholic and Anglican Gospels in Year C. The clergy will know exactly what Sunday it is, just ask them, or your parish office. If in doubt, get the Bible reference from your priest, look it up in the Index of Biblical References, and you'll find the right script.

Other Christian churches also follow the lectionary we've based this book on, so the material will be useful for them as well.

Copying and Printing

After you've established what Gospel you're going to do, gather the toys and props during the week, and photocopy or print the script for any leader without a book. You might also like to copy the sections of the Kyries (the 'Lord have mercy' prayers) on three separate strips of paper for individual children to read out.

If there are pictures involved, find the set suggested on the CD-Rom and print them up as large as possible. All the pictures that make a 'scene' are provided separately, so you can copy them on to A4 (or A3 if you've got the resources) and combine them on an A1 sheet of paper.

Getting Ready

- Set up the hall on the day, with all the objects and scripts you'll need to hand.
- Read the script through and agree with the other leader on who says what.
- Alert the children's music group (if you have one) to the hymns on offer.
- Some scripts call for help from a couple of children, find your volunteers and run through their contribution (it's always very easy).
- That's it, you're ready to go.

Following the Scripts

The scripts follow a simple format. Each section is headed up in bold and, as long as there are no lines for you to speak in the section, the font looks normal.

Like this:

SET UP

- A list of props, extra people, etc.
- A crook (a walking stick will do).
- Toy sheep, etc.

If a section contains remarks by you, your lines stay in normal font, but any instructions now appear in italics, like this:

Put the toy sheep on the floor, and grasp the crook

Leader   OK, now there are a couple of things you need to know about sheep.

Any question you ask the children comes with the expected answer in bold font, enclosed in round brackets.

Leader	Today we're thinking about sheep – and the people who look after them.
	Anyone know what they were called?
	(**Shepherds**)

The only other font change happens when you pray. Prayers said by one person come in normal font, prayers said by everyone are in bold.

Lord have mercy
Lord have mercy
Christ have mercy
Christ have mercy

God's Capital H

You'll notice that God's personal pronoun (He, Him or His) always has a capital H. In the pilot sessions for this book we found this a helpful way of remembering just who we were talking about (especially when doing the liturgy at speed).

A Typical Script, Section by Section

SENDING OUT

The first thing you need to do is organize your exit from the church. Ask if you can place the children's Gospel book on the altar and gather your troupe together. At a given moment (usually after the entrance hymn) the celebrant hands the Gospel book to one of the children (chosen in advance) and sends them out. The whole team processes out, following the Gospel as it is held aloft.

You'll probably find that you pick up stragglers and shy kids as you leave church.

WELCOME

Once you're all in the hall, welcome the children. Keep it brief and go straight into:

THE SIGN OF THE CROSS

If this is not a usual devotion in your church, you may find it helpful to run through the Sign like this:

1 ✠ **In the Name of the Father,** – *on 'Father' you touch your head, that's the Father in Heaven*
2 **and of the Son** – *bring your hand down – the Son came down to earth*
3 **and of the Holy Spirit.** – *touch your heart, the Spirit lives in our hearts*
4 **Amen** – *finish the Shape of the Cross by touching your right side*

A little cross ✠ in the text flags up the times it is usual to make the Sign of the Cross.

Making the Sign of the Cross can have an extraordinarily quietening effect on children. However, if they *are* slightly chatty at the beginning, do the old trick of going silent yourself until they get unnerved and stop talking. Reinforce this by saying things like, 'Thank you Charlie' to any phenomenally well behaved child.

One leader I knew surprised everybody one Sunday by asking the children to make the Sign of the Cross very quietly (he had a hangover). The kids looked sideways at one another. 'How do you do a *noisy* sign of the cross?' you could see they were thinking – even so, a breathless hush ensued.

THE KYRIE

Preface the Kyrie with a brief, 'Let's look back at the week – is there anything we wish we hadn't done? Anything we'd like to say sorry for?' Keep it light.

If you've got three children prepared to read the three petitions of the Kyrie, have them at the front, give them a hand if necessary, and join the children in the response:

Lord have mercy
Christ have mercy
Lord have mercy

It's extremely important that all grown-ups in the room take part in the prayers and follow the proceedings as seriously as the children. Gossiping mums at the back should be politely banned.

PRAYER FOR FORGIVENESS

This is the 'layman's absolution' and can be said by a leader, or repeated by everyone. If the children don't know it, you may ask them to repeat it after you, line by line.

OPENING PRAYER

The moment when the theme of the day starts to appear.

BEFORE THE GOSPEL

A huge change of gear takes place as you prepare for the Gospel reading. The idea is that the children should be able to follow the Gospel when they hear it and to achieve this the scripts try everything: games, mini-dramas, startling demonstrations (like how stupid it is to build a wall out of jelly). Anything to get them going.

It's here that you begin to interact with the children. Ask them questions, the simpler the better. Children love putting their hand up (some toddlers do it automatically but all you get from them is a sweet smile).

As soon as the Gospel Book has been set up, move into:

THE GOSPEL PROCESSION

Obviously the Sunday Gospel is the dynamo of the whole session. Everything – songs, prayers and games – derives from it and, when it's read, it either sets up the message for the day, or clinches it. Either way Jesus calls the shots.

To make this apparent to the children it's helpful to read the Gospel with some ceremony.

Depending on how your space is shaped, you can place the Gospel Book on its own special lectern, or table, at the back of the hall and process it to the front, or you can place it down the front and process it into the middle of the children. Or you can just move it from a small table at the front to a lectern beside it. The point is, it should be moved.*

You can't replicate the solemn reading of the Gospel in church (unless you have a deacon or priest present) so don't top and tail it with the customary acclamations. You can, however, set it apart. Hold the Gospel Book up as it's processed – Jesus is present in His Word, just as He will be present later on in the Bread and Wine of the Eucharist. Flank it with candles – you'll have no lack of volunteers – and invest in some hand bells. Dinging the bells as the Gospel is processed is a marvellous job for very small kids.

If you're blessed with a music group you might like to sing some 'Alleluias' as the Gospel is processed.

There is no Gospel Procession in Advent or Lent. This is not something we've taken over from church – actually Gospel Processions happen all year round – but it's a helpful way of marking these seasons with the children. You'll see the rationale for this change when you do the sessions.

---

* The Eastern Orthodox invented the Gospel Procession to dramatize Jesus' wanderings through Galilee: they directed that the Gospel, and its reader, should process from the altar, 'wander' through the church and land up in the midst of the people.

THE GOSPEL

Normally you read the Gospel straight; however, keep an eye on the script because in some cases we give you a paraphrase to read out instead. All our paraphrases contain at least one sentence (usually many more) of a recognized translation of the Bible. The children must hear the genuine Word of God.

If you are reading straight from the Bible, think of ways of making it accessible: make the dialogue sound real, cut verses not dealt with in the session, change *denari* into pounds or *tunics* into shirts. Having said that, it is often appropriate to offer the kids an old-fashioned phrase as part of their cultural heritage. Many of them know already one shouldn't hide one's light 'under a bushel', or that the Rich Fool said to himself that he could 'eat, drink and be merry'. Take a view: stylistic gear changes are part of the modern Christian package.

AFTER THE GOSPEL

You wrap the Gospel up: sometimes in a pithy sentence or two, more often in an extended activity. This might be a game, or a devotion, or some music. The activity always includes a rehearsal for a presentation back in church (if you're doing one).

DIY ART

Colouring pictures is not a major feature of this book. When it happens it appears as a group activity, and is usually timed – so the children produce art work at speed (this seems to motivate the less arty). However, some of the pictures on the CD-Rom are in black and white, to give the kids who like to colour in a chance to show their skill.

There are many occasions when the children can make their presentation as well as perform it, particularly if the presentation involves pictures. There's no reason, except time, why they should hold up versions of the pictures on the CD-Rom. The congregation is going to be much more interested in stuff the children have produced themselves.

GAMES

All the board games can be played either by a group of children crowded round the board, or a large group, split into teams, who play via a representative. In the latter case, most members of the team get a chance to roll the enormous Children's Church dice.

Energetic games which normally require rushing around have been offered in two versions. One for spaces in which children *can* run around, and another for more restricted venues.

Jesus appears to have been deeply uninterested in people who came first, so make sure you cheer the losers.

MUSIC

Hymns, traditional and modern, are a wonderful way to finish the session, but they depend on somebody having the musical confidence to lead them. If you can't rustle up a piano or guitar player, you can download karaoke style music for many popular hymns via the internet, and there are CDs available with children's songs on. Any member of the team who works in a local church school is invaluable here as they'll know what songs the kids sing in assembly.

If you are intending to sing, think about the words: writing them up on a flip-chart is quicker than children fiddling round with hymn books. (On the other hand, if you've got the time, some kids find it thrilling to look up 'number 143'.)

REHEARSING THE PRESENTATION

The congregation deserve to hear what the children have been up to. Choose good readers and run the presentation through with the kids. It's almost bound to be fun, try to get it slick and well timed as well.

PRAYER

You won't be able to have an extended session on prayer every Sunday, but get the children used to the idea of a prayer circle. Put a large candle in the middle (the sort that can stand on its own base) as a focus of attention. Or pass round one of the many objects suggested in the scripts.

Give the children alternatives to verbal prayer, sprinkle them with water, bless them with incense. Let them wave their arms about to the movements of an interactive hymn, or reflect on the power of the Holy Spirit by feeling a fan blowing in their faces. Explore the Catholic tradition: most children like bells, icons, holy book-

marks and statues, and they are usually up for making some of these objects them-selves. (Like the Free Trade Rosary, made by knotting a decade of the rosary in a bit of string.) Give the children a chance to pray privately.

Quiet music in the background is a help, but keep the sessions fairly short. There is a moment beyond which even the most pious child can't concentrate.

Every now and then these sessions will provoke a distressing revelation. A child might be anxious about a sick relative, or show an awareness of a family grief they only dimly understand, like a miscarriage. In the immediate situation, give the child time to talk (or add the stories for kids in distress from Year A, p. 309) afterwards, have a private word with the parents.

THE FINAL PRAYER

Make sure you gather for a formal prayer before you go back to church: a brief 'Glory Be . . .' is fine.

COMING BACK TO CHURCH

When you come back depends on your priest and the number of children who re-ceive Holy Communion. Some parishes like the children to help with the Offertory procession, others prefer them back at the moment when the people are coming to the altar.

Depending on numbers, you may want the children to rejoin their parents or (if this is too disruptive) reserve a couple of pews for them down the front. Their presentation happens either at the Offertory or, more usually, after Communion.

Do your best to promote a 'guaranteed success' atmosphere in the church – and congratulate the kids yourself.

EXTRAS

Mass/Holy Communion/Eucharist

Anglicans and Catholics use different names for this great sacrament – this book uses all three.

Gender

The sessions acknowledge that Jesus and the Apostles were male, the Virgin Mary and many of Jesus' disciples female, and that Angels, though technically neuter, often appear as 'a young man in white'. However, though the pronouns are gender specific, there's no reason for the kids to be. You'll find that most girls are happy to play St Peter or the good Samaritan, boys don't mind being angels, and everyone enjoys being sheep, lepers and so on. Do your best to cast the children even handedly.

Health and Safety

Obviously anybody leading an organized activity for children needs to be aware of Health and Safety. All these scripts have been test run three times with no problems, but venues differ (as do children). Look at each script beforehand to work out potential flash points. Script 42 (*Trusting in God*), for example, suggests a leader falls to the floor, and Script 48 (*Fire!*) explores the fascination of fire, from a simple candle flame to a bonfire in a brazier. Take a view on what's feasible and follow the Health and Safety protocols of your own church.

Saints' Days

Sometimes a major saint's day falls on a Sunday – or your priest decides to celebrate All Saints' Day on the nearest Sunday to 1 November. The last script in the book (Script 64) is a 'filler' session, which can be adapted to cover practically any saint in the calendar.

Frequently Used Prayers

The Sign of the Cross

✠ In the Name of the Father,
and of the Son
and of the Holy Spirit.
Amen

The Prayer for Forgiveness

May God our Father
Have mercy upon us
✠ Forgive us our sins
And bring us to eternal life.
Amen

The Lord's Prayer

Our Father, who art in Heaven,
hallowed be thy Name,
thy Kingdom come,
thy will be done,
on Earth as it is in Heaven.
Give us this day our daily bread.
And forgive us our trespasses,
as we forgive those who trespass
against us.
And lead us not into temptation,
but deliver us from evil.
For thine is the Kingdom,
the power and the glory,
for ever and ever.
Amen

Modern Version of the Lord's Prayer

Our Father in Heaven,
hallowed be your name,
your Kingdom come,
your will be done,
on Earth as in Heaven.
Give us today our daily bread.
Forgive us our sins
as we forgive those who sin
against us.
Lead us not into temptation
but deliver us from evil.
For the Kingdom, the power,
and the glory are yours
now and for ever.
Amen

Glory Be

Glory be to the Father, and to the Son, and to the Holy Spirit:
as it was in the beginning, is now, and ever shall be, world without end,
Amen

Hail Mary

Hail Mary full of grace,
the Lord is with thee.
Blessed art thou among women
and blessed is the fruit of thy womb, Jesus.
Holy Mary, Mother of God,
pray for us sinners now
and at the hour of our death.
Amen

Script 1   Stay Awake!

Advent 1

St Luke 21.25–26, 36

THEME

The Christian year begins with Jesus' description of the end of the world. The alarming imagery – stars falling from the sky and so on – never appears to bother children, especially once they realize it's not necessarily going to happen tomorrow. Christmas, however, is another matter. That feast *is* imminent and this session concentrates on Jesus' first coming, rather than His second, with a story about the clueless King Basil.

SET UP

- The liturgical colour is Purple.
- Flag up the change of colour in church by wearing some purple – tie, scarf, socks, anything.
- Write out the shopping list on page 3 and put in your pocket.
- Three paper crowns.
- A small Bible, a fourth crown (too small to wear) and a gravestone – see template on CD-Rom crammed into Basil's pockets.
- Insert the text of today's Gospel into Basil's Bible.
- Leader 2 plays King Basil, all other parts can be played by the children.
- A couple of pairs of binoculars, telescopes (toy ones are fine), opera glasses, anything a star gazer might look through.
- Star puppet, made from the CD-Rom template.
- Optional Advent Wreath.

An Advent Wreath helps define the Sundays in Advent. Traditionally there are three Purple candles (for Sundays 1, 2 and 4), a Pink candle for the cheerful Sunday (number 3) and a White candle in the middle for Christmas Day. There is no Gospel Procession in Advent.

WELCOME *the children and lead them in* **The Sign of the Cross** ✠ (**p. xxxvi**).

Leader	This week the colour has changed in church. Did anyone notice what colour the priest was in today? (**Purple**)

Pick up on any purple you can see around you

What colour is my scarf? (**Purple**)
Yup, the church has gone purple.
When things go purple in church it means we're getting ready for something. Does anyone know what that might be?

If they don't, pull out your 'shopping list'

I've got a shopping list here. Hmm …
I've got to get a turkey
And some wrapping paper
And a box of crackers …
What am I getting ready for? (**Christmas!**)
Exactly, the Church is getting ready to welcome Jesus when He comes as a tiny child on Christmas Day. One way to do that is to ask God to forgive us for the things we've done wrong, we'll do that now.

THE KYRIE	Lord Jesus, you came to Earth to tell us how much God loves us, Lord have mercy **Lord have mercy**

Lord Jesus, you came to Earth to help us say sorry
Christ have mercy
Christ have mercy

Lord Jesus, you came to Earth so our sins could be forgiven
Lord have mercy
Lord have mercy

Ask the children to repeat **The Prayer for Forgiveness** *after you* (**p. xxxvi**).

OPENING PRAYER	God our Father Thank you for bringing us together. Help us to be very wide awake this morning And ready for anything. **Amen**

OPTIONAL ADVENT WREATH

Introduce the Advent Wreath if you've got one. Run through the candle colours and help a child light a Purple candle for the first Sunday of Advent.

BEFORE THE GOSPEL

Four Kings

Place four chairs down the front. Leader 1 stands to one side of them, with the props (see below) to hand. Leader 2 shambles off to the back, ready to play King Basil

Leader 1	Right, well this Sunday we're going to hear about a bunch of kings who were also getting ready for Christmas. They were …

As you say each name, choose a child to be a king, give them a crown, and ask them to stand at the front

	King Caspar King Melchior King Balthazar, and King …
Look round	Where is he? Basil!
Basil	Hullo?
Leader 1	We want you down here …
Basil	OK. *(Leader 2 (aka Basil) joins the others)*
Leader 1	Here he is, King Basil. King Basil is a great bloke, but kinda forgetful. Where's your crown, Basil?
Basil	Ah, I left it too long in the washing machine … *(Pulls very small crown from his pocket)* It shrank.
Leader 1	What else have you got in your pocket?
Basil	Well, I've got a gravestone for one of my favourite knights, he died
CD1.1	last week … *(hold it up)* May he rust in peace … And, of course *(hold it up)* my Bible.
Leader 1	Basil never went anywhere without his Bible. He didn't read it very often, but he was always meaning to …

Basil opens the Bible, nearly reads it, decides against it and puts it back in his pocket

Leader 1	Well, he and the other kings were great friends.

Basil joins the others – slaps their backs or something friendly. The three other kings do what Basil does in the following section

	They inspected the troops together.

All four kings stand very straight and look keenly at the audience

They waved to the public together.

They all do a royal hand wave

	And they went to the cinema together. *(They sit down)*
	What's your favourite film, Basil?
Basil	'King Kong.'
Leader 1	But sometimes they would go outside, climb up as high as they could, and watch the stars together …

The kings stand on their chairs. Pass them up the binoculars

Basil loved watching the stars – but he was completely useless.
He could never remember which end of the telescope to look through and, because you can only watch stars at night, he was always falling asleep.

Basil sits down on his chair and falls asleep

CD1.2	One night the other three kings were very excited, they saw a wonderful new star …
CD1.3	*Enter kid holding up the star puppet*

moving across the sky.

The three kings watch the progress of the star across the room

And they jumped down. *(They do)*
And woke Basil … *(The star goes behind them)*
'We've seen an amazing new star!' they said. 'Look!'
And they pointed up into the sky.
'Where?' said Basil, and he got up. 'It's behind you!' they said.

Run the 'look behind you' panto joke
Basil appeals to the kids

Basil	'Can you see the star?' (**YES! It's behind you!**)

But he never turns round fast enough

Leader 1	Well, all the kings decided to follow the star.
	Caspar ran off to get a rucksack. *(Exit Caspar)*
	Melchior ran off to get the passports. *(Exit Melchior)*
	Balthazar ran off to get some camels. *(Exit Balthazar)*
	And Basil agreed to meet them at the camel parking place.
	Where's that, Basil?
Basil	It's in my royal city – Camelot …

Leader 1   I should have guessed.

Well, Basil looked at his watch, and decided he just had time to have a little kip before the others returned. *(Basil settles down again)*

And he slept, and he slept and he slept.

The sun came up – and Basil woke up and looked round. There was nobody there …

He rushed over to Camelot.

Basil runs to the other end of the room

Nobody there either. The others had gone.

'Rats!' said Basil, 'Why do these things always happen to me?'

He was so fed up that he hunched his shoulders and put his hands in his pockets and discovered – his Bible. *(Basil does this)*

'Useless book!' he said to himself.

'Oh well, I may as well read it. There's nothing else to do.'

And he opened the Bible and began to read …

Basil walks slowly down the room, reading. He stops suddenly

Basil   Oh no!
Leader 1   What's up?
Basil   Look at this – why didn't I read this before?

Hands the book over to Leader 1

Leader 1   Basil had found the Gospel for today. Let's see what it says …

Emphasize the 'Stay awake!' as you read it

THE GOSPEL   *St Luke 21.25–26, 36*

Jesus said to His disciples,

'There will be signs in the sun and the moon and the stars,

people will be frightened and the Heavens will be shaken.

When this happens, stay awake, and pray for strength, so that you may be ready for my coming on the clouds of Heaven.'

Leader 1   So what does Jesus want us to do? (**Stay awake**)

Yup, He wants Christians to be the sort of people who are on the ball, ready for anything. King Basil had better buck up …

(If you've got the time …)

GAME

Keeping Basil Awake …

Leader 2 sits with his back to the children and a crown – any crown, quite a stiff one – behind him. Basil apparently goes to sleep and a child, cued in by Leader 1, tries to sneak up to steal the crown. If Basil hears the kid he points in the direction the child is coming from, and the child has to retreat. Play this game with a view to variety. Let some kids get very close before 'hearing' them, and allow some very small children to win.

Practise the message you are going to take back to the grown-ups – 'WAKE UP!'

Leader	To finish we are going to say our Advent Prayer. It's a very old prayer – and it's very short: Come, Lord Jesus, Amen. **Come, Lord Jesus, Amen.**

BACK IN CHURCH

The children line up down the front

Leader	Today the children have come back with a special message for the whole church. *(Turn to the children)* What is it kids?
Children	**WAKE UP!**

If for some reason the children don't shout this at full power, look round at the congregation, shake your head and say to the kids

Leader	You know, I don't think they quite got that. I think we'll have to tell them again …
Children	**WAKE UP!**

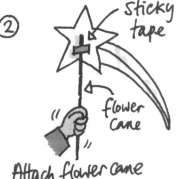

Shooting Star template

① Print star as large as possible

② sticky tape
flower cane
Attach flower cane to the back

(CD1.3)

Sample cartoons for this script

Script 2   John Gets a Name

Advent 2

St Luke 3.1–3

> **THEME**
>
> St John the Baptist makes his traditional appearance on the second Sunday of Advent. Year C is the year in which St Luke's Gospel is used at Mass so, for this session, we turn back to Chapter 1 and discover a story *only* found in Luke – how John got his name.

SET UP

- The liturgical colour is Purple.
- Pictures from the CD-Rom.
- A black marker pen.
- Optional Advent Wreath (see p. 1): the first Purple candle should be lit before the session begins.
- Some large soft balls (look at the game below to gauge how many you will need). Older children can probably catch any ball thrown at them; little ones will need something large and soft.

WELCOME *the children and lead them in* **The Sign of the Cross** ✠ (p. xxxvi).

Ask the children if they noticed the colour in church – highlight anything in the hall that's purple. Bring forward any kids who are wearing purple (however minimally)

Leader	We're in Purple time. It's called Advent.
	Purple is a dark serious colour. Christians think it's a good idea to be serious sometimes, especially when they think about the things they've done wrong. Fortunately we know that we only have to say sorry for God to forgive us. Let's say sorry now.
THE KYRIE	Lord Jesus, we're sorry for the times we've forgotten you,
	Lord have mercy
	Lord have mercy

Lord Jesus, we're sorry for the times we've been unkind,
Christ have mercy
Christ have mercy

Lord Jesus, we thank you for never forgetting us,
Lord have mercy.
Lord have mercy

Ask the children to repeat **The Prayer for Forgiveness** *after you* (**p. xxxvi**).

OPTIONAL ADVENT WREATH

Help a child to light the second candle on the Advent Wreath – another purple one.

OPENING PRAYER

Lord God
We thank you for Advent
(And for our Advent Wreath)
Open our hearts
So that we will be ready to greet your Son
When He comes as a tiny child on Christmas Day. **Amen**

BEFORE THE GOSPEL

VIPS

Leader
OK, today I want to talk about VIPs. *(Write it up)*
Does anyone know what VIP means? (**Very Important Person**)
What sort of person is Very Important? Anyone know?

See what the children come up with – allow a few local celebrities, but try to steer them to really important people like HM The Queen, the Prime Minister, the Pope, the President of the USA

How about their names – what is the Queen's name? (**Elizabeth**)

Write up a couple of others: keep it snappy

OK, well the Gospel this morning starts off with a list of Very Important people indeed. We'll write them up as we hear them …

Leader 2 should have a marker pen and be ready to do so
There is no Gospel Procession in Advent, ask someone to bring up the Gospel book

THE GOSPEL   *St Luke 3.1–3*

Read the Gospel using the following text
Leader 2 writes up the names as you say them

Leader   This story starts in the fifteenth year of the reign of the Emperor
                  Tiberius.

Leader 2 writes up Tiberius

                  When Pontius Pilate was governor of Judea ...

Leader 2 writes up Pontius Pilate

                  and Herod was tetrarch of Galilee.

Up goes Herod – look up and tell the children that a tetrarch is a mini king*

                  Herod's brother Philip was another tetrarch ...

Write up Philip

                  and Lysanias was another one.

Write up Lysanias

                  And, while all these people were ruling Palestine, the Word of God
                  came to John the son of Zechariah, who was living in the wilderness.
Leader 2   *(Leader 2 looks up)* Do I write those names as well?
Leader 1   Yeah, why not? *(Leader 2 writes John and Zechariah)*
                  So John preached by the River Jordan, urging people to be baptized
                  and repent of their sins.

AFTER THE GOSPEL

Leader 1   OK, let's look at these names ...
                  This lot (the first five) were all VIPs once.
                  Anyone heard of Lysanias? *(A rhetorical question)* Nope?

Put a cross by him

                  Or Herod's brother Philip? Nope?

Another cross

                  How about Herod?

---

* 'Tetrarch' means 'ruler of a fourth': the Holy Land was split into four parts and a local ruler was put in charge of each section. In this list you can see Herod and Lysanias have a part each, while Philip, Herod's brother, has two. Even so, Herod (the Great) was richer and more powerful than his fellow tetrarchs.

Go with the flow – the older children may remember the Three Kings visited him and he ordered the Massacre of the Innocents. Put a cross or tick according to the mood of the room

> Pontius Pilate?

Throw it open – whatever the kids say Pilate gets a tick because he's in the Creed

> How about Tiberius?

Probably a cross, unless they've seen a re-run of the television programme I Claudius

> OK, what about John? We know him as John the Baptist – hands up anyone who has heard of him.

Make sure that all the grown-ups present put their hands up, John has to have a tick

> None of these guys – *(indicate the Famous Five)* – would have guessed that John was a VIP, but he's the man who baptized Jesus and became one of the most famous saints in the world.

Circle John's name

> How about Zechariah? *(A rhetorical question)*
> Well Zechariah was St John's father, and there's a story about him in the Bible. Let's see if he's a VIP …

The Birth of St John the Baptist

Settle the children for a story. One Leader tells the story, another puts up the pictures with some help from the kids

Leader 1	A long time ago there lived an aged couple,
CD2.1	Zechariah
CD2.2	and his wife, Elizabeth.
	They were so old that Zechariah needed a walking stick when he went out. *(Ask a child to draw one in)*
	Zechariah and Elizabeth had been married for ages – but they'd never had any children.
	Well, one day, Zechariah was in the Temple. He was a priest and it was his job to offer incense to God. So he went up to the altar to offer incense …
CD2.3	*Attach thurible picture to Zechariah and draw in the outline of a cloud of smoke, big enough to contain the next picture*
	When suddenly, standing in the smoke, he saw …
CD2.4	*(Picture of Angel) – ask the children what it is*

Quite right, an Angel.

And the Angel said to Zechariah,

'Zechariah, God has listened to your prayers and is going to send your wife Elizabeth a son. He is going to be one of the great prophets and, listen to this bit, you are to call his name …

CD2.5   *(Put up speech balloon)* JOHN.'

'Hmm,' said Zechariah. 'Well, I don't see how that's going to happen – my wife's far too old.'

There was a silence. The Angel couldn't believe his ears.

'Hey!' he said. 'You just listen to me! My name is Gabriel and I've come from Heaven to talk to you. It doesn't make any difference whether you believe me or not because it'll happen anyway. BUT, as you haven't believed me, you won't be able to say a word until all these things come true!'

And from that moment Zechariah was dumb.

CD2.6   *Add padlock to Zechariah's mouth*

And the Angel left.

Take off Angel, and speech bubble

And Elizabeth *did* have a son.

Ask a child to stick the baby picture **(CD2.7)** *to Elizabeth*

Everybody was delighted – especially Zechariah, though he couldn't say anything of course.

Well, all Elizabeth's friends and relations said the baby should be called Zechariah like his father.

'No,' said Elizabeth. 'His name is John.'

'But nobody's called John in your family!'

At which point Zechariah made signs that he wanted to write – so they handed him a tablet.

CD2.8   *Stick up the tablet picture*

And he wrote down the baby's name.

What do you suppose he wrote? (**John!**)

Exactly –

Ask a child to write the name on the tablet

And, as soon as he'd done this – Zechariah's speech came back!

Take the padlock off the mouth

And Zechariah and Elizabeth and baby John lived together very happily.

And when John grew up, he became the last great prophet of Israel, John the Baptist.

CD2.9   *Last picture of John the Baptist*

Sum up

Leader   So do we think Zechariah is a VIP? *(This can go either way)*
Well, it doesn't matter. God knew all about him and wanted him to be the father of one of His greatest saints.
Everyone is a VIP as far as God is concerned.

GAME

Name Game

Gather the children into circles of six.
Ask the children to toss the ball to each other, saying their names as they catch it. A grown-up makes a note of the order in which the ball was thrown and asks the kids to remember the name of the person who threw it to them.
After the ball has been caught by everyone, ask them to throw it in reverse order.
If they get very good at this, combine two circles and run it again.

Optional Twist

Start the ball going in the original order, and then throw in another ball going in reverse order. The game normally collapses when one person gets both balls thrown at them.

REHEARSAL

Practise your presentation for when you go back into church (see below).

Leader   We're going to finish by asking St John for his prayers.
The response is
'Pray for us'

FINAL   Holy John
PRAYER   **Pray for us**

Holy John, cousin of Jesus
Pray for us

Holy John, the Baptizer
Pray for us

Holy John, last of the prophets
Pray for us

God our Father,
We thank you for sending your servant John,
to prepare us for the coming of your Son.
Help us this Advent to heed his word,
so that we will be ready to greet Jesus when He comes again,
For Jesus' sake. **Amen**

BACK IN CHURCH

Leader	Today we heard about the important people who used to rule Palestine.
	There was …
Child 1	*Standing very straight, hands on hips*
	Lysanias!
Leader	But we'd never heard of him.
	And …
Child 2	*Just as straight, hands folded across the chest*
	Philip!
Leader	We hadn't heard of him.
	And …
Child 3	*Hand held high in an Imperial wave*
	the Emperor Tiberius!
Leader	And most of us hadn't heard of him either.
	Then we heard of a person we did know.
	He was poor and hungry and lived in the desert and his name was …
All the children	**John the Baptist!**
Leader	Why do we remember John?
Child 4	Because he's the man who told us to get ready for Jesus.

*Sample cartoons
for this script*

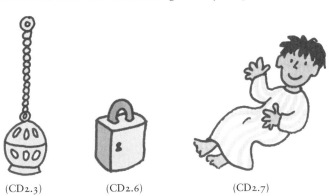

(CD2.3)   (CD2.6)   (CD2.7)

Script 3 'Cheer Up!'

Advent 3

St Luke 3.10–14, 18

THEME

Advent 3 is *Gaudete* Sunday, the moment when Advent lightens up. Gaudete means 'rejoice' and is the first word of the Entrance Antiphon (the verse that starts the service in some churches). St Paul writes to the Christians at Philippi, telling them to cheer up, and St John the Baptist preaches the Good News to the crowds that gather round him (an excellent moment to tell the kids what 'Gospel' actually means). Traditionally, the vestments for Gaudete are rose-coloured but, as not everyone has a rose set, the priests may still be in purple. Still, there's no reason why the children shouldn't be liturgically correct! See if you can find something pink to wear.

SET UP

- The liturgical colour is Pink.
- Bring in a doom-laden newspaper story, not too harrowing – cars stuck in mud, a tree blown down, something like that. Supplement it with *The Daily Gloom* on the CD-Rom.
- St Paul's letter – on the CD-Rom – in an envelope. Leader 2 should be ready to enter with it just BEFORE THE GOSPEL (see below).
- Some large sheets of paper, pens and glue for the kids to make their own newspaper (template on the CD-Rom).
- Set up tables with the materials listed above.
- One black marker pen.
- Optional Advent Wreath (see p. 1): two Purple candles should be lit before the session begins.

WELCOME *the children and lead them in* **The Sign of the Cross** ✠ **(p. xxxvi).**

THE KYRIE Lord Jesus, we're sorry for the times we've forgotten you,
Lord have mercy
Lord have mercy

Lord Jesus, we're sorry for the times we've been unkind,
Christ have mercy
Christ have mercy

Lord Jesus, thank you for never forgetting us,
Lord have mercy
Lord have mercy

Ask the children to repeat **The Prayer for Forgiveness** *after you* (**p. xxxvi**).

PINK SUNDAY

Remind the children about Advent

Leader   We've been in Purple for nearly three weeks now, but today we lighten up.
The right colour for today is …?
Let's see if you can guess.

Bring forward some kids dressed in pink, show them your pink tie …

Yup, it's Pink.
Purple seasons always have one Pink Sunday in them, to cheer us up.

OPTIONAL ADVENT WREATH

Leader   OK, given it's Pink Sunday, which candle shall we light? (**Pink!**)

Help a child to light the Pink candle

OPENING   *Ask the children to repeat this prayer after you*
PRAYER   **Lord Jesus**
Help us to rejoice today
As your birthday
Gets nearer and nearer. Amen

BEFORE THE GOSPEL

News

Leader 2 leaves the room quietly – with St Paul's letter in his/her pocket

Leader   Well, it's Sunday, so I've brought in some Sunday papers. *(Flap your newspaper sheets at them)* I haven't had time to read them yet.

What have we got? *(Quick scan)* Oh dear, look at this ...

Show them a real headline

And what about this?

CD3.1   *Read out the stories from* The Daily Gloom, *and show the children the pictures*

Isn't it odd how all the stories in a newspaper are about bad news?

Scrunch up the newspapers

Well, it's Pink Sunday, I want to cheer up. Isn't there any happy news?

Leader 2 knocks at the door

CD3.2   Hallo, who's that? *(Enter Leader 2)*
Leader 2   We've got a letter ... *(Hands it over)*
Leader 1   *Read the address on the envelope*
                To the Christians at *Name (your town/village or church)*

A Message from St Paul

Ask a child to open the envelope and take out the letter

Leader   Goodness, it's from St Paul, what's he got to say?

Ask a child to read it

Kid   Dear Christians,
                I want you to be happy at all times.
                Cheer up and don't worry about anything –
                the Lord is coming soon.
                Best wishes,
                PAUL
Leader 1   Well that's very kind of St Paul, and the Lord certainly is coming soon. How long is it to Christmas? (x *number of days*)
                Only x days! We'd better crack on and read the Gospel.

There is no Gospel Procession in Advent: ask a child to bring the Gospel book up to the front.

THE GOSPEL   *St Luke 3.10–14, 18*

Optional Paraphrase

Crowds of people turned up to listen to John the Baptist.

They asked him, 'Teacher, what must we do?'

John said, 'Anyone with two shirts must share with the one who has none, and anyone who has got enough to eat must share his food. If you are a tax collector, don't cheat people, and if you are a soldier, don't be a bully.'

In many different ways John preached to the people – and told them the Good News.

AFTER THE GOSPEL

Leader 1	*(Read the last sentence again)* 'In many different ways John preached to the people – and told them the Good News.'
	What Good News? *(A rhetorical question probably)*
	John was there to tell everyone that the Saviour who God was going to send was on His way.
	Who was that? (**Jesus**)
	Quite right, Jesus.
	And Jesus arrived with more Good News – that God loved everyone and was going to put everything right.
	In fact our faith is all about Good News, we have a special word for it.
	Does anyone know? *(Hold up the Gospel)*
	It's called 'Gospel' – 'Gospel' means Good News.*
	So, as this is Pink Sunday, I think we ought to get going on some Good News. Let's make a cheerful newspaper.

ACTIVITY

Good News

The kids are about to produce their newspaper. Talk through good news. Be very specific

Leader 1	Anyone here got a new baby?
	Great – that'll make a good story – we want his/her name, and a picture.

Get a kid to look out of the window

What's the weather like?

---

* The original Greek word for Gospel is Euaggelion, 'good news'. The English word 'Gospel' comes from two Early English words, 'good spell' (good story). We use Gospel as a synonym for Good News.

Try to make the weather sound OK – sun is easy, so is snow, rain is good for filling up the reservoirs, and anyway kids like splashing in puddles

> We'll need a picture of people enjoying the weather.

If desperate, ask them to draw a picture of a couple of cheery ducks

> What about sport? Any good sporting stories? Did anyone's team win?
>
> Anyone had a birthday? Great, we'll want to hear about that.
>
> Anything nice happen in school – anyone get a gold star?
>
> Are you doing a carol concert?
>
> How soon are the holidays – that would be a good story – only eight days to go …

Assign each story to various groups of children and get your newspaper into production

You could use the template on the CD-Rom **(CD3.3)**

Make this activity quite snappy – real journalists have to work to deadlines – towards the end ask them if they can think of a title for their newspaper – maybe Good News, St *(Name of your church)* Times, Pink Sunday Special *(Londoners may suggest* The Pink 'Un)

Stick the stories and pictures on an A3 sheet, write in the title with a black marker pen, and leave a gap at the bottom

Admire the result

Stop Press

Leader 1 That's brilliant – we've left a gap at the bottom in case any more news comes in at the last moment. If you get late news you stop the printing presses to put it in, so it's called Stop Press.

Label the gap 'Stop Press'

> I don't think we've got a Stop Press, have we?

Leader 2 Yes we have! What about the Gospel? Jesus is coming!

Leader 1 You're right. Could someone put that in for me?

A child writes in 'Jesus is coming'

> OK, now we've got a complete newspaper.

REHEARSAL

Practise your presentation for when you go back into church (see below).

FINAL PRAYER	*Gather the children round the newspaper*
	Let's just sit still for a moment and think about all the happy news in our newspaper. I think you've done really well.
	Especially that last bit of news – 'Jesus is coming'.
	Let's pray that He will turn up very soon in the words of our Advent Prayer.

ADVENT PRAYER	Come, Lord Jesus, Amen
	Come, Lord Jesus. Amen

BACK IN CHURCH

The children line up down the front

Leader 1	Today we got a letter from St Paul. *(Hold up the letter)*
	What did he say, kids?
Children	**Be happy!**
Leader 2	Then we heard that St John preached the 'Gospel'. *(Hold up the Gospel)*
	I've forgotten what Gospel means …
Children	**Good News!**
Child	Then we wrote our own newspaper, full of good news.

Another child holds the newspaper up

Leader 1	And we think that the message for this Sunday is –?
Kids	**Cheer up!**

Place the newspaper at the back of the church so that the adults can read it at the end of the service

The Daily Gloom

Katie's cat eats her goldfish

Tibby speaks to the Press

(CD3.1)

Sample cartoon for this script

Script 4   Mothers

Advent 4

Luke 1.39–44

THEME

History is full of great mothers. Some are formidable, like various Spartan and Roman mothers, some are simply devoted – like St Monica, whose story we hear today. It leads up to the quiet story appointed for Advent 4, the visit of Our Lady to her kinswoman, St Elizabeth.

SET UP

- The liturgical colour is Purple.
- Pictures from the CD-Rom.
- Black, red or pink marker pens.
- The 'Hail Mary' jigsaw on the CD-Rom – stuck on thin card, if you've got the time.
- Optional Advent Wreath – for once, leave all the candles unlit.

WELCOME *the children and lead them in* **The Sign of the Cross** ✠ **(p. xxxvi).**

Leader	Well, this is the last Sunday of Advent.
	That must mean it's nearly …? **(Christmas!)**
	When is it? *(Let them tell you)*
	Fantastic, Christmas is coming.
	Let's be ready for it by leaving behind all the silly and wrong things we did last week.
THE KYRIE	Lord Jesus, you came to Earth to tell us how much God loves us,
	Lord have mercy
	Lord have mercy
	Lord Jesus, you came to Earth to help us say sorry,
	Christ have mercy
	Christ have mercy

> Lord Jesus, you came to Earth to bring us God's forgiveness,
> Lord have mercy
> **Lord have mercy**

Ask the children to repeat **The Prayer for Forgiveness** *after you* (p. xxxvi).

OPTIONAL ADVENT WREATH

Leader	Which Sunday in Advent is this? (**Four**)
	Four! Well, we'll need four children to light these candles …

This is the countdown: have four children lined up and ask everyone to count each candle as it gets lit

Everybody	1 … 2 … 3 … 4!
Leader	We're nearly there!

OPENING PRAYER	Lord God
	You sent an Angel to tell the Virgin Mary she was going to be the mother of your Son.
	Help us to join with all the angels and saints this Christmas
	To welcome Jesus, the newborn King. **Amen**

BEFORE THE GOSPEL

Leader 1	We're going to think about mothers today.
	There've been some very tough mothers down the centuries.
	I think the toughest were the Spartan mothers.
	They lived hundreds of years ago in Greece.
CD4.1	And they used to send their sons off to battle saying … *(picture of Spartan mother)*
CD4.2	'Either come home with your shields, or *on* them …' *(picture of Spartan returning on his shield)*

The picture is obvious. What these appalling mums were saying was, come back victorious – with your shield – or dead – on it. People who ran away always ditched their shield, it got in the way

Leader	*(Look at picture* **CD4.1** *again)*
	She does look grim, doesn't she?
	I'd like to tell you about another sort of mother – St Monica.

Settle down into story-telling mode, ask another Leader to put up the pictures as you go

St Monica

There was once a very famous family that lived in North Africa in 400 AD – 1,600 years ago …

They were Berbers – that's a North African race – and their names were

CD4.3	Patrick
CD4.4	Monica
CD4.5	and Augustine.

Augustine was just a baby, and his parents loved him so much they used to stand in the doorway and watch him as he lay asleep …

Draw a door frame round Patrick and Monica, and ZZZZs from Augustine

CD4.6   But unfortunately Augustine grew up.

He was a clever boy, and his parents still loved him, but he was a worry. He used to go scrumping and steal pears from people's gardens.

Add pear to Augustine's hand

CD4.7   Then he became a teenager.

CD4.8   He was moody and difficult and wouldn't go to church.

Add 'shan't!' to thought balloon by Augustine's head

CD4.9   Then he became a young man.

By now he was very clever, and did well at university, but he still didn't go to church. And he started to have unsuitable girlfriends …

Draw some obvious lipstick kisses on Augustine's cheeks (use a red or pink marker pen)

CD4.10   And his mother Monica was in despair.

CD4.11   She went to see the bishop.

Then she went back, and back again. The bishop got quite nervous about her – especially as every time she came she burst into tears.

Draw in a halo of teardrops round Monica

Until the bishop said, 'Don't worry, Monica, a young man who has had so many tears shed over him is bound to turn out all right.'

So Monica went home to pray – and Augustine

CD4.12   eventually calmed down, and became a Christian.

CD4.13   And then a bishop. *(Add picture of mitre to cartoon)*

And eventually a great saint. *(Draw in a halo)*

And he said afterwards that it was his mother's love and prayers that put him right.

If anyone asks what happened to Patrick tell them that he died while Augustine was quite young. Take a moment to think about the story

Has anyone here got a mother like that?

(A rhetorical question: you could add a version of the sort of thing I usually say – 'My mother used to think I was a genius, I didn't really believe her, but it was nice to know somebody thought that')

The world is full of loving mothers, thank goodness, and we're going to hear about two mothers today.

THE GOSPEL   *St Luke 1.39–44*

Whatever version you use, ensure that the words of Elizabeth's greeting are the same as the ones we use in the Hail Mary – 'Blessed art thou among women, and blessed is the fruit of thy womb.'

AFTER THE GOSPEL

Leader 1

So today we heard that the Virgin Mary went on a visit to one of her relatives, Elizabeth.

Mary was already pregnant – what was her Baby going to be called? **(Jesus)**

Elizabeth was pregnant too. Does anyone know who her baby would be? **(John the Baptist)**

And something odd happened, as Mary greeted Elizabeth, little St John moved in his mother's womb. It's as if he knew that Mary and Jesus were near him.

Then Elizabeth greeted Mary, and she used words we still say today.

Produce the pieces of the Hail Mary jigsaw **(CD4.14–4.22)**

Stick up this bit of the Hail Mary jigsaw: 'Blessed art thou amongst women, and blessed is the fruit of thy womb'

The script splits here – for those who know the Hail Mary, and those who don't

FOR KIDS WHO KNOW THE HAIL MARY

Leader 1   Does anyone know where these words come from? (**The Hail Mary**)
                  Yup, but that's not how the prayer starts – can you tell me what I
                  need to put here?

Indicate the spaces before the first 'Blessed'

                  (**Hail Mary, full of grace**)
                  Quite right. *(Add that)*
                  And the next bit? (**The Lord is with thee**) *(Add that)*
                  Does anyone know who said that?

See if they do – it was the Angel Gabriel when he came to give her God's message

                  Now Elizabeth didn't know the name of Mary's Baby, but we do, so
                  we'll add that … Can anyone find it?

Get a child to add the 'Jesus' piece

                  And then there's the second half of the Hail Mary, the bit where we
                  ask for her prayers, let's put that up as well …

Ask some children to finish the jigsaw

FOR KIDS WHO DON'T KNOW THE HAIL MARY

Leader 1   Ever since Elizabeth greeted Mary, we've used her words in a very
                  ancient prayer called the Hail Mary.
                  It starts off 'Hail Mary, full of grace, the Lord is with thee'.
                  Can anyone find those pieces for me?

The children find the pieces and stick them up

                  Does anyone know who said that?

See if they do – it was the Angel Gabriel when he came to give her God's message

                  Now Elizabeth didn't know the name of Mary's Baby, but we do, so
                  we'll add that here.

Indicate the last word, 'womb'

                  Can anyone find it?

Get a child to add the 'Jesus' piece

                  Then the prayer finishes with us asking the Virgin Mary to pray for
                  us.
                  It starts with her name – who can find that?

A child finds 'Holy Mary' and sticks it up

                  Then whom she is Mother of – see if you can find that.

Another kid finds 'Mother of God'

Then we ask for her prayers, I'll do that …

Stick up 'Pray for us sinners now and at the hour of our death'

OK, and how do we end a prayer? (**Amen**)
Brilliant,
Name, (choose a small child) can you find that word for me?

Stick up 'Amen'

REHEARSAL

Practise your presentation for when you go back into church (see below).

BEFORE THE FINAL PRAYER

Leader 1   We're going to finish by praying the Hail Mary.
And, as we do so, we'll remember St Elizabeth who gave us some
of the words.

FINAL PRAYER

Finish with the **Hail Mary** *… (see p. xxxvii).*

BACK IN CHURCH

The children come into church with the Hail Mary jigsaw: make sure that – whatever order the congregation sees the pieces – the prayer will eventually read in the right order

Leader   Today we heard how St Elizabeth greeted the Virgin Mary.

The children with the 'Blessed art thou among women' and 'blessed is the fruit of thy womb' jigsaw pieces hold them up

Then we remembered how the Angel Gabriel greeted Our Lady.

The children with the 'Hail Mary, full of grace, the Lord is with thee' pieces hold them up

Then we added the name of Mary's Baby.

A kid with the 'Jesus' piece holds it up

Then we asked Our Lady for her prayers.

The kids with the remainder of the pieces of the prayer hold them up (keep the 'Amen' back)

And we'd like to pray this with you now:

Recite the Hail Mary, and make sure the 'Amen' is held high at the right moment

Script 5 Jesus Gets Lost

Christmas 1

St Luke 2.41–52

THEME

The only story about Jesus the kid. He's 12 years old and gets lost. Adults reading this story usually empathize with Mary and Joseph and find Jesus' self-possession exasperating. 'Why were you looking for me?' He says. 'Didn't you realize I must be in my Father's house?'

The trouble is, He's right. Of course He's in His father's house and, should we ever lose Him, that's where we shall find Him too.

SET UP

- The liturgical colour is White or Gold.
- Set Leader 2 up with string on his or her gloves, hat, and any other garment you can think of, that might conceivably get lost.
- Pictures from the CD-Rom.
- Board game from the CD-Rom, printed up as large as you can.
- Either buy an inflatable (or bouncy) die from a party/joke shop or make one by covering a box with stiff white paper and drawing on the dots.

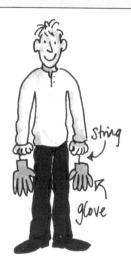

string

glove

WELCOME *the children and lead them in* **The Sign of the Cross ✠ (p. xxxvi).**

THE KYRIE Lord Jesus, you came to Earth to tell us how much God loves us,
Lord have mercy
Lord have mercy

Lord Jesus, you came to Earth to help us say sorry,
Christ have mercy
Christ have mercy

Lord Jesus, you came to Earth to forgive us,
Lord have mercy
Lord have mercy

Ask the children to repeat **The Prayer for Forgiveness** *after you* (**p. xxxvi**).

OPENING	God our Father
PRAYER	We thank you for Christmas
	For the fun we had
	For the food we ate
	For our families and friends
	And, most of all, for the birth of your Son,
	Jesus Christ. **Amen**

BEFORE THE GOSPEL

Leader	*Talk through Christmas*
	Did Father Christmas arrive?
	What did he give you? *(Run with that for a moment)*
To Leader 2	Did you get a Christmas present, *Name*?
Leader 2	I certainly did – a nice ball of string.
Leader 1	A ball of string! Did you want a ball of string?
Leader 2	Yes I did. I've put string on my gloves *(show the kids)* to stop me losing them.
	And on my hat *(show them)* to keep it on my head.
	And round my socks …
Leader 1	You lose your socks?
Leader 2	All the time …
Leader 1	Well, you've done better than Mary and Joseph – I mean, you just lose your socks, they managed to lose Jesus …
Leader 2	You're kidding!
Leader 1	No, we're going to hear about it now.

THE GOSPEL PROCESSION

As this will be the first Gospel Procession since before Advent, run through the procedure with the children. (See p. xxix in the Introduction.)

THE GOSPEL   *St Luke 2.41–52*

Whatever translation you use, make sure that Jesus says … at verse 49

'Why did you have to look for me? Didn't you know that I'd be in my Father's House?'

AFTER THE GOSPEL

One Leader goes through the Gospel, as the other one puts up the pictures from the CD-Rom

Leader 1   So this is a story from when Jesus was 12. **(CD5.1)**
                He'd gone up to the Temple in Jerusalem with His parents – and a whole load of friends and relations.
                The roads were dangerous, so it was sensible to travel in a crowd – and anyway, it'd take several days to get to Jerusalem and it's more fun to camp with lots of other people.
                Quite often the men and boys would thunder on ahead, and the women would follow behind with the little kids.
                The trouble is, when you're 12, are you a big kid, or a little grown-up? You can imagine Mary walking back, thinking Jesus was old enough to be at the front with Joseph, and Joseph striding ahead, thinking Jesus was with His mum.
                Then they compared notes …

CD5.2   *(Mary and Joseph discuss the situation, head to head)*

                'Where's Jesus?' said Mary.
                'I don't know – isn't He with you?' said Joseph.
                'No!'
                'Well He must be with Uncle Reuben.'
                'Well He isn't …'
                'Oh blimey! I don't believe it!'
                And back they went to Jerusalem. It took them three days to find Jesus and, when they did, where was He? **(In the Temple)**
                Yup, there He was, as calm as could be, listening to the Jewish teachers, asking them questions – having a great time.

CD5.3   Mary and Joseph made straight for Him. *(Picture of them rushing up)*
                'Jesus!' they said.
                (Turn to the kids) Has this ever happened to you?
                What happens when you've worried your parents out of their minds? **(Yeah, they are furious)**

CD5.4   But Jesus said, '*Why* did you have to look for me?' *(Picture of Jesus looking impervious)*
                'Didn't you know that I'd be in my Father's House?'
                Which sounds a bit annoying, but actually He was right.
                Jesus wasn't lost at all, He was in His Father's House.
                Who was Jesus' real Father? **(God)**

I think St Joseph must have thought, 'Of course, I should have guessed Jesus would want to be near His real Father.'

And perhaps Our Lady thought, 'Oh yes, I should have guessed I'd find my Son here.' She never forgot that moment, but treasured it in her heart.

I think that's the story we ought to remember too.

Because sometimes *we* lose Jesus – He doesn't seem to be around – we seem to have left Him behind somewhere.

Well there's one place we'll always find Him – in His Father's House. You can go into any church, and kneel, and find Jesus waiting to talk to you.

Let's see how good we'd be at finding Jesus.

GAME

Finding Jesus

Depending on numbers, either gather the kids round a table and play the board game **(CD5.5–6)**, *or stick it up, divide the kids into two teams, and call up various representatives to throw the dice, move the tokens – and see if they can find Jesus. (Instructions and counters for the game are on* **CD5.6**.)

REHEARSAL

Practise your presentation for when you go back into church (see below).

FINAL PRAYER

Leader	Jesus called God 'His Father' – and He told us to do the same.
	Let us say together the prayer that He taught us:
	Our Father… (see p. xxxvi).

BACK IN CHURCH

Child 1	Today we heard how, when Jesus was a little boy, He got lost.
Child 2	His parents looked for Him everywhere.
Child 3	And they found Him in His Father's House.
Child 4	Jesus wasn't lost at all!
Leader	Sometimes we feel we've lost Jesus – but we can always find Him again.
	Where do we know Jesus can always be found, kids?
Everyone	**In His Father's House!**
Leader	It's why we've come back to church.

Script 6   **Light in Darkness**

Christmas 2

St John 1.1–5, 9

THEME

Today's Gospel is from the poem that starts St John's Gospel. It's not an obvious passage for children, but they are good at telling light from darkness, which is what we've gone for this session.

SET UP

- The liturgical colour is White or Gold.
- A blindfold.
- Three sheets of black paper, one sheet of white.
- Yellow marker pen.
- Glue or Sellotape.
- Pictures from the CD-Rom – they should be cut out ready to be stuck on to the paper.
- Set up the pictures and the sheets of paper on a large table.
- A large prayer candle, the sort that can stand on its own base.
- Matches and taper.
- Hand-held candles in candle holders.

WELCOME *the children and lead them in* **The Sign of the Cross** ✠ **(p. xxxvi).**

THE KYRIE	Lord Jesus, you came to Earth to tell us how much God loves us, Lord have mercy **Lord have mercy**
	Lord Jesus, you came to Earth to help us say sorry, Christ have mercy **Christ have mercy**
	Lord Jesus, you came to Earth to forgive us, Lord have mercy **Lord have mercy**

Ask the children to repeat **The Prayer for Forgiveness** *after you* (**p. xxxvi**).

OPENING PRAYER	God of power and life Fill the world with your splendour And bring everyone into the light of your truth. **Amen**

BEFORE THE GOSPEL

Blindman's Buff

Leader 1	Good morning. On a nice/miserable *(this depends on the weather)* day like this, I thought we'd start with a game. It's called Blindman's Buff – we blindfold someone.

Blindfold another Leader

Then we circle him/her. *(Everyone circles the Blindman)*
And he tries to catch us …
If he catches us, we stand still and he tries to guess who we are.
If he gets it right, then we get the blindfold. Otherwise, he has to carry on.

Run this a couple of times – a degree of cheating helps this game along, the blindfolded Leader should catch someone old enough to be unfazed by being the Blindman.
Let a couple of small children have a go eventually, circle them closely – so they've got a chance of catching someone – and give them some outrageous hints as they try to guess whom they've caught. (Make it really obvious: 'Oh no! I've been caught! I hope she doesn't guess I'm Sarah …')

Darkness

Get the kids to sit round the table

Leader 1	Rushing round in the dark is quite fun, isn't it?
	But there are times when it's kinda scary.
	Why is the dark scary?

Take all answers, indicate it's not silly to be frightened of the dark: as not being able to see can be dangerous

When I was little, I was scared of the dark. Look this is me …

CD6.1   *Stick cartoon on a sheet of black paper*

But fortunately, my mum and dad gave me a little night light.

CD6.2   *Stick cartoon on the sheet*

Some people work in the dark – like this miner.

CD6.3   *Stick him on another sheet of black paper*

Can anyone see what sort of light he needs?

CD6.4   *(They should spot the miner's helmet) – stick it on*

CD6.5   And if this singer didn't have a light on her we'd never see her at all. *(A greyed-out singer, stick her on another sheet of black paper)*

CD6.6   *and ask the children to find the spotlight she needs*
                Stick that over her

With a spotlight on she'll not only be seen, she'll come into colour as well.

CD6.7   *(The singer in glorious technicolour) – stick her over the greyed-out singer, and in the spotlight*

But most important of all, the whole world needs light, so that things can grow and people don't freeze to death.

Pull forward the sheet of white paper

What is the enormous light we all need? (**The Sun**)
Would someone draw that for me?
And let's draw some of the things that happen when the sun comes out.

Ask the children to draw trees and flowers, people looking happy, bees buzzing about (Go through the pictures)

Light stops you being frightened,
And it shows you where you're going
And gives you colour,
And warmth and life.
God loves light.
The first thing He says in the Bible is 'Let there be light!'
OK, now you've got to imagine God looking down from Heaven and seeing our world. And, to God, it looks dark. Not because the sun isn't shining – but because evil has taken over and people are frightened and miserable.
What these people need is Light, thinks God.
So what does He do? We're going to find out in the Gospel.

THE GOSPEL PROCESSION

THE GOSPEL   *St John 1.1–5, 9*

Any translation will do – including the King James version

Leader 1   *Before you start, look up and say*
In this bit of the Bible Jesus is called the Word*. So when you hear me talking about the Word, you'll know I mean Jesus.

AFTER THE GOSPEL

Leader 1   *Go through the Gospel with the children*
Before the world began, the Word – Jesus – was with God.
He was the True Light, that shines on everyone in the world.
Let's think about that as we pray.

Form the kids in a prayer circle, dim the lights, set the large prayer candle in their midst

God sent Jesus into the world to clear away the darkness.
And He did.

Light the candle

And everyone who believes in Him – that's us – is called a Child of Light.
We get our light from Jesus, just as we can get a flame from this candle. It looks the same as Jesus' light, only smaller.

---

* Strictly speaking Jesus Christ, as the Word *made flesh*, doesn't come to exist until the incarnation. The Son of God is always God's Word and only after the incarnation is He Jesus Christ. It's a reasonable shorthand, however, to say that when John talks about the Word he is talking about Jesus.

Dish out the little candles (give any small child's candle to its attendant grown-up) and light them, with a taper, from the prayer candle

God our Father
You sent Jesus to be the Light of the World
The light shines in the darkness
And the darkness cannot put it out.
Help us to be lights in the world as well. **Amen**

MUSIC

The obvious hymn here is 'Lord the light of your love is shining' ('Shine, Jesus, shine').

REHEARSAL

Practise your presentation for when you go back into church (see below).

BACK IN CHURCH

Go back into church with the Leader holding the prayer candle. (You might have to tip out its hot wax before you go.) Depending on numbers, either ask the children to bring their (unlit) candles into church, or designate a few kids to be token 'lights of the world'
Line up down the front, the kids with candles nearest the prayer candle
Leader 1 holds the prayer candle, Leader 2 is ready with a lit taper

Leader 1   Before the world began, the Word was with God.
He was the True Light, that shines on everyone in the world.

Leader 2 lights the prayer candle

God sent the Word into the world to clear away the darkness.
And everyone who believes in Him – that's us – is called 'a child of light'.

Light the children's candles from the prayer candle

So now we can say:

All the children   Jesus is the Light of the World.

Ask the kids to blow out their candles as they return to their seats

(CD6.1)
Sample cartoon for this script

Script 7   Epiphany

St Matthew 2.1–11

THEME

For this session we give the Three Kings their Biblical name of Magi – wise men. The trio were intellectuals, men who observed the stars or, as they would have put it, watched the heavens. The difference is important as our ancestors supposed they had access to a beautiful and ordered world when they gazed into the night sky. The stars, they felt, were mysterious objects whose motions could influence the affairs of men. (Sadly, all that's left of this ancient idea is the astrology column in the newspaper.) This morning we turn into star-gazers and watch the sky with the Magi – especially the mysterious star which rises in the East.

SET UP

- The liturgical colour is White or Gold.
- An image of Baby Jesus from a crib (a Bambino).
- Small pieces of black paper on which the kids can prick out constellations (see templates on CD-Rom).
- Some sharp pencils.
- Star sheets from the CD-Rom: make several copies of each (see below).
- A large sheet of black paper.
- One large transparent sheet taped lightly, on one side, over the black paper.
- A packet of stick-on silver stars, all sizes. Reserve the largest for the Bethlehem Star.
- Two strips of transparent paper: one has a small star stuck on it, the other has the Bethlehem Star.
- A large cut-out star taped to a stick (see template on CD-Rom).

- Set up a large table with all the craft objects listed above set out.
- A cut-out star on a stick, quite simple, something for the children to process behind when they walk back into church.

WELCOME *the children and lead them in* **The Sign of the Cross** ✠ (**p. xxxvi**).

THE KYRIE   Lord Jesus, you came to Earth to bring us back to God,
Lord have mercy.
Lord have mercy

Lord Jesus, you came to Earth to heal us from our sins,
Christ have mercy
Christ have mercy

Lord Jesus, you came to Earth to tell us how much God loves us,
Lord have mercy
Lord have mercy

Ask the children to repeat **The Prayer for Forgiveness** *after you* (**p. xxxvi**).

BEFORE THE OPENING PRAYER

Leader 1   *Holding the Bambino reverently*
Hi, before we pray this morning, I'd like to think about any cribs you have seen. Baby Jesus is always in the middle *(show the image gently to the children)* and there are all sorts of people gathered round.
Who are they? (**Mary, Joseph, shepherds**)
Quite right.
Name, (to a female Leader) could you be Mary for a moment?

Leader 2 comes forward and kneels

And *Name*, could you be Joseph?

Any male Leader or older child comes forward, and kneels

Name, (to a child) could you be a shepherd?

Bring them forward and ask them to kneel

That's what a crib looks like, lots of people kneeling before Baby Jesus. Why did they do that? *(See what the children think – sum it up …)*
People knelt before Baby Jesus to see Him – He was so little – and to worship Him – He was the Son of God.
Let's kneel as well …

| OPENING PRAYER | Lord God,
On Christmas Day
Mary and Joseph and the shepherds
Knelt before your Son,
To worship Him and show how much they loved Him.
We kneel before you this morning
To worship you and thank you
For sending us Jesus Christ into our world. **Amen** |

BEFORE THE GOSPEL

Stars

Leader	*Ask the children to sit down* Right, today we're going to think about the stars. Where do you see them? (**In the sky**) Oh good, so if I go out shall I see some? (**No!**) Why not? (**It's daytime, too much light**) – *(Anything they come up with)* Yup, you're right. I think if we're going to see any stars we'll have to make some ourselves. Let's have a go.
CD7.1	*Go over to the table – pick up the Plough star sheet* OK, when we look at the sky at night, we see stars. But – I expect you know this – they don't just whizz round the sky, they stay together in groups. We call the groups 'constellations'. This is the constellation of the Plough. Now hundreds of years ago, shepherds and people like that, would sit out at night looking up at the sky, and they'd see a constellation like this – and imagine what it would look like if you joined up the lines. Like this …
CD7.2	*Go through the Plough sheet (**CD7.1**) with the children. Then move on to the Swan and Orion sheet (**CD7.2**) and follow the instructions on the sheet*

*Dish out copies of **CD7.3** and show the children how to make constellations*

| CD7.3 | OK, we're going to make our own constellations – like this. |

Place the star sheet on a piece of black paper, and use a sharp pencil to punch through the dots so as to make holes in the black paper underneath. Hold the black paper up to the light, it looks a bit like the night sky, the holes reading as stars. Help the kids make some constellations and admire the results

OK, now I want to make a really big night sky. We're going to need it for the Gospel.

ACTIVITY

Star-gazers

Lay out the large sheet of black paper

Leader 1   Right, this is going to be the night sky as it appeared over 2,000 years ago.

In those days the night sky looked incredibly beautiful, because there were no neon lights or tall buildings – and you could get out into the countryside and see millions of stars.

Really clever people watched the stars. The sort of chaps who knew the difference between a star and a planet, and who could work out their movements.

Let's give them something to look at.

Slide the star sheets under the transparent sheet to act as a guide as you put on the silver stars. Slide out the star sheets and admire your night sky

That looks good …

Of course stars move round the sky, just like the moon.*

Un-tape the transparent sheet and rotate it a little

People loved watching them slowly move across the heavens; they felt they were watching a very slow and wonderful dance.

And if a flying star suddenly shot across the sky …

Zip the small star you have prepared across the sky

they'd be worried that there was something wrong.

You see, they felt one of the reasons God made the stars was to tell us when something important was about to happen.

So a comet, there goes another one, *(zip the flying star across again)* might mean there was going to be an earthquake or a flood.

The Bethlehem Star

Well one night, three wise men – like these chaps – saw a large and beautiful star rising in the East …

Place the Bethlehem Star on the right-hand side of the sheet

And move slowly across the sky.

---

* You could add a rider on the fixed North Star, but not if the children are small.

Move it in an arc over to the other side of the sheet

> They were very excited.
>
> 'Such a beautiful star must be the sign that something fantastic is about to happen,' said one. 'Perhaps a hero is going to be born?'
>
> 'It's such a big star, I think it's more likely to be a king,' said another.
>
> 'Look!' said the third, 'It's stopped over the Holy Land. It must be a Jewish king – let's follow it ...'
>
> And so they did. Let's hear what happened next in the Gospel.

THE GOSPEL PROCESSION

THE GOSPEL   *St Matthew 2.1–11*

(Leave out verses 5b and 6 if you wish.)

AFTER THE GOSPEL

Leader   Hands up anyone who knows that story? *(Look impressed)*
I thought so ...
What are the three men called? (**Wise men, kings**)
Correct, we called them 'wise men' this morning.
Sometimes people call them 'the Magi' – that's just 'wise men' in Latin.
They followed the star, until they found it shining over the place where Baby Jesus, and Mary and Joseph were staying. Then they went in and knelt before Him.
Guys, we started this session kneeling, and that's how we're going to end it, but we're going to do it in a special way, quite fast.

Genuflecting

It's a way of kneeling when you honour something very holy – and keep moving.
It works like this.
Here's Baby Jesus again. *(Pick up the Bambino reverently)*
And *Name* wants to go to the other side of the room.
She thinks it's right to honour the image of Jesus, so she does it like this ...

Leader 2 crosses the room, genuflecting to the Bambino on the way

You see how easy it is, you go down on your right knee – make sure it touches the ground – and then up again.
Can anyone else do that?

See if another grown-up or teenager will lead the way

> In the Bible it says, 'At the Name of Jesus, every knee shall bow.'
> Listen out for the Name of Jesus in our last prayer, and see if you can do a fast kneel.

FINAL PRAYER

Lord God Almighty
Today three wise men
Found your Son and knelt before Him.
Help us to find Him too.
Holy Jesus *(genuflect)*
We worship you. **Amen**

REHEARSAL

Leader   Now you know how to genuflect, you can practise the presentation. *(See below)*

BACK IN CHURCH

The children gather at the back of the church with a star on a stick; two of them come to the front

Child 1   Today we heard that three wise men followed a star to find Baby Jesus.

Child 2   And when they found Him, they knelt before Him.

Child 1   This morning we've followed a star back into church.

The children follow the star down the aisle

Child 2   We know that we shall find Jesus here.

The kids line up, facing the altar

Leader   So we are going to kneel before Him, before we go back to our seats.

The children genuflect together, and go back to their seats

Script 8 Baptism of Jesus

Epiphany 1 (Church of England) or Ordinary Time 1 (Roman Catholic)

St Luke 3.3, 7a, 21–22

THEME

This Sunday we celebrate Jesus' Baptism by John the Baptist in the River Jordan. This session looks at the way we baptize people and discovers that what we do in church links up with the Gospel.

SET UP

- The liturgical colour is White or Gold.
- Holy water stoup and an aspergillum or a small bowl of holy water and a little bunch of rosemary – or similar.
- A large transparent bowl.
- A large jug of water.
- A scallop shell (optional).
- A baby doll.
- A couple of large towels.
- Print the Baptism Jigsaw from the CD-Rom, either as a large jigsaw – if you want to do it as a group exercise, or in small copies – if you want to dish it out among small groups of three or four children.

WELCOME *the children and lead them in* **The Sign of the Cross** ✠ (p. xxxvi).

BEFORE THE KYRIE

Leader	Today we're going to say a short Kyrie, just 'Lord have mercy' and 'Christ have mercy'.
	Can anyone tell me what 'Lord have mercy' means?

This might not get any answers; establish that we are asking God to forgive us

	Right, but what are we asking God to forgive us from? (**Our sins, the things we've done wrong**)

And does He forgive us? (**Yes**)
OK, well let's say that Kyrie right away!

THE KYRIE   Lord have mercy
Lord have mercy

Christ have mercy
Christ have mercy

Lord have mercy
Lord have mercy

Ask the children to repeat **The Prayer for Forgiveness** *after you* (**p. xxxvi**).

BEFORE THE OPENING PRAYER

Leader 2 stands ready with the aspergillum

Leader 1   As we say our Opening Prayer, *Name* is going to splash us with holy water. It's a good way to remind ourselves how quickly God washes away our sins.

As you start the prayer, Leader 2 splashes everyone with holy water – the other Leaders, the children, any grown-up in range. Cross yourself as you are splashed – and make sure that someone splashes Leader 2 at the end

OPENING   Lord God,
PRAYER   Friend of Sinners,
You have given us the gift of water
To refresh us
To wash us
And to splash people with.

Pause here to give Leader 2 time to splash a few more people

Thank you for your gift,
And help us to remember how swiftly you wash away our sins,
Through Jesus Christ our Lord. **Amen**

BAPTISM PRACTICE

Move over to the jug and pour half the water into the basin from a great height

Leader   Water is really important in church – can anyone tell me what we use it for?

*Take everything that comes: washing things, making the Sign of the Cross as we come
in, filling up flower vases, washing the priest's hands during Mass, and so on
Steer the answers to Holy Baptism – a remark like 'Babies get wet as well, don't they?'
will do it*

Hands up anyone who's seen a baptism.
Did the baby like it? *(It doesn't matter what they say)*
Did the priest drop the baby? *(Don't wait for disaster stories)*
I bet the priest didn't – they're trained to baptize babies properly –
and they start with a doll.

Produce the doll; Leader 2 stands ready with a towel

The secret when baptizing a baby is to tuck it firmly under your
armpit like this *(follow the
illustration here)* and, however
much they wriggle *(make sure the
doll puts up a spirited resistance)*,
hold on tight and pour water on
its head three times like this.

*Dip the shell – or your hand – in the water and douse
the baby*

The baby is probably yelling by
now.

Sound effect from Leader 1

	But if you dry her very firmly *(do so)* and bounce her up and down.
To the doll	There, that was all right, wasn't it?
	You can probably fool her into thinking it was just an ordinary bath. *(Hold the doll up)*
	Look – she's smiling …
	Would anyone like to try?

Wrap any volunteer in a towel and let them loose on the doll

BEFORE THE GOSPEL

The River Jordan

OK, let's put away this very baptized doll and think about what we've done.

Stand by bowl and be ready to scoop and pour water from the shell as you recite the Persons of the Holy Trinity

	We didn't drop the baby – that was pretty good – and we poured water on it, how many times? (**Three**)
	Yes, if we'd been saying the words, we would have baptized it in the Name of the Father *(pour some water)*
	And of the Son *(pour some water)*
	And of the Holy Spirit *(pour some water)*
	Did you notice how I poured the water?
Do it again	One of the rules about Holy Baptism is that the water must be running water. *(Pour it again)*
	You can't just dip your hands in the bowl, you must pour it over the baby.
	Running water is the sort that runs in streams and brooks and rivers – it's clean water, alive and fresh.

Leader 2 goes to the back of the room

'Running' is really important.
The River Jordan 'ran' through the Holy Land.
People 'ran' to John the Baptist to get baptized.
Christians have to be good at running, let's have a practice.

Get the kids to run on the spot

Yup, not bad, I think those knees could go higher.

One of the Leaders does an exaggerated running step

Can you do that? Let's see … *(After a very brief time)*
Stop! Stand still.

It's time for one of my really good jokes.
Are you ready?
If we go on like this we're going to run out of time …

Other Leaders groan

It's Gospel time, let's hear about John the Baptist.

Leader 2 quietly tips away the water while you're sorting out the procession

THE GOSPEL PROCESSION

THE GOSPEL   *St Luke 3.3, 7a, 21–22*

Optional Paraphrase

Crowds of people came out to be baptized by John and eventually Jesus Himself came to be baptized. Once He was baptized, and while He was praying, the Heavens opened, and the Holy Spirit came down upon Him in the bodily form of a dove. And a voice came from Heaven, 'You are my Beloved Son, with you I am well pleased.'

AFTER THE GOSPEL

Leader	*(Go through the Gospel)* Whom did John the Baptist baptize? (**Jesus**)

Do you think He tucked Him under His arm? (**No!**)
No, but I'm sure He made sure Jesus got very wet.
What else happened?

Read through the passage again if they're not sure

(**The Holy Spirit, a dove, came down over Jesus – and a Voice spoke to Him**)
Have you ever seen a dove turn up at a baptism? *(A rhetorical question)*
I never have.
But you know, the Holy Spirit does come to every baptism, we just don't see Him. *(Go back to the bowl)*
You see, the priest pours in the water – would someone do that for me?

A child pours in what's left in the jug; encourage the child to do it from a height

OK, there's the water. It's just ordinary water but, at a baptism, the priest asks God to make it holy.
He does that by praying to God, and calling on the Holy Spirit.
There are lots of ways of doing that.
The priest may breathe on the water, like this …

Breathe on the water and make the Sign of the Cross … (Use your whole hand to make the Sign of the Cross in the water)

And say, 'Bless this water by the power of the Holy Spirit.'
The Holy Spirit will always arrive if we ask Him, so we know He'll turn up.
And what about that Voice?
Whom do you suppose that was? (**God**)
Yup, God the Father. Well *He's* at every baptism too.
God the Father accepts the new Christian as a beloved child.
In some churches we greet the new Christian by saying,
'We are children of the same Heavenly Father, we welcome you.'
There are lots of bits to baptism, aren't there?
Let's put them all together.

ACTIVITY

CD8.1–9   *The children put together the Baptism Jigsaw.*

REHEARSAL

Practise your presentation for when you go back into church (see below).

FINAL PRAYER

Gather the children round the bowl of water, put a hand in, and let the water run very gently through your fingers

Leader   Jesus started out just as we do, by getting baptized. And, the moment He came out of the water, He heard His Father's voice saying, 'You are my Beloved Son.'
Jesus told us that God was our Father too. Let's say the prayer He taught us together,

Our Father … (p. xxxvi).

MUSIC

'Abba, Abba Father, you are the potter …' *works well here.*

BACK IN CHURCH

Take in the bowl and jug (now filled up with fresh water) and go down the front with the kids
Leader 2 holds the bowl

Child 1   Today we learnt how important it was to baptize people in running water …

Leader 1 pours in the water from a height

Child 2   It reminded us how the River Jordan runs through the Holy Land.
Child 3   It reminds us how people ran to John the Baptist to get baptized.
Child 4   We'd like to show you how important running is …
Child 5   We're going to run back to our places for the rest of Mass. *(They do)*

(CD8.1)

(CD8.6)

(CD8.7)

Sample cartoons for this script

Script 9   Happiness

Epiphany 2 (Church of England) or Ordinary Time 2 (Roman Catholic)

St John 2.1–11

THEME

A very simple message this morning, God wants us to be happy – as we can see from Jesus' wonderful first miracle at Cana.

SET UP

- The liturgical colour is White or Gold, though some churches may already have changed to Green. Check with your priest.

For the Gospel

- Glass or transparent cup in a plastic holder, to conceal the spot of red food colouring or Ribena on the bottom. If you can't find a plastic holder, hold the glass by its base with the napkin round it when you pick it up.
- You'll need to bring in another splash of food colour with you for the presentation.
- Large clear glass jug of water.
- A waiter's napkin.

For the party

- Anything you think suitable for a party – party crackers, disco music, balloons, fruit juice, tiny bits of party food. Set up any game you know that goes down well: you'll find some party games and templates on the CD-Rom.

WELCOME *the children and lead them in* **The Sign of the Cross** ✠ (p. xxxvi).

BEFORE THE KYRIE

Happiness

Leader	Ages ago, children were taught the Christian faith by learning the answers to a list of questions in a book called *The Penny Catechism*. The first question was easy, I bet you know the answer.

Question 1: Who made you? (**God**)
Quite right, the kid would reply: 'God made me.'
OK, how about Question 2?
Question 2: Why did God make you?

Take all answers – because He likes making things, because He loves me, or (quite often) I don't know why He made me – and use them as a springboard for the specific answer you are going to give

The answer in the catechism is: 'God made me to know Him, love Him and serve Him in this world, and to be happy with Him for ever in the next.'
That's a good answer, God made us to know, love and serve Him – and to be happy.
Christians are very keen on people being happy. The whole Christian story is about Jesus making us happy, it's why we call it the 'Good News'.
So, what makes us happy?

Take all answers – home in on games, food, parties: if the suggestions don't come naturally, make sure another Leader volunteers them

Games, music, nice food – most of that happens in a party. Perhaps we should have a party this morning.
But first, we need to remember what makes us unhappy? *(A rhetorical question)*
That can happen when we've done something wrong.
Let's get rid of any of that sort of unhappiness now.

THE KYRIE

Leader   God our Father, you are always ready to forgive our sins,
              Lord have mercy
              Lord have mercy

              Lord Jesus, you came to save us from our sins,
              Christ have mercy
              Christ have mercy

              God the Holy Spirit, help us to be sorry for our sins and ask for forgiveness,
              Lord have mercy
              Lord have mercy

Ask the children to repeat **The Prayer for Forgiveness** *after you* (**p. xxxvi**).

OPENING PRAYER	God our Father You made us to know you Love you, and serve you. You made us to be happy. Thank you for your kindness to us. Help us to be happy, In the way you want us to be, Through Jesus our Lord. **Amen**

BEFORE THE GOSPEL

Leader	Right, well today we're going to hear about Jesus' first miracle. Did He walk on water? Did He still a storm? Did He catch lots of fish? Nope, He made 40 gallons of wine – just to make people happy. Let's hear it.

THE GOSPEL PROCESSION

THE GOSPEL   *St John 2.1–11*

Read the Gospel freely, it's a very good story; have the spiked glass ready and a large jug of water: pour the water (from an immense height) at verse 8: 'He said to them, "Now pour it out …"' Then add the line, 'The water had become wine.'

If you make sure the 'servant' doing the pouring flourishes the napkin over his arm, the children are so fascinated by the napkin they don't inspect the glass.

A grown-up washes out the glass and refills the jug, ready for the presentation Back in Church.

AFTER THE GOSPEL

Leader   That's one of my favourite Gospels. Jesus saved a wedding feast at
          Cana by turning water into wine.
          I bet that feast turned into one of the happiest and noisiest wedding
          parties they'd ever had in Cana.
          Well, Jesus liked parties – so I guess Christians should.
          Why don't we have a party?

Party Time!

Run the party.
CD9.1–3 *Keep the games quite slick so the children don't feel aimless. (Ideas on the
CD-Rom.) Leave time to rehearse the presentation Back in Church.*

REHEARSAL

Practise your presentation for when you go back into church (see below).

FINAL PRAYER

*Gather the kids into a circle, put some of the party stuff in the middle – balloons,
crackers (now pulled), anything you've got*

Leader   Well, that was a great party. I think we should thank God for it.
          We're going to do a Litany of Thanks – the response is:

          Blessed be God
          Blessed be God

          For friends to play with
          Blessed be God

          For games to play
          Blessed be God

          For all the happy times we have together
          Blessed be God

          God our Creator,
          We thank you that your Son, Jesus Christ,
          performed His first miracle at a party.
          Help us to be like Him this week
          And bring happiness to others wherever we go. **Amen**

BACK IN CHURCH

Take in the newly spiked glass, napkin and jug of water

Leader   Today the children in church learnt a very useful trick – how to turn
                    water into wine. Watch this:
                    Here's an empty glass.

Child holds up the glass, concealing its splash of food colour

                    And here's a jug of clear water.

Another child holds up the jug

                    And now the impressive moment when …

The kid pours the water into the glass

                    water turns into wine!

Acknowledge any applause
Turn to the children

                    Did we really turn water into wine, kids? (**No!**)
                    No, it was a trick – but Jesus did.

Child   It was the first miracle Jesus ever performed.

Script 10   The Bible

Epiphany 3 (Church of England) or Ordinary Time 3 (Roman Catholic)

St Luke 4.16–21

THEME

The setting for Jesus' first sermon is His local synagogue. He reads from an Isaiah scroll and speaks as 'all the eyes in the synagogue were fixed on Him'. Jesus' roots (humanly speaking) were His Jewish faith and His neighbours in Nazareth. This session gives the children a taste of that faith, especially the Jewish passion for the scriptures, exemplified by the story of Hillel and the window sill.

SET UP

- The liturgical colour is White or Gold, though some churches may already have changed to Green. Check with your priest.
- A Bible.
- Make an Isaiah scroll (template on the CD-Rom – **CD10.1**), wrap it in a nice scarf and place it in a box. (A shoe box is OK, but if you've got anything more solid, use that.)

or

- Contact the educational supplier, TTS, who sell a miniature Western-style Torah scroll for £11 (at the time of writing). It comes complete with cover and pointer. Their website is www.tts-shopping.com, and you'll find the Torah in the RE/Judaism section.
- A votive light.
- A music stand or lectern.
- Cast Leader 2, or any kid who is good at reading, as Jesus. This person should have seen the script beforehand.
- Pictures from the CD-Rom.

WELCOME *the children and lead them in* **The Sign of the Cross** ✠ (**p. xxxvi**).

THE KYRIE   God our Father, you are always ready to forgive our sins,
            Lord have mercy
            Lord have mercy

            Lord Jesus, you came to save us from our sins,
            Christ have mercy
            Christ have mercy

            Holy Spirit, you help us be sorry for our sins and seek forgiveness,
            Lord have mercy
            Lord have mercy

Ask the children to repeat **The Prayer for Forgiveness** *after you* (**p. xxxvi**).

OPENING   God of Abraham and Isaac,
PRAYER   We thank you for our elder brothers in Faith, the Jewish people.
          Help Christians and Jews
          to know each other,
          and love each other,
          as we join in the worship
          of the One True God. **Amen**

BEFORE THE GOSPEL

The Jewish Faith

Leader   Today we prayed to the God of Abraham and Isaac.
Pick up a Bible   Those guys lived thousands of years ago. We find them

Rifle through the Old Testament

            right at the beginning of the Bible.
            They were the first people to get to know God and try to do His will.
            We owe them a lot.
            Does anyone know what people Abraham and Isaac belonged to?
            Were they British? (**No**)
            What were they? (**Jewish**)*
            Quite right, they were Jews – and very famous ones.
            Can you think of any other famous Jews?

*The answers, if any, will depend on the kids' ages: take what comes and, if they don't
get to the New Testament, put up cartoons 10.1 and 10.2*

---

* Actually Abraham started off as a Sumerian, but he is the father of the Jewish race.

CD10.2	Who have we got here? (**Mary and Jesus**)

Who have we got here? (**Mary and Jesus**)
What nationality are they? (**Jewish**)
Yep, Mary was a Jew and
Jesus was a Jew.
The Jews were God's chosen race, and He sent His Son to them.
So Jesus was brought up in a Jewish family and He went, with the other kids, to the synagogue every Saturday, and there He prayed and listened to the Bible.
Jesus would have called the Bible, the 'Torah'.*

Write up 'Torah'

He loved it.
Actually all Jews love the Torah. They feel when they're reading it, they're really getting to know God. Some Jews spend years studying the Torah, I'm going to tell you a story about one of them.

The Story of Hillel

Leader 1 tells the story, Leader 2 puts up the pictures. The snow (**CD10.8**) *goes over Hillel as he sits on the sill*

CD10.3   There was once a poor Jewish student called Hillel.
He was training to be a rabbi, so he went to college, and the thing he
CD10.4   loved learning about most was the Torah.
But to get into college you had to pay a couple of pennies to the porter at the gate, and one day Hillel searched all his pockets and discovered he hadn't any money at all.
The porter shut the door on him and Hillel looked at the college and
CD10.5   felt quite desperate.
There was the college, and inside all the other students were hearing about the Law, and he couldn't get in. So he began to climb up the
CD10.6   building …
And when he got to his classroom, he sat on the window sill, pressed
CD10.7   his ear to the glass, and sat there –
Listening …
Then it began to snow.
An hour or so later, the students inside couldn't understand why the day had gone dark so quickly. 'It must be the snow,' they thought. 'Oh yes, look, there's a great lump of it leaning against the window.'

---

* Strictly speaking, 'Torah' means 'law' and can only be taken to apply to the first five books of the Old Testament. But the Jews also use it in a wider sense to apply to the Old Testament, which is the way it is used here.

CD10.8   So they opened the window – and discovered Hillel, covered in snow and completely unconscious. *(Put the snow over* **CD10.7***)*
He had been listening so hard, he hadn't noticed the snow falling, and now he was completely frozen.
But the students brushed the snow off, got him into the warm, and eventually Hillel thawed out. And the moment he could sit up, he said,

CD10.9   'Right, let's go on hearing about the Torah!'
That's how much he loved the Bible.
Well, Jesus was a Jew and He loved the Bible too.
In fact, His very first sermon was in the local synagogue, with all His neighbours sitting round.

The Synagogue

Leader 1   Now, to get a feel of the Gospel this morning we need to rearrange this room.
Jesus started off His preaching in a synagogue – so I think we'll make ourselves a synagogue.
Synagogue just means 'meeting place'. It's like a church without an altar.
Instead it has an Ark. *(Hold up your box)*
The Ark is a chest and in it *(open the box and show them)* it has the Torah, wrapped up in a beautiful scarf.
The Ark should be on the Eastern side of the synagogue, where's East?

Work it out   It should be quite high.

Place a chair on a table and ask a child to put the Ark on it vertically; the Torah should be standing up

And there should be a light burning in front of it.

Get the children to place the votive light before the Ark, and light it

OK, now we have to sort out the chairs.
They are placed in a square round the other important part of the synagogue, the reading desk. It's called a 'Bimah'.

Ask Leader 2 to set a lectern or music stand in the centre of the room and arrange the chairs in a square round the Bimah. Leave a space in the row in front of the Ark, you need room for a procession from the Ark to the Bimah
While you are doing this, move your Gospel table to the side of the room facing the Ark, and make a space between the chairs that side as well, for the Gospel Procession

Excellent. Now I'd like you all to sit down.*

Everyone sits, the person playing Jesus as well, and Leader 1 goes to the Bimah

Of course this is only a pretend synagogue, so we'll welcome the Gospel as we normally do.

THE GOSPEL PROCESSION

THE GOSPEL   *St Luke 4.16–21*

Leader 1   When Jesus came to Nazareth, where He had been brought up, He went to the synagogue on the Sabbath day, as was His custom. He stood up to read.

Jesus gets up and goes to the Bimah

And the scroll of the prophet Isaiah was given to Him. *(Look up)* That means the Ark would have been opened and the Torah taken out. The Torah was so holy that everyone stands in its presence.

Ask a child to open the box, unwrap the Torah and bring it to Jesus
Everyone stands

He unrolled the scroll and found this place …

Jesus unrolls the scroll and reads

Jesus   The Spirit of the Lord is upon me,
because He has anointed me
to bring good news to the poor.
He has sent me to proclaim release to the captives
and recovery of sight to the blind,
to let the oppressed go free,
to proclaim the year of the Lord's favour.

Leader 1   He rolled up the scroll and gave it back to the attendant

The scroll goes back to the Ark

Jesus sat down. So do we … *(All sit)*
And the eyes of everyone in the synagogue were fixed on Him. Then He said to them,

Jesus   Today this scripture has come true …

---

* The boys and girls sit together; men and women were not necessarily separated in first-century synagogues.

AFTER THE GOSPEL

Leader 1   That was an amazing sermon. Jesus picked up the Torah and said,
'The Torah is alive – it's coming true, right now.'

Hold up the Bible

It's always been wonderful to read the Bible but, since Jesus has
come on Earth, you have to be careful when you open it – *(open it
and jerk the book)* – It's alive!
OK, let's put the room back to normal.

REHEARSAL

Practise your presentation for when you go back into church (see below).

FINAL   Our final prayer is taken from Psalm 18.
PRAYER   The response is
Your words are alive, O Lord
Your words are alive, O Lord

The Torah of the Lord is perfect
It refreshes my soul
Your words are alive, O Lord

The rule of the Lord is to be trusted
It gives wisdom to the simple
Your words are alive, O Lord

The teaching of the Lord is right
It gladdens my heart
Your words are alive, O Lord

MUSIC

*The Jewish folk song 'Shalom my friends' works well here. The lyrics vary, but one
excellent version is:*

Shalom* my friends, Shalom my friends
Shalom, Shalom
The Peace of God I give you today
Shalom, Shalom

You can find the tune on YouTube

---

* Shalom is Hebrew for 'peace'.

BACK IN CHURCH

The children go in with the Ark and the Isaiah scroll

Leader 1   Today we hear how Jesus went to the synagogue, and a scroll of the prophet Isaiah was handed to Him.

One child opens the Ark
Another unwraps the scroll
Another hands it to 'Jesus'

Leader 1   Jesus unrolled the scroll and read from it …

He unrolls the scroll and reads

Jesus   The Spirit of the Lord is upon me,
              because He has anointed me
              to bring good news to the poor.

Leader   Everyone in the synagogue looked at Him, and Jesus said …

Turn to the kids

              What did He say, children?

Everyone   **Today this scripture has come true!**

(CD10.4)

(CD10.3)

Sample cartoons for this script

Script 11   Candlemas

Epiphany 4 (Church of England)

St Luke 2.22. 24–33, 36a, 38

THEME

Candlemas is the very last day of Christmas: if you haven't taken your decorations down by now, you never will. It is also the day Jesus was presented in the Temple (not circumcised – that had happened when He was eight days old). Every first-born Jewish boy was deemed to belong to God, rather than his parents, and was supposed to be 'redeemed' by them, in the Temple, for the price of 5 shekels. The obligation was totally optional and it is a tribute to the piety of Mary and Joseph that they bothered to trek up to Jerusalem to present their son. It was there they met Simeon and Anna and the peculiar character of this feast was established. Simeon hailed the Child as 'a light to lighten the Gentiles' and the Church has been dishing out candles on this day ever since.

SET UP

- The liturgical colour is White or Gold.
- Pictures from the CD-Rom.
- Birthday candles.
- Cheap ready-made birthday cake – or a lump of plasticine, if hard pressed.
- Three candles, already lit before the session begins.
- Hand-held candles with wax guards, one for each child – make sure that very small children have theirs held by their parents.

- Matches and a taper.

Materials for a Christingle

- A vegetable knife for the leader to make a hole in the top of the fruit – to stick in the candle
- Each child needs:
  - a clementine
  - a candle to stick in the top
  - a red ribbon
  - four cloves
  - and some dolly mixture or glacé fruit on cocktail sticks.
- Have an orange ready to make a monster Christingle to take back into church.

BEFORE THE WELCOME

Try to dim the lights in the hall, and have the three candles lit at the front.
Matches and a taper to hand.

WELCOME *the children and lead them in* **The Sign of the Cross ✠ (p. xxxvi).**

BEFORE THE KYRIE

Leader	Today is Candlemas.
	And we've got three candles lit already – we're going to use them for the Kyrie.

This week the Leaders say the Kyrie.

THE KYRIE	God our Father,
	Every time we forget you, we walk into the dark,
Snuff a candle	Lord have mercy
	Lord have mercy
	Lord Jesus
	Every time we do something wrong, we turn out a light,
Snuff a candle	Christ have mercy
	Christ have mercy
	Holy Spirit
	Every time we forget you, we put out the flame you have lit in our hearts,
Snuff a candle	Lord have mercy
	Lord have mercy

Leader 1   But every time we ask for forgiveness, your light fills our hearts.

Light all three candles again

Ask the children to repeat **The Prayer for Forgiveness** *after you* (**p. xxxvi**).

OPENING	*Ask the children to repeat this after you*
PRAYER	**Lord Jesus,**
	You are the Light of the World
	Thank you for taking the darkness away.
	Amen

BEFORE THE GOSPEL

Leader 1   OK, let's think about candles.

Hold up some birthday cake candles

What sort of candles are these? (**Birthday candles**)
Anybody here ever blown out a birthday candle?

Stagger back at the response

Anyone blown them out in one go?

Look sceptical   Oh yeah? I'd like to see that …

Who's blown out ten candles? *(Or whatever age, in the upper limit, you think feasible)*

Ask the candle blower to come forward

OK, we'll put ten candles on this cake. Light them … *(Do so)*
Take your time – let's see you blow them out.

Congratulate the kid, whatever the result

How about the little ones? Is there anyone here who's five? *(Or even younger if you've got toddlers present)*
Have you blown out candles?
Would you like to try?

If a little group presents themselves, get them to circle the cake and stick in a representative amount of candles – three for Jimmy, two for Kate, and so on

OK, 1, 2, 3 Blow!
Fantastic! I like candles.

BEFORE THE GOSPEL

Leader 1 — Now in church at this moment, the grown-ups are holding candles for the Gospel. So I thought we'd do the same here.
But first let's work out why we're so keen on candles today.
It's all to do with Jesus' first visit to the Temple.
Mary and Joseph took Him there when He was tiny, to present Him to God. It cost 5 shekels – unless you were very poor: poor people paid with two turtle doves.

CD11.1 — Well, here are the Holy Family.
What do you think? Are they rich or poor? (**Poor**)
When Mary and Joseph and the Baby got to the Temple they were
CD11.2 — met by an old woman, Anna,
CD11.3 — and an old man, Simeon.
What happened next is in the Gospel, let's welcome it with light.

Light the children's candles – put the grown-ups on candle watch …

THE GOSPEL PROCESSION

THE GOSPEL *St Luke 2.22, 24–33, 36a, 38*

Optional Paraphrase (*with the order of the verses slightly changed*)

Mary and Joseph brought Jesus to the Temple to present Him to God, offering a sacrifice of two young turtle doves.
An old woman was in the Temple when they came. Her name was Anna and she was 84 years old. As soon as she saw Jesus she thanked God for Him.
An old man called Simeon joined them. God had promised him that he would not die before he saw the Saviour. And as soon as *he* saw Jesus, he took Him in his arms and said, 'You can take me now, Lord, for I'm a happy man. I have seen your Saviour at last. This child will be a light to lighten the Gentiles, and will be the glory of your people Israel.'

AFTER THE GOSPEL

Ask the kids to blow out their candles and sit down

Leader   So Simeon said, 'This child will be a light to lighten the Gentiles.'
                What's a Gentile? *(A rhetorical question probably)*
                It's someone who is not Jewish.
                That's us.
                Gentiles are so glad to hear that Jesus was sent to be a 'light to
                lighten us', that we've lit candles on this day ever since.
                We're going to make some special candles now – let's get round this
                table.

Take them to a table where the Christingle materials are laid out

ACTIVITY

Construct the monster Christingle in front of the children

Leader   This orange is the world.
                It is surrounded by God's love.

Tie the ribbon round the middle

                And it's full of wonderful things,
                these are the fruits of the world ...

Stick on the dolly mixture or glacé fruit

                God loved the world so much that
                He sent Jesus down to die for it ...

*Stick the four little cloves round the top (they
represent the nails that crucified Christ)*

                And Jesus became the Light of the
                World.

Stick in the candle and light it
Help the children make their Christingles, then gather them into a circle

REHEARSAL

Practise your presentation for when you go back into church (see below).

FINAL PRAYER

Ask the children to hold their Christingles so everyone can admire the way the candle flame shines on the child holding it

Leader   Jesus is the Light of the World, we are His people,
                and He wants us to be lights in the world too.
                Let us pray,

                Lord Jesus Christ
                You have called us to be lights in the world
                Grant that we may so shine,
                That people may see the good we do
                And praise Almighty God. **Amen**

BACK IN CHURCH

Scripts for kids in church. One child reads the first bit, another holds up the Christingle – make sure it is lit! – another points out the bits

SCRIPT

Reader 1   Today is the day after Candlemas, and we have been thinking about
                Jesus the 'Light of the World'.
                We've made a Christingle to show you how Jesus is the 'Light of the
                World'.
                It looks like this …

One kid holds up the orange – another goes through the bits

Reader 2   The orange is the world.
                The ribbon shows God's love surrounding the world.
                The sweets are the fruits of the world.
                God loved the world so much He sent Jesus down to die for it.
                The cloves are the nails that crucified Jesus.
                The candle shows that Jesus is the Light of the World.

Script 12   Stilling the Storm

2 before Lent (Church of England)

St Luke 8.22–25

This is a Sunday when Anglicans and Catholics have different Gospels. Check with your priest first, but most Anglicans will be hearing this one, the 'Stilling of the Storm' (*St Luke 8.22–25*), while Catholics will be listening to *St Luke 4.21–30*, which you'll find in *Script 13*. (The RC Church does not single out a Sunday two weeks before Lent for special observance. In the CofE use this script, rather than the one with a 'proper' number for this particular date.)

THEME

St Luke's version of this famous incident strips the story down to its bare essentials: the disciples are caught in a violent storm, Jesus is fast asleep, their desperate cries wake Him and He stills the storm. Our Lord's sole remark in this account is 'Where is your faith?' and the disciples subside into awe. For an adult Christian, this terse recital has resonances with critical moments in our own lives when we appear to have lost God, but children enjoy the story as a straightforward adventure. It seems unfair to take the gloss off Luke's uncomplicated approach and in this session we concentrate on the actual boat, the danger, and the escape.

SET UP

- The liturgical colour is Green.
- Foil trays that the children can turn into boats (template on the CD-Rom).
- Plasticine, Blu Tack or modelling clay.
- Bamboo or wooden skewers.
- Sail-shaped pieces of paper (see template on CD-Rom).
- A pile of pennies and small stones.
- Bowls of water – about one per four children. (Or a large bowl for you to give a demo to the entire group.)
- A couple of large towels.
- If you have the time, run the boat-sinking activity beforehand, so you know how many coins or stones it takes to sink a boat.
- If anybody has got a model boat they could bring in, it would work well in the final prayer.

WELCOME *the children and lead them in* **The Sign of the Cross** ✠ (**p. xxxvi**).

THE KYRIE   Lord Jesus, you came to bring us back to God,
Lord have mercy
Lord have mercy

Lord Jesus, you came to heal us from our sins,
Christ have mercy
Christ have mercy

Lord Jesus, you came to tell us how much God loves us,
Lord have mercy
Lord have mercy

Ask the children to repeat **The Prayer for Forgiveness** *after you* (**p. xxxvi**).

Leader   Today's Gospel is about Jesus and His friends going for a sail in a boat. It's a good Sunday for thinking about sailors, fishermen and anyone who's sailing the high seas.
Let's remember them to God our Father.

OPENING   Eternal Father,
PRAYER   Lord of Sea and Sky
Bless and protect all sailors and fishermen
As they go about their daily work at sea.
Be with them in storms and tempests
And bring them safely back to harbour,
we ask this through Jesus, your Son. **Amen**

Boats

Leader 1   Today we're going to talk boats – in fact, we're going to *make* boats
– let's get cracking …

Take the children over to a table where you've set up the foil trays, canes, paper and so on. Using the template on the CD-Rom (**CD12.1**), *show the kids how to pinch the trays into a boat shape, thread on the sail, and fix the mast on the boat*
Then launch your fleet
Admire them for a moment, and then turn to the bowl where your own ship is floating

Of course this all looks very nice while the water is calm – but suppose the weather changes (*gently wobble your bowl*), the boat will begin to rock …
Perhaps some water will get in the boat (*splash some in*) – that could be serious. I wonder how much extra water these boats can take?

Sinking Boats

Dish out penny coins and small stones to the children
Ask them to put them, very carefully, one by one into their boats (Start with the coins)
How many can the boat take before it sinks?
Do this yourself with your boat and get it to crisis point – low in the water, but not actually sinking
Go round, inspect the wrecks, and show the kids your boat

Leader	This boat is on the verge of sinking: look how low in the water it is – one more penny or a big wave – and it will go …
	Well, that's all right with a toy boat. But supposing you were on a boat like that? The water filling up, the waves getting higher – how would you feel? (**Frightened**)
	You're right – very frightened I should think.
	The Gospel today is about a boat, and 12 very frightened men. We'll hear it after we've mopped up a bit …

Salvage the boats and pennies, and dry off anyone who needs it

THE GOSPEL PROCESSION

THE GOSPEL   *St Luke 8.22–25*

AFTER THE GOSPEL

Run through the story

Leader	So there were the disciples on the boat – and a storm blew up – and the boat began to fill with water and they were all terrified.
	Actually one person wasn't terrified. Who was that? (**Jesus**)
	What was He doing? (**He was asleep**)
	Yes, you know, I don't think Jesus was having a nap. I think He must have been incredibly tired to sleep through a storm.
	Anyway, He didn't wake up fast enough for His friends and they began yelling at Him.

Optional Section for Older Children

> Have any of you had that feeling?
> Has anyone wanted to say, 'Come on, God, hurry up!'

(This might turn out to be a rhetorical question)

Sometimes people feel that God has disappeared for a moment.
The disciples felt like that.
'Where's Jesus?' they yelled. 'Master! we're dying!'
And He was there all the time, very quiet, very still, but deep in the storm – with His disciples.

BEFORE THE FINAL PRAYER

Hold up a model boat, or one of the boats the children have made

Sometimes people think that our life is like a journey on a boat.
We start off from one harbour when we're born.

Start moving the boat

And often the weather is fine and we have a great time – and then sometimes there's a wave or two.

Rock the boat

Or there may even be a storm.

Really rock the boat

But, we're in that boat with our mates – that's good to know – and somewhere on that boat we'll find Jesus.
He might be very quiet – but He's there, ready to help.

Ask the children to repeat the final prayer after you

FINAL	Lord Jesus
PRAYER	Help of Christians
	Hear us when we call you.
	Save us from trouble and danger,
	And bring us safely
	To our final harbour,
	Our true home in Heaven. Amen

MUSIC

Nothing beats the traditional hymn 'Eternal Father, strong to save' *on a Sunday like this.*

REHEARSAL

Practise your presentation for when you go back into church (see below).

BACK IN CHURCH

The children line up with their model boats

Leader   Today we heard about Jesus and his disciples sailing their boat in a
                storm.
                We made our own boats.

The kids hold them up

                And we thought that our life was like a boat journey.
                We sail off the moment we are born.

The kids move their boats

                And sometimes there's a wave or two.

The kids rock their boats

                And sometimes there's a storm.

The kids really rock their boats

                But somewhere on that boat we'll find Jesus.
                He might be very quiet, but He's there.

The boats go still

                We prayed to Jesus by one of His great titles this morning.
                The children will tell you what it was.

Kids   **Lord Jesus,**
                Help of Christians.

(CD12.1)

Script 13   Jesus Annoys His Neighbours

Ordinary Time 4

St Luke 4.16–22, 24, 28–30

This is a Sunday when Anglicans and Catholics have different Gospels. Check with your priest first, but Catholics will be hearing this one, 'Jesus Annoys His Neighbours' (*St Luke 4.21–30*), while Anglicans will be listening to *St Luke 8.22–25*, which you'll find in *Script 12*.

THEME

Jesus' first sermon in Nazareth went well, but there came a moment – probably a little later (St Luke seems to have combined two incidents) – when people stopped being amazed that Jesus could preach so well, and began to listen to Him. It was at this point that they got annoyed, so annoyed they wanted to kill Him. This session introduces the children to Simon, an imaginary next door neighbour, as we try to understand this reaction. It also teaches them to 'freeze' – a useful skill anyway, and essential for this re-telling of the Gospel story.

SET UP

- The liturgical colour is Green.
- Pictures from the CD-Rom.
- Audio player and dance music to accompany a game of 'Statues'.
- The box, scarf and Torah scroll from last Sunday (*Script 10* The Bible). If you didn't run that script then, look it up for instructions on how to make the scroll.
- Cast Leader 2 as Simon and find two good readers among the kids. One has to play Jesus, the other interjects a line into the Gospel. Both should look at the script beforehand – but they read their lines, there's nothing to memorize.

WELCOME *the children and lead them in* **The Sign of the Cross** ✠ **(p. xxxvi).**

THE KYRIE   Lord Jesus, you came to bring us back to God,
Lord have mercy
Lord have mercy

> Lord Jesus, you came to heal us from our sins,
> Christ have mercy
> **Christ have mercy**
>
> Lord Jesus, you came to tell us how much God loves us
> Lord have mercy
> **Lord have mercy**

Ask the children to repeat **The Prayer for Forgiveness** *after you* (**p. xxxvi**).

OPENING   Lord God, Father of all
PRAYER   As we hear the Gospel today
              Help us to welcome it with open hearts
              So that we may believe you sent your Son, Jesus Christ,
              into the world to save us. **Amen**

BEFORE THE GOSPEL

Freezing

Leader 1   Good morning everyone – just to start with, I want to talk about films. I expect you've all watched DVDs, haven't you?
Yes, I thought so.
Hands up anyone who's ever pushed the 'Pause' button?
What happens? (**The DVD pauses**)
What does it look like? (**Everything stops mid-action**)
Can you show me?
Let's have an action moment on a DVD.

Ask two children to come forward and mime an imaginary quarrel – arms waving, fingers pointing, then shout

              PAUSE!

The children should freeze – run it again if they don't

              If you were doing that on stage, I'd shout FREEZE!
              Let's see how many of you can 'freeze' when I ask you to.
              Stand up everyone.

Get the kids to run on the spot, then shout

              FREEZE!
              Yup, good – but wobbly. We need to freeze halfway through the Gospel today – perhaps we'd better practise.

GAME

Statues

Play a game of Statues. Ask the children (and grown-ups) to dance to the music on your audio player. The moment the music stops they should freeze like a statue. (If the children are not keen on dancing, ask them to walk round the room like a monster – you usually get a crop of robots and King Kongs.) Don't bother to play the game competitively, sympathize with the wobblers, and run it again. Give them about three goes.

	Well, I think we're all pretty good at freezing. Now, before we read the Gospel we need to meet someone …
CD13.1	**Simon Next Door**
CD13.2	*Put up the first picture*
Leader	We don't actually meet this chap in the Bible, but he's somebody Jesus might have known, he was Jesus' next door neighbour. We've decided to call him 'Simon'.
CD13.3	Simon was a chap who talked to Joseph over the fence.
CD13.4	And said hello to Our Lady as she hung out the washing. Of course he knew Jesus. He could hear Jesus playing round the
CD13.5	house.
CD13.6	And he watched Him grow up. And naturally Simon was in the synagogue on the day Jesus gave His first sermon.

Jesus in the Synagogue

Adapt this section in the light of what you did last week. The key feature of Script 10 is that Jesus went to His local synagogue and was given a Bible scroll to read

Leader	Jews go to the synagogue every Saturday to listen to the Bible and pray together. They call the Bible, the 'Torah' – and the Torah is written on scrolls, like this –

Show them the Torah scroll

It is very holy, and kept wrapped up in a box called the 'Ark'.
I'll wrap this scroll up and put it away.

Name (choose a child)

Would you look after the Torah for me and bring it up when I want it?
OK, I think we're ready to hear the Gospel – no, wait a minute, we haven't got Simon.

Leader 2   I'll be Simon.

He/she goes and sits very obviously among the kids
As the Gospel Procession forms up, ask the child playing Jesus to stand beside you

THE GOSPEL PROCESSION

THE GOSPEL   *St Luke 4.16–22, 24, 28–30*

Optional Paraphrase

Leader 1   Jesus went with everyone else to the local synagogue on Saturday.
                There He was asked to read from the Torah and somebody handed
                the Bible scroll to Him …

Ask a child to open the Ark, unwrap the scroll, and bring it to 'Jesus'

                Jesus unrolled the scroll and read. *(He does so)*
Jesus   The Spirit of the Lord is upon me,
                because He has anointed me
                to bring good news to the poor.
Leader 1   Then He rolled up the scroll and gave it back to the attendant.

The scroll goes back into the Ark and is handed back to its keeper

                The eyes of the whole congregation were fixed on Him – and He
                started His sermon with these words,
Jesus   Today this scripture has come true …
Leader 1   Then He began to preach.
                Everyone was amazed. Simon couldn't believe his ears.
Simon   *Getting up and looking round*
                I don't believe it!
                See that bloke? I've known Him since he was a kid …
Leader 1   Someone else said,
Child 2   I know Him! He's the son of Joseph.
Leader 1   They couldn't believe Jesus could speak so well, and they listened in
                astonishment. Then they began to realize what Jesus was saying …
Jesus   The scripture says:
                'The Spirit of the Lord is upon me.'
                That means me – the Spirit of the Lord is on me.
                I'm the one who has come to preach good news to the poor.
Simon   *Standing up*
                Oi! Jesus!
                That's not right!
                You're just a carpenter's son.

Jesus	I thought this would happen.
	Prophets are never welcome in their home town.
Simon	Who says you're a prophet?
	Get Him, lads!
Leader 1	And the whole synagogue got up.
	Everyone get up!
	They were furious.
	Be angry, shake your fists …
	Now watch this bit, when I say 'go' – come forward, and when I say 'freeze' – freeze!
	And they grabbed Jesus and tried to throw Him down a cliff.
	Go! *(and almost immediately)* Freeze!
	Stay frozen …
	And Jesus slipped away.

The child playing Jesus weaves through the frozen kids and goes to the end of the room

Leader	Unfreeze!
	Everybody looked at each other in bewilderment – but Jesus had gone.

AFTER THE GOSPEL

Ask the children to sit down

Leader 1	Why was everyone so cross?

Take all answers, and establish that they didn't believe Jesus because they knew Him too well

It's like hearing *Name (choose some kid)* is going to be the next Pope – or that *Name* has just won 'Britain's Got Talent'.

Of course it *might* happen to them – but it would take a lot of believing.

REHEARSAL

Practise your presentation for when you go back into church (see below).

FINAL
PRAYER

Our last prayer comes from Psalm 70.
It was written by someone who had trusted God since he was a kid:
I think Jesus knew this psalm very well.
The response is

In you, O Lord, I put my trust
In you, O Lord, I put my trust

In you, O Lord, I put my trust,
pay heed to me and save me
In you, O Lord, I put my trust

Be a rock where I can take refuge,
a mighty stronghold to save me
In you, O Lord, I put my trust

It is you, O Lord, I long for,
I have trusted you since I was a child.
In you, O Lord, I put my trust

Let my mouth be filled with your praise
That I may tell of your glory all day long,
In you, O Lord, I put my trust

Glory Be ... (see p. xxxvii).

BACK IN CHURCH

Leader 2 and the children go to the front and bunch up on one side as Jesus' indignant neighbours. The Jesus character stands with Leader 1

Leader 1   Today we heard how Jesus

Bring him forward

annoyed His neighbours.

Wave a hand in the direction of the mob

That lot over there.
Jesus told them that the Bible has come true, and He was the one sent by God to preach the Gospel to the poor.
They were furious ...

The kids shake their fists

And rushed forward to grab Him.

The children rush forward – and FREEZE just before they get to Jesus

> And Jesus slipped through them and went away.

Jesus slips through the crowd and ends up on the other side
Everyone unfreezes and faces front

To the kids	Why were Jesus' neighbours so cross?
Child 1	Because they knew Him.
Child 2	They thought He was just a carpenter.
Leader 1	Were they right?
All the kids	No!
Child 3	Jesus was the Son of God.

(CD13.3)

(CD13.4)

Sample cartoons for this script   (CD13.6)

Script 14 The Transfiguration of Jesus

1 before Lent (Church of England) or Lent 2 (Roman Catholic)

St Luke 9.28–36

If you are using this session for Lent 2, the liturgical colour will be Purple and you should use the opening sequence of prayers provided on pages 98–9 for Script 17.

THEME

Peter, James and John accompany Jesus to the top of a mountain. They knew from the scriptures that Moses and Elijah had climbed up mountains to meet God, and sure enough they see (and hear) Him too. But the experience is deeply unsettling. Jesus is transfigured before their eyes and they hear God the Father acknowledging His Son. The next minute Jesus reverts to His everyday self – the ordinary Jesus who has been with them in Galilee. They didn't have to go mountaineering to see God, He was there all the time.

SET UP

- The liturgical colour is Green.
- Pictures from the CD-Rom.
- Rucksack packed with climbing or walking gear: put in anything you think looks feasible – a slab of chocolate, torch, light blanket, compass, whistle.
- A length of rope. Leader 2 starts the session with the rope coiled up and slung over her shoulders.
- A walking stick – a high-tech walker's stick if you've got one, but any stick will do.
- A tiny Union Jack.
- Mark two 'crevasses' on the floor with lines of coloured tape. Crevasse 1 should be just wide enough for a kid to jump over, Crevasse 2 is quite impossible.
- A plank or a ladder, anything the kids could use to walk on – on the flat – a long strip of cardboard is fine. It must be wide enough to clear Crevasse 2.

- Ask an older child to help with the rope at the end of the mountaineering session. Go through their 'wobble' moment beforehand (see below).
- Marker pen to draw a mountain on the flip chart.

WELCOME *the children and lead them in* **The Sign of the Cross** ✠ **(p. xxxvi).**

THE KYRIE   God our Father,
You always hear those who say they are sorry,
Lord have mercy
Lord have mercy

Lord Jesus,
We are sorry for the times we have forgotten you,
Christ have mercy
Christ have mercy

God, the Holy Spirit
Be with us in the coming week, as we try not to sin again,
Lord have mercy
Lord have mercy

Ask the children to repeat **The Prayer for Forgiveness** *after you* (**p. xxxvi**).

OPENING   Lord Jesus
PRAYER   You are always with us.
Help us to recognize you
In the Gospel this morning.
Help us to hear you
As we pray,
And help us to see you
in the Bread and Wine of the Altar. **Amen**

BEFORE THE GOSPEL

Climbing Kit

Leader 1   Today we are going to think about mountain climbing.

Bring forward Leader 2

Name here is very good at climbing mountains.
You can see she's got a rope and – what else have you got?

Leader 2 unpacks her rucksack and talks through its contents

Leader 1   What do you need the rope for?

Leader 2	Ah, that's very important, I'll show you. Anyone want to come mountaineering with me?

Line up the volunteers (you sometimes find they all volunteer – have a grown-up on hand to help the little ones)

Mountaineering

Turn the hall/room into a mountain. The children follow Leader 2 round the room doing everything she tells them

Leader 2	The most important rule in mountain climbing is following your leader. Right, I know the mountains round here – follow me … Hmm – here, for example, we've got a narrow ledge. Put your back against the mountain like this …

This is a blank wall, the children inch along it, with their backs to the wall

Do some patter	Don't look down! The ground's miles away … don't wobble … only six inches of ledge here … OK, I've got to the end – hold my hand as you jump off.

Grasp each kid's hand as he or she jumps back into the room
Leader 1 places a couple of chairs in the middle of the room

Leader 2	Right, now what? Ah, boulders – the first one's easy …

Everyone climbs over the first chair. Leader 2 stops at the second one

Hmm, tricky, I'll need my stick for this.

Place stick on chair and climb up, pass the stick back so the kids do the same

Fantastic, on we go – Oh no!

Stop at the first 'crevasse'

Look in	This is a crack in the mountain, a crevasse. It's unbelievably deep. Can we jump it? I'll go first.

Leap over Crevasse 1. The kids follow, insist they do it one by one – make sure no toddler falls into the abyss

Brilliant and now – oh no!

Stop at Crevasse 2

Another one! This is impossible …
OK, this is where I need my faithful plank.

Leader 1 hands over the plank/ladder or strip of cardboard
Leader 2 lays it across the crevasse and crosses with exaggerated care

Now, before you chaps do it – we're going to make sure you're really safe. Who can catch a rope?

Leader 2 throws one end of the rope over the crevasse to the kid you've cast for this difficult job. Leader 2 fastens the rope round her waist and gets the kid to do the same
Hold the rope taut between and ask the children to go over the plank, one by one, using the rope as a rail
The kid with the end of the rope goes over last, wobbles off, does a mock 'Aaargh!' and is pulled to safety by the Leader

That's why we need a rope …
And now the summit!

Look up as Leader 1 places a chair on a table

Aha, just room to put a flag at the top, to show we've got there.

Put Union Jack on the top of the chair

Brilliant – now we'll clear this mountain out of the way and sit down.

Old Testament Mountaineers

Once the children have settled

Leader 1   Why do you think people climb mountains?

Take all answers, establish things like it's fun, exciting, great view, etc

Yes, you're right. And some people, when they get to the top of a mountain, find it's so beautiful and still that they say their prayers. God can seem very close to you on a mountain.
People in the Bible were convinced that, if they wanted to meet God, a mountain was a good place to start.

CD14.1   Moses went up Mount Sinai, and there, amid thunder and lightning, he talked to God.

CD14.2   Elijah went up Mount Sinai as well and when *he* got to the top, he found that God talked to him as well,
but this time God spoke in a small, still voice.
Well, Jesus and three of His friends climbed a mountain too – we'll hear what happened to them in today's Gospel.

THE GOSPEL PROCESSION

Process the Gospel if you are reading this on the Sunday before Lent; no Gospel Procession if you are reading it in Lent.

THE GOSPEL   *St Luke 9.28–36*

Optional Paraphrase

Leader 2 draws a mountain and places the pictures

Leader 1   One day Jesus took His disciples, Peter and James and John, up a high mountain to pray …

CD14.1/CD14.2   *Stick up the pictures of Moses and Elijah. Draw in a mountain to stick up between them – they should appear to be hovering on each side*

Place **CD14.3**, *normal Jesus, on the top of the mountain*

And, as He was praying, His face shone, and His clothes became dazzling white.

Place **CD14.4**, *the transfigured Jesus, over* **CD14.3**

And Moses and Elijah appeared beside Him. *(Indicate those two)* Peter, James and John were so bewildered that they fell asleep, but as Moses and Elijah began to leave,

CD14.5   Peter called out,
'Lord, shall we make some tents for you and for Moses and Elijah?' (He didn't really know what he was saying.)

CD14.6   As he spoke a bright cloud overshadowed them and a Voice from the cloud said, 'This is my beloved Son, listen to Him!' Peter, James and John fell flat on their faces, but Jesus came down to them, touched them, and said, 'Don't be afraid, get up …' And Peter, James and John looked up, and found that everything had gone back to normal –

Remove cloud, Voice, Elijah and Moses, and transfigured Jesus

and they were alone with Jesus on the mountain top.

AFTER THE GOSPEL

Leader 1   So Peter, James and John went up a mountain with Jesus. Did they find God at the top?

Take all answers, establish that they did

They heard God the Father and they saw God the Son.

Hold up the transfigured Jesus

Then everything went back to normal, and they saw Jesus looking ordinary again.

Hold up normal Jesus

> And as they went down the mountain, I think they must have realized that they didn't need to go up a mountain to find God. God was Jesus, and He'd been with them all along.

REHEARSAL

Practise your presentation for when you go back into church (see below).

BEFORE THE FINAL PRAYER

> Well, Jesus has gone back to Heaven, but He's still with us.
> We don't have to climb mountains to find Him.
> We can find Him in the Bible, in our hearts and, especially, in the Bread and Wine of the Eucharist.

FINAL PRAYER

> Let us pray
> Lord Jesus
> Your friends, Peter, James and John
> Saw you in all your glory on the top of a mountain
> Help us to see you this morning
> As we kneel before the bread and the wine of the altar. **Amen**

BACK IN CHURCH

Go back in with the pictures of Moses, Elijah and the two pictures of Jesus

Leader   Today we heard how Moses

Child holds up Moses picture

> and Elijah

Another child holds up Elijah

> climbed mountains to meet God.
> We also heard how Jesus took three friends up a mountain
> and there they saw Him transfigured.

A child holds up the transfigured Jesus

> But, as they came down, Jesus went back to looking quite ordinary

Child holds up normal Jesus

> and Jesus' friends realized they didn't have to climb mountains to see God. He had been with them all the time.

Script 15   The Devil Tries It On Again …

Lent 1

St Luke 4.1–13

Lent

It is a good idea to get children used to the variety of the Church year by giving some seasons a special character. Christmas and Easter have such strong traditions they always stand out, but the 'Purple' seasons that set them off are another matter. Lent particularly benefits from having its own traditions (such as a mini-desert, Lenten prayers and so on) that turn up year after year. You'll find that the children often do a mock wail when their candles and bells are emphatically buried on Lent 1 but, next Lent, they'll look forward to burying them again.

THEME

This session marks the break between Lent and the rest of the year as we follow Jesus into the desert at the start of His ministry. A lay 'ashing' is provided in this session if you think some of the kids weren't ashed on Ash Wednesday. Check this out with your priest first. The Gospel is the classic Temptation of Jesus story. To give it context you might like to alert the children to the Devil's wicked ways by prefacing the Gospel with the story of his temptation of Adam and Eve in the Garden of Eden. Shape this session in the light of the time available to you. There's a lot to get through; setting up the desert and reading the Gospel are the main priorities.

SET UP

- The liturgical colour is Purple.
- Try to wear a purple top, or tie – even socks will do.
- Stuff to make a desert:
  - A deep baking tray filled with sand.
  - Some rocks or large stones.
  - Mini cacti, or candle cacti from a florist.
  - And any suitable extras – like a toy camel.
  - Plus a large candle, that will stand by itself in the sand, to represent Jesus.

- A large box to bury your candlesticks and bells in: covered with purple paper if you've got the time.
- Halloween props for the Devil, horns and a pitchfork – always go down well. It's no bad thing to make him look ridiculous.
- An apple.
- Picture from the CD-Rom.

Optional

- Ash – either see if there is any left over from Ash Wednesday, or make some by burning the charcoal used for incense (it'll take a good 15 minutes) or by burning up some small dry twigs. Cool the ash down with water. (You'll need a spot of water anyway to add to the ash and make it stick.)

WELCOME *the children and lead them in* **The Sign of the Cross** ✠ (p. xxxvi).

Leader	Did anybody notice the colour in church today? (**Purple**)
	What colour are my socks [or whatever ...]? (**Purple**)
	Yup, we're in Purple time.
	Purple is a dark, serious colour, and the church always goes into
	Purple when we're about to get ready for something –
	What are we getting ready for?

Give some hints – it's almost impossible to trigger the word 'Easter' without mentioning chocolate (**Easter**)

Absolutely, Easter – ages away, not for another six weeks.

But Easter is so important that we start getting ready six weeks before.

Those six weeks have a special name – does anyone know it? (**Lent**)

OPTIONAL ASHING

Leader	Lent started last Wednesday and people came to church to be 'ashed'.
	We start Lent by putting a cross on our foreheads – it's made of ash.

Show them the ash

We do this to show:

this is Lent;

we're sorry for the things we've done wrong;

we're going to return to God.

This is how you ash somebody ...

Another Leader ashes you with the words 'Return to God'

Leader   **Amen.**

Ash the children

'Return to God.'
Amen.

Finish with the Prayer for Forgiveness (below)
If you aren't going to ash the children, say the Kyries as normal

BEFORE THE KYRIE

As we start the holy season of Lent, let us call to mind the things we've done wrong and ask God to forgive us.

THE KYRIE   Lord Jesus, you came to call us back to God,
Lord have mercy
Lord have mercy

Lord Jesus, you fasted in the desert,
Christ have mercy
Christ have mercy

Lord Jesus, you told sinners how much God loved them,
Lord have mercy
Lord have mercy

Ask the children to repeat **The Prayer for Forgiveness** *after you* (**p. xxxvi**).
There is no Opening Prayer, go straight into the Lent procession

Leader   OK, Lent is such a serious time that we get rid of some of the fun things we do in church.
This morning we're going to bury our bells and candles in that box over there …

Somebody holds up the box at the other end of the room
Dish out the bells and candles and practise killing the sound of the bells by cueing the children in, and stopping them with the 'kill that!' cue (a finger across throat). Make sure you give the cue bang in the middle of a ding
Set up a procession of kids to take the bells and candles to the box

LENT PROCESSION

The children hold the candles high and ring the bells. Give the 'kill it!' cue as they arrive at the box; everything goes silent as the bells go into the box

Leader	Right, Lent has begun.
	Today we are going to hear how Jesus went into the desert and met this guy ...

Either introduce Leader 2 with horns and pitchfork, or show them cartoon 1

CD15.1	Who is it? (**The Devil**)
	Yup, the Devil. I don't know if he really looks like this but, whatever he looks like, he's a nuisance.

Either go straight on to the Gospel, or preface it with an optional session on

The Garden of Eden

Leader 1	Way back, when the whole world was new, the Devil turned up in the Garden of Eden. There were only two people in the world then – Adam and Eve.

Ask a boy and a girl to come forward

	God placed them in the Garden and gave them everything in it – except one tree: an apple tree.

Put an apple between the boy and girl

	God wanted Adam and Eve to remember Him, even when He wasn't there, so He told them they could eat everything in the Garden – except the apples on *that* apple tree. Then God went back to Heaven. And in came the Devil.

Leader 2 sidles in

	He snuck up behind Eve and said,
Leader 2	That's a nice apple – why don't you eat it?
Leader 1	And Eve said, no, she couldn't, God had told them not to.
Leader 2	Oh, I wouldn't worry about that – God can't see you ...
Leader 1	Is that true, kids? (**No!**)
	Quite, God *could* see her, but Eve didn't realize that.
Leader 2	Go on, have a bite ...
Leader 1	And Eve did ... *(Eve bites the apple)*
	Then she gave it to Adam. *(Eve hands it over)*
	And he had a bite. *(He does this)*
	And from that moment Adam and Eve – and the rest of the human race – were in deep trouble.
	The Devil thought he'd been very clever ...

Exit Devil, looking pleased with himself

	But then he came up against Jesus ...

There is no Gospel Procession in Lent, ask a child to bring the Gospel up from the back

THE GOSPEL   *St Luke 4.1–13*

Gospel for Narrator and Devil: the Devil stands just behind and insinuates his temptations into the Narrator's ear ...

Narrator	Filled with the Holy Spirit, Jesus was led into the desert.
	He was there for 40 days and ate nothing. And when the 40 days were up, He was hungry. Suddenly, the Devil spoke to Him:
Devil	If you are the Son of God, do some magic,
	command this stone to become bread.
Narrator	Jesus answered him,
	'It is written, "Human beings do not live by bread alone."'
	Then the Devil took Jesus up and showed Him all the kingdoms of the world in a single instant, and he said:
Devil	Look! here's the whole world,
	I can give it all to you – if you fall down and worship *me*.
Narrator	Jesus said to him in reply, 'It is written:
	"You shall worship the Lord, your God, and serve only Him."'
	Then the Devil led Him to Jerusalem and placed Him on a parapet of the Temple, and said to Him,
Devil	Prove you're the Son of God:
	throw yourself down from here. God is bound to save you,
	it says in the Bible, 'God will command His Angels to save you – lest you dash your foot against a stone.'
Narrator	But Jesus said to him in reply,
	'It also says, "You shall not put the Lord, your God, to the test."'
	When the Devil had finished every temptation,
	he gave up and left Jesus.

Exit Devil with a very bad grace, he ad libs: 'Rats! ...'

AFTER THE GOSPEL

Leader	Well, that sorted the Devil out.
	Jesus knew how to deal with him, and we need to know how to deal with him too; because he's always up to his tricks.
	We call it 'Temptation'.
	Anytime you feel something say to you, 'You don't have to go to church, have a nice lie in', that's a temptation.
	Or perhaps you give up chocolate for Lent – and you get this feeling

that perhaps one Mars bar would be OK.
That's a temptation.
You have to be like Jesus, and say
'Nope I'm going to Mass' or 'Go away, I'm keeping my Lenten
promise – Bog off, Devil!'

Scrunch up **CD15.1**, *or tell Leader 2 to clear off – he/she slinks off, and puts the Devil
props to one side*

ACTIVITY

Leader   So this Lent, we're going to go into the desert with Jesus,
                knowing that He'll be with us and keep us safe from all the tempt-
                ations of the Devil.
                Let's make our desert.

Bring the 'Desert Tray' forward filled with sand only

                This is our desert ...

Run the sand through your fingers

                It's very dry ...
                The only things you'd see there would be **rocks** ...

Get the kids to put in the rocks

                The only things that grow would be **cactuses** ...

A child puts in the cactus

                And the only animals that could live there would be creatures like
                camels.

In goes the camel

                It's very rocky, very lonely – but Jesus is there, in the middle. *(Put in
                the Jesus candle)*

FINAL PRAYER

Leader   *Light the candle*
                Let's say together the prayer Jesus taught us – particularly the line
                about 'and lead us not into temptation'.

Our Father ... (see p. xxxvi).

REHEARSAL

Practise your presentation for when you go back into church (see below).

BACK IN CHURCH

The children come in with the 'desert', one of the Leaders brings in the lighted Jesus candle

Child 1   This Lent we are going to follow Jesus into the desert ...

Bring the 'Desert Tray' forward

Child 2   This is our 'desert' ...
Child 3   It's very dry and rocky.
Child 4   It's very lonely.
Child 5   But Jesus is there in the middle ...

The Leader puts in the lighted Jesus candle

(CD15.1)

Script 16   Cities

Lent 2 (Church of England)

St Luke 13.33–35, plus St Matthew 24.2

The Gospel read in the Roman Catholic Church today is the Transfiguration, *St Luke 4.1–13*; you will find it in *Script 14*.

THEME

As Jesus sets His face towards Jerusalem, He foresees that He will be rejected and the city itself destroyed. (Jerusalem was razed to the ground by the Romans 40 years later in AD 70.) Taking a line based on Abraham (who appears in the first reading), this session looks at God's love for people and cities – and Jesus' calm acceptance of what Jerusalem was liable to do to Him.

SET UP

- The liturgical colour is Purple.
- No candles or bells.
- 'Desert Tray' plus the Jesus candle to hand.
- About 20 cardboard boxes from the local supermarket. They don't have to be the same size, but should be fairly firm (wine boxes are best).
- Cast Leader 2 as Abraham for the play below; he or she will need sun glasses.
- Some scrunched-up balls of paper.
- Toy bricks – not Lego, you want the sort that will fall over.
- Five cards labelled 'Carthage', 'Troy', 'Rome', 'London' and one with the local city on it. *(If you live in London or Rome, add 'New York' or some other city as the final card.)*

WELCOME *the children and lead them in* **The Sign of the Cross** ✠ **(p. xxxvi).**

THE KYRIE   Lord Jesus, you came to call us back to God,
Lord have mercy
Lord have mercy

Lord Jesus, you fasted in the desert,
Christ have mercy
Christ have mercy

Lord Jesus, you told sinners how much God loved them,
Lord have mercy
Lord have mercy

Ask the children to repeat **The Prayer for Forgiveness** *after you* **(p. xxxvi).**

Leader   *Run a brief résumé on Lent – the colour in church and the fact we're getting ready for Easter*
This Lent, we're thinking about Jesus, praying in the desert.

Bring the 'Desert Tray' forward

This is our desert. *(Run the sand through your fingers)*
It's very dry,
Very rocky,
Very lonely,
But Jesus is there in the middle. *(Place the Jesus candle)*
Jesus prayed in the desert
So let's copy Him

Light the candle and ask the children to repeat after you:

OPENING   **God our Father**
PRAYER   **This Lent, help us to return to you,**
pray to you
and love you.

Help us to see you more clearly,
love you more dearly,
and follow you more nearly,
day by day. Amen

BEFORE THE GOSPEL

Cities

Leader   We're going to think about cities today.
What's our nearest city? *(You may be living in it of course)*
Have you been there? Do you like it? *(Go with the flow)*
OK, well I'm going to ask you to build some cities.

Produce the toy bricks – look at them

Hmm, you can't build a whole city.
Could you build some towers? About five I think.

Get five children to build some brick towers, get them as high as possible. If one crashes, build it again – and stop at the critical point. Admire the towers

Right, I'm going to give these cities names.

Lean a card against each one

Carthage, Troy, Rome, London and *Name. (The local city)*
Well, Carthage was destroyed …
Can anyone knock it down?

Knock over Carthage

So was Troy.

Knock it down

Rome is still with us – but Ancient Rome was destroyed.

That gets knocked down as well

London is fine – but one day even London will fall.

Knock down London

And what about *Name*? I'm afraid even that will go one day.
Knock it down That's what happens to cities.
Anyone who loves a city knows, deep inside, that one day it will be destroyed.
But we love them anyway.
God loves cities too.
Let's think about a couple He was very interested in.
Centuries ago, He looked round the Earth, to see whether there was anybody who'd be prepared to be His friend, and He saw the ancient city of Ur …
Let's build it …

Clear the toy bricks and use the cardboard boxes to make the walls of Ur
Place it down the front, slightly to the side
Leader 2 drifts in behind its walls. He/she is a cool dude and wears shades

The City of Ur

Leader 1   That looks very good.
Ur was the capital city of Mesopotamia, and it was there that God found Abraham. He said, 'Abraham! I want you to leave your native land and follow me.'

| Abraham | *Looking all round, to see where the voice is coming from*
Wow! Weird … |

He takes his shades off to see better and puts them on the walls of Ur

| Leader 1 | Follow me! said God. |

Abraham leaves Ur, remembers his shades, and goes back for them

| | Leave Ur behind! |
| Abraham | If you say so, God. |

He quickly puts his shades on and comes out of Ur and walks into the centre

Leader 1	And God said, 'Abraham, look up at the sky. Can you count the stars?'
Abraham	*Pushing his shades back as he looks up, tries to count them, and gives up very quickly* No …
God	That's how big your family is going to be. Look at the desert …

Abraham moves across to the Lent 'Desert Tray'

	Can you count how many grains of sand are at your feet?
Abraham	*Sifting some sand through his fingers* No way …
God	That's how many descendants you are going to have. I'm going to bless you, and your family – and through you everyone in the whole world will be blessed.
Abraham	Cool …

Exits looking pleased with life

Leader 1   Abraham became the founder of a great nation, the Jews. And his descendants built an even greater city than Ur – it was called Jerusalem.
Let's build that – I'm afraid we will have to knock down Ur and recycle the boxes …

Use all the cardboard boxes to build Jerusalem on the other side of the room to Ur
Put the scrunched-up balls of paper inside

Jerusalem

Leader   Jerusalem was a beautiful city. The Jews lived in it.

Can we have some Jews living inside? Invite three or four kids to become Jerusalemites

Sometimes they listened to God – and sometimes they didn't.
God sent them prophets, and every now and then they would welcome them.
Name, (to a kid) could you be a prophet for me?

Send the kid across to Jerusalem; the inhabitants shake him by the hand and let him in

But more often they threw stones at them.
Can anyone cope with that? What sort of stones have you got there?

One of the kids holds up a scrunched-up ball of paper

Anyone want to risk it?

Send Leader 2 across, plus any brave volunteer

OK, here come two more prophets.

The kids inside throw the balls of paper at them – the two prophets retreat

Yup, Jerusalem was a dangerous place to go to.
Jesus knew that.
In the last weeks of His life, He walked steadily towards Jerusalem – knowing He'd be killed there – but loving the city all the same.
We'll hear about that now in the Gospel.

Settle the children and ask one of them to bring up the Gospel book

THE GOSPEL   *St Luke 13.33–35, plus St Matthew 24.2*

Optional Version

Jesus said, 'I must be on my way. O Jerusalem, Jerusalem.
You kill the prophets and stone the messengers God has sent you! How often I have wanted to put my arms round you and your children – just as a hen gathers her chicks under her wings. But you would not let me!

And now your Temple will be abandoned, and the day will come when not a stone on your buildings will be left standing on another.'

AFTER THE GOSPEL

Leader   Jesus didn't storm off to His death in Jerusalem, looking furious. He went, loving the place, even though He knew what the city would do to Him.
Jesus' love for Jerusalem shows us how much God loves us, and the cities we build.

FINAL PRAYER

Leader   Jerusalem is still a place where people quarrel and fight – but that doesn't stop God loving it. Let us pray for the peace of Jerusalem.

(From Psalm 122)

The response to the psalm is:
Pray for the peace of Jerusalem
Pray for the peace of Jerusalem

I was glad when they said to me,
We will go to the house of the Lord
Pray for the peace of Jerusalem

Our feet shall stand in your gates, O Jerusalem
Pray for the peace of Jerusalem

O pray for the peace of Jerusalem,
they shall do well that love you
Pray for the peace of Jerusalem

Peace be within your walls and plenty within your palaces
Pray for the peace of Jerusalem. Amen

REHEARSAL

Practise your presentation for when you go back into church (see below).

BACK IN CHURCH

Child 1	Today we heard how greatly Jesus loved Jerusalem.
Child 2	Jerusalem is still a place where people fight each other.
Child 3	But God loves it.
Leader	So we've come back with this prayer from Psalm 122.

A grown-up, or very good child reader, says the psalm; the others say the response

I was glad when they said to me,
We will go to the house of the Lord
Pray for the peace of Jerusalem

Our feet shall stand in your gates, O Jerusalem
Pray for the peace of Jerusalem

O pray for the peace of Jerusalem,
they shall do well that love you
Pray for the peace of Jerusalem

Peace be within your walls and plenty within your palaces
Pray for the peace of Jerusalem. Amen

Script 17   Extra Time

Lent 3

St Luke 13.6–9

THEME

The Gospel today is a dialogue between Jesus and His audience. Two tragedies are discussed in St Luke 13.1–5 and Jesus warns His listeners not to assume that, just because someone is unlucky, they've got their just deserts. None of us gets our just deserts, fortunately, and Jesus extends the discussion to show the amazing patience of God. We're like the fig tree in His parable, never producing fruit, but always being granted a bit more time. The idea of a 'bit more time' is well known to children, especially at bedtime. We do our best to 'beat the clock' in this session so that we will end up able to appreciate the Gospel message: God gives us extra time.

SET UP

- The liturgical colour is Purple.
- No candles or bells.
- 'Desert Tray' plus the Jesus candle to hand.
- Pictures from the CD-Rom.
- As many alarm clocks and timers as you can muster.

WELCOME *the children and lead them in* **The Sign of the Cross** ✠ (p. xxxvi).

THE KYRIE   Lord Jesus, you came to call us back to God,
                Lord have mercy
                Lord have mercy

                Lord Jesus, you fasted in the desert,
                Christ have mercy
                Christ have mercy

                Lord Jesus, you told sinners how much God loved them,
                Lord have mercy
                Lord have mercy

Ask the children to repeat **The Prayer for Forgiveness** *after you* (**p. xxxvi**).

Leader   *Run a brief résumé on Lent – the colour in church and the fact we're*
                getting ready for Easter
                This Lent, we're thinking about Jesus, praying in the desert.

Bring the 'Desert Tray' forward

                This is our desert. *(Run the sand through your fingers)*
                It's very dry,
                Very rocky,
                Very lonely,
                But Jesus is there in the middle. *(Place the Jesus candle)*
                Jesus prayed in the desert.
                So we'll copy Him.

Light the candle and ask the children to repeat after you:

OPENING   God our Father
PRAYER   This Lent, help us to return to you,
                pray to you
                and love you.

                Help us to see you more clearly,
                love you more dearly,
                and follow you more nearly
                day by day. Amen

BEFORE THE GOSPEL

Bedtime

Leader   Good morning. How are you all – did you sleep well?
                How about you, *Name*? *(Leader 2)*
Leader 2   *(Yawning)* I had a terrible night.
Leader 1   What time did you get to bed?
Leader 2   Oh – about 2 o'clock …
Leader 1   2 o'clock? Disgraceful.
                What time did you lot get to bed?

Take all answers – some of them are bound to boast that they were up until midnight
Pick up the clock

                OK, now I remember when I was a kid. My mum would tell me
                to go to bed at 7 o'clock *(turn the hands to 7)* and I would make
                excuses and muck about – and wouldn't actually get to bed until 8.
                (Turn the hands to 8)

Has anyone here ever done that? *(Clock up the show of hands)*

Ah – well you'll sympathize with my brother Andrew. *(Substitute any other name of course)*

CD17.1   He was a genius at not going to bed.

Lay out the blank speech balloons from the CD-Rom so you can write on them

CD17.2   What excuses do you think he made? *(Six speech bubbles)*

See what they come up with – and write them in. Standard ones are
  Oh, just five minutes more
  Can I finish watching this film?
  I haven't done my homework
  Can you tuck me up?
  Can you read me a story?
  Can I have a glass of water?
(Limit the children to six)

So my parents would be sitting down at last, and there'd come a knock on the door.

It was Andrew and he'd say ... *(Put up one of the excuses from the speech bubbles above)*

Then there'd be another knock – it was Andrew again.

Put up another excuse, and run this – getting quicker and quicker – until you get to the last one

After that, they really thought they'd got rid of him, but at 11 o'clock – just as Mum and Dad were thinking they'd go to bed themselves – there was another knock.

'WHAT IS IT THIS TIME?!' said Dad.

And Andrew came up with his final excuse:

CD17.3   'I'm a Shepherd in the nativity play tomorrow and I haven't got a costume ...'

We thought that was the best ever mega excuse we'd ever heard – and my poor mother never got to bed at all ...

I'm sure none of you have ever done that. But it is nice to get extra time sometimes.

*The kids have now got to shut their eyes and **not** see you set up the* Beat the Clock *game. Small groups could perhaps go outside for a moment. But if this is not practical, either get the kids to put their hands to their eyes and count to 50 or – if you're not totally convinced you can trust them – say*

OK, we're going to play a game about Time – but we need to set it up. So I want you all to lie down on your tummies – excellent – rest your head on your hands – yup – shut your eyes, and count to 50. Do it out loud so we know how much time we've got.

Set the clocks to go off in 3 minutes – or 5 if you've got some really nifty hiding places – and hide them round the room

Beat the Clock

The children have got to find all the clocks and timers before they go off. One clock should be un-findable; make sure Leader 2 has it in his pocket. Have some grown-ups on hand to switch the clocks off if the kids don't know how.
Panic them (slightly) by giving them a minute-by-minute countdown.
After the time has expired, it may be that only Leader 2's clock is left; if that's the case, say

There's only one clock left – Hurry!

Or if there are a few others, say

We've still got a few to go … hurry up!

Whatever happens, the ring of Leader 2's alarm clock should finish the game. He pulls it out of his pocket.

Leader   Ah, here's the last one. We needed more time …
                Well, God gives us a lifetime to get things right –
                but we'd always like a bit more. Jesus told a story about that.

Ask a child to bring the Gospel to you

THE GOSPEL   *St Luke 13.6–9*

AFTER THE GOSPEL

Leader   What happened in that story?

A farmer found his fig tree wasn't producing fruit and wanted to cut it down, but his gardener said, give it another year …

                Whom do you suppose God is in that story – the farmer or the gardener? *(See what they think)*
                I think it's both.
                On the one hand, there's God, looking at His watch, wondering when any of us is going to behave properly – perhaps He ought to give up on us …
                Then He thinks, 'No, I'll give them a bit more time – *and* I'll give them some help as well.'
                Thank goodness.

Well, Lent is one of the things God gives us to help us do better.
Let's thank Him for Lent in our last prayer.

FINAL PRAYER

A Lent Litany   The response is:
We thank you Lord
We thank you Lord

For the time of Lent
We thank you Lord

For our Lent desert
We thank you Lord

For our Lenten promises
We thank you Lord

For your great patience
We thank you Lord

For the promise of Easter
We thank you Lord

Lord God, we thank you for the holy season of Lent.
Help us to use the time you have given us
To grow in faith,
And hope, and love. **Amen**

REHEARSAL

Practise your presentation for when you go back into church (see below).

BACK IN CHURCH

A couple of alarm clocks are set so they will ring the moment Leaders 1 and 2 twiddle the minute hand round. The children go down the front

Child 1   Today we played a game against the clock.
Child 2   But we ran out of time.

The Leaders set off the alarms – and kill them quickly

Child 3   Then we read the Gospel.
Leader 1   And discovered that God is always prepared to give us extra time – how did we feel about that, kids?

The children punch the air cheerfully

It cheered us up a lot.

Script 18 The Prodigal Son

Lent 4

St Luke 15.11b–32

THEME

Today is a 'Pink' Sunday, a moment when the liturgy lightens up and any church that possesses a Rose set of vestments swaps them for the usual Lenten Purple. The traditional sentence that begins Mass today starts with Laetare, the Latin word for 'Rejoice!', and this Sunday is sometimes known as Laetare, but it's just as likely to be called the Fourth Sunday of Lent or Mothering Sunday or Refreshment Sunday. It's also the Sunday when we hear one of the best stories Jesus ever told, 'The Prodigal Son'. It's only found in St Luke's Gospel and this session homes in on all the people involved – the farmer, the Prodigal and, of course, the pig …

SET UP

- The liturgical colour is Rose, though churches that haven't got a Rose set will still be in Purple. Flag up the change of colour: drape the Gospel table in pink, wear a pink garment, choose a child wearing pink as a Kyrie reader.
- 'Desert Tray' plus the Jesus candle to hand.
- A doctored newspaper with a new heading on the front page and a news flash about the Missing Pig Boy stuck somewhere in the middle (inserts on the CD-Rom).
- Two people prepared to play Mr Hodge, the farmer, and Hog, the pig: they'll need to see the script beforehand. They can either ad lib their parts, or act with the Script in their hand.
- A prop for the farmer, a hoe perhaps, or a battered hat.
- A couple of chairs, one of which is labelled 'Pig Sty'.
- Make the note that goes in Mr Hodge's pocket and the post-card for Mr Hog. (The texts for both of these are in the script below.)
- Large soft ball.
- Either a large purse or wallet you are prepared to let the children use in the presentation, or some 'pirate doubloons'. (You can get these from party shops, or via the Internet. At the time of writing, 40 plastic coins cost £2.50.)

WELCOME *the children and lead them in* **The Sign of the Cross** ✠ **(p. xxxvi).**

THE KYRIE   Lord Jesus, you came to call us back to God,
Lord have mercy
Lord have mercy

Lord Jesus, you fasted in the desert,
Christ have mercy
Christ have mercy

Lord Jesus, you told sinners how much God loved them,
Lord have mercy
Lord have mercy

Ask the children to repeat **The Prayer for Forgiveness** *after you* **(p. xxxvi).**

Leader   We're in Lent, there are no candles or bells today, instead
we've got our own desert. *(Bring the 'Desert Tray' forward)*
We've been in the desert for three weeks.
It's very dry *(Run the sand through your fingers)*
Very rocky
Very lonely
But Jesus is there in the middle. *(Place the Jesus candle)*
Jesus prayed in the desert.
Let's copy Him.

Light the candle and ask the children to repeat after you

OPENING   **God our Father,**
PRAYER   **This Lent help us to return to you,**
pray to you,
and love you.

Help us to see you more clearly,
love you more dearly,
and follow you more nearly
day by day. Amen

Leader   Well, it's still Lent ...
But something's changed today, what is it?
Yes, the table *(or whatever)* is draped in pink.
I'm in pink, *Name* is wearing his pink socks, *Name* is in pink, and
so is *Name*. *(Choose any children you see in pink)*

It's a Pink Sunday, there's one in Advent and one in Lent.
It's the moment in Lent when we cheer up.
Some people are feeling very cheerful today – can anyone guess who?

Give some hints

Did anyone get a card today, or some flowers? (**Our mothers**)
Yes, it's Mothering Sunday, the card shops call it Mother's Day.
It's time to chill out – I'll read the newspaper.

Pull up a chair and flourish the doctored newspaper

CD18.1   Here's my newspaper – it's called *The Farmer's Weekly.*
Did you know I was interested in farming? Yup, I love it.
And here, in the centre, there's a big story about a pig farm.

Open up the paper to the doctored headline 'Pig Boy Goes Missing'. Ask someone to read it out –

'The whereabouts of Mr Hodge's pig boy was still a mystery last night. The youngster went missing yesterday, shortly after he'd given the pigs their breakfast. Police followed a trail of husks, possibly left by the boy, from the pigsty down to the river bank. "We are taking this extremely seriously," said a police spokesman. Meanwhile the Hodges are devastated. "He was like a son to me," said Mr Hodge. The boy was last seen wearing muddy jeans and a T shirt and anyone who thinks they may have seen him should contact the police or Hodge's Farm immediately.'

CD18.2   *Show the children the 'photograph'* (**CD18.2**) *in the paper, point out the desolate pigs*

Leader   That looks interesting, let's check it out.
               Ah, here's Mr Hodge …
Enter farmer Hello, Mr Hodge, I hear you've lost your pig boy?
Farmer   *(A slimy individual)* That's right, mate. Here we are in the middle of a famine, nobody's getting anything to eat – and that stupid pig boy's gone missing.
               What's his problem? He was getting three good meals a day.
               And who's going to look after my pigs!?
Leader   Sounds odd, when did he arrive?
Farmer   A couple of weeks ago …
               Thin as a stick, no money.
               But I'm all heart – I gave him a job, and as much as he wanted to eat.
Leader   Then what happened?

Farmer	Well, he did the job OK.
	The pigs were happy – and then, yesterday, I found this note.

Produces note – the Leader reads it

Leader	'Goodbye, thanks for the husks, gone back to Dad.'
Farmer	And I haven't seen him since.
Leader	*(To the kids)* I must say it all sounds very strange.
	I think I'll go down and look at the sty.

Moves across the room to the sty

Ah, there it is – and what luck – one of the pigs is at home ...

Pig acting from Hog (a few 'oinks' should do it)

Leader	Hello, piggy wig!
Hog	Actually, my name's Hog.
Leader	Sorry, Hog. Can you tell us anything about this mysterious disappearance?
Hog	*(Looking round)* Can you keep a secret?
Leader	Certainly.
Hog	OK, come over here ...

They move into the middle of the kids

Hog	That lad who turned up two weeks ago – he was in a right state. And old skinflint there ...
Leader	You mean ... *(Nods his head in the direction of Hodge, who is now reading* The Farmer's Weekly*)*
Hog	Yup, well he thought, here's where I get something for nothing. So he told the boy he could look after us pigs and get his meals free.
Leader	That sounds all right.
Hog	Yeah, except his meals were anything we left over ...
Leader	I didn't know pigs *did* leave anything over.
Hog	Yeah, well, no we don't. But we shared all our meals with him. But that boy was a fussy eater: we gave him potato peel and apple cores, and things scraped off people's plates – you know, all the best bits – but he didn't fancy them. The only things he could manage were husks.
Leader	Husks?
Hog	Bits of fruit peel and stuff. So, I said to him – listen, mate, this is no life for you. Where do you come from? And then he told me how he'd upset his father and run away. And I said, 'Well, your father would be even more upset to see you living

	with us pigs – you go home and say you're sorry … So he did.'
Leader	And then?
Hog	*(Getting closer)* Ah well, I got a postcard from him only this morning.
Producing card	Don't tell him. *(Referring to Hodge)*
	You can read it if you like. *(Hands it over surreptitiously)*
Leader	Wow, a scoop! Let's hear what the boy has to say …
Leader 2	*(Or any responsible person not playing Hog)*
	OK – but after the Gospel!
Leader	You're kidding …
Leader 2	*(Firmly)* The Gospel comes first.

Ask a child to bring the Gospel book to the front
The Leader sits down to read it, and Hodge and Hog sit with the children

THE GOSPEL   *St Luke 15.11b–32 (with interjections from the pig)*

Jesus said,

There was once a man who had two sons, a serious elder son and a happy-go-lucky younger son. He loved them both very much.

One day the younger son said to him,

'Dad, you know all that money I'm going to get when you die? Why don't you give it to me now – I want to go off into the world and have adventures.'

So the father gave the boy a great bag of money and off he went, very pleased with himself.

He travelled to a far country and stayed in a big city. He made lots of friends and he spent his time partying and dancing and drinking. He had a super time until he found he'd spent all his money – at which point his new friends disappeared.

And if that wasn't bad enough, the country began to suffer from a famine. There was not much food around – and none at all for him.

The boy had to look round for a job. *(Look up at Hodge to cue him)*

Hodge	Ah, that's when I met him.
Narrator	And he got a job looking after some pigs. *(Look at Hog)*
Hog	That's us!
Narrator	The boy watched as the pigs ate their grub – potato peelings, apple cores, left-overs, all mixed up. And he was so hungry, he began to eat husks.

Well, at last (Jesus said), 'He came to himself'.

'This is ridiculous,' he said to himself. 'My Dad's servants get more to eat than I do – and here am I about to starve! I'll get up and go back to him and say, "Father, I have sinned against God and against you. I'm no longer fit to be your son – let me come back as one of your servants.'"

So he got up and started the long journey back home.

Hog   Hey, I know the rest of this – he sent me a postcard!

Leader   So he did! *(Pull out postcard)* It says:

'Dear Hog

Thanks for the tip. I went back, like you said, and I was working out what I was going to say to Dad when – before I got to the front door – he rushed out. And I said, "Look, I'm sorry, Dad" and he just hugged me. We're about to have a feast!

Cheerio – keep eating those nice potato peelings ...'

Check this out by referring to the Bible

Yup, that's just what happened.

The boy's father had been watching the road ever since he'd run away and, when he saw him come back, he was so happy he ran to meet the boy, and kissed him.

The boy said, 'Father, I've sinned against God and against you, I am not worthy to be called your son ...'

But the father said, 'Don't worry about that!' And he called his servants, 'Hurry up! Get a feast ready, give my son here some new clothes, put a ring on his finger – let's celebrate!'

You might want to stop here, but if you've got some older children, go on and finish the story

Leader   But of course, there was another son.

The one who had stayed at home. He worked hard and took himself very seriously. And, though He was a good chap, he was not quite as good as he thought he was. (Jesus was always very interested in people like that.) The elder son thought it was deeply unfair that the runaway was getting a feast and he said to his father: 'Hey, Dad, I've worked for you all my life, you've never made any fuss about *me*.'

'But you are always with me', said his father. 'You have everything of mine. Don't just think of yourself, come and be happy with us. For your brother was dead, but now he is alive, he was lost, but now he is found.'

AFTER THE GOSPEL

Talk through the story, and establish that

Leader   This is a story about parents and kids – it's a very good one for Mothering Sunday.

Even though the father had been badly treated by his younger son, he never stopped loving him.

As soon as the boy turned back, there was his father, running down the road to greet him.

Jesus said, that's what God is like.

However badly we treat God, He never stops loving us – He knows the *moment* we turn round *and* He runs down the road to greet us.

If you've done the complete story

But what about the older son – do you think it was fair for the father to make such a fuss of the younger boy?

Take all answers – kids are very hot on things being fair, and we all like people to get their just deserts – especially if it's not us – whatever they come up with, try to get them to think about generosity

Generosity is not about clocking up every good thing you do, and every bad thing the other person does. It's about loving people in spite of their faults.

The father in the story was generous. The older son was not.

Jesus is telling us that God our Father is generous. Of course God is also *just*.

He knows when we've done wrong and He doesn't pretend we're nicer than we are but, like the father in the story, He loves us anyway. Thank goodness …

GAMES

Piggy in the Middle

After all this listening, the children will welcome a game. 'Piggy in the Middle' is the obvious choice. Use a large soft ball (so the small children have a chance of catching it) and start with two grown-ups throwing the ball out of reach, to make sure the kids rush around for a minute or two.

Baby Pig

If you have limited space you can play a quiet pig game. One child is designated Mummy (or Daddy) Pig and goes out of the room. Choose another child to be Baby Pig. Huddle the kids in a circle, faces to the floor, and call Mummy/Daddy Pig back. The Baby Pig says 'oink' very quietly, now and then, and its parent has to locate him, by tapping him on the shoulder, in 1 minute, or 30 seconds if that's too easy. (Two wrong taps and the Mummy Pig is out and the child playing Baby Pig gets to go outside.)

REHEARSAL

Practise your presentation for when you go back into church (see below).

FINAL PRAYER

Leader	Our last prayer today will be the one Jesus taught us. What is that? (**Our Father**) Excellent. As we say it, let's remember what a generous father God is, and how happy He is to forgive us our trespasses.

Our Father … (see p. xxxvi).

BACK IN CHURCH

The children come down to the front: two stand on one side (they are the father and the son), a group stands in the middle, the rest bunch up on the other side. (If you have a limited number of children the group in the middle can dash over to the other side as the story proceeds)

Leader	Today we heard a story Jesus told about a boy who asked his Dad for a bag of money and left home …

The father gives the boy a purse, they shake hands, and the boy walks off

The boy got to a large town, and suddenly made loads of new friends.

The group in the middle pat him on the back, shake hands with him, and somehow relieve him of his money

And he found all his money had disappeared. So he had to get a job. Nobody wanted to help him – but eventually he got a job looking after pigs.

The group on the side go down on all fours and start 'oinking'. The boy walks over to them

The pigs were friendly.

They rub their shoulders against him

But the food was terrible, and the boy decided to go home. He turned back towards his father's house.

The boy does this very deliberately

And began to walk home slowly – he was wondering what on earth he could say to his father.
But his father saw him in the distance.

The father shades his eyes as he peers across the church

And ran to greet his son. The son barely had time to say sorry when his father hugged him and hurried him home.

Father and son hug and go off together

Jesus told that story to show us how generous God our Father is. Just like the father in the story, God knows immediately when one of His children is coming back to Him – and He rushes out to welcome them home.

Pig Boy still missing!

The whereabouts of Mr Hodge's pig boy were still a mystery last night. The youngster went missing yesterday, shortly after he'd given the pigs their breakfast. Police followed a trail of husks, possibly left by the boy, from the pigs' sty down to the river bank. "We are taking this extremely seriously" said a police spokesman. Meanwhile the Hodges are devastated. "He was like a son to me," said Mr Hodge. The boy was last seen wearing muddy jeans and a T shirt and anyone who thinks they may have seen him should contact the police or Hodge's Farm immediately.

Mr Hodge's pigs

(CD18.2)

Sample cartoon for this script

Script 19   Two Sinners

Lent 5

St John 12.3–8 (Church of England) or
St John 8.2–11 (Roman Catholic)

THEME

There are two possible Gospel readings this Sunday, so check which one you are doing with your priest. Both stories have a very similar plot. A woman is publicly condemned by self-righteous accusers and is defended by Jesus, who takes the opportunity to condemn her critics. It's interesting to notice that, though Jesus welcomes thieves, cheats and other dodgy characters, there is one sort of sin He can't stand: self-righteousness. This Sunday is the start of Passiontide. Everything in church will probably be covered up – statues, crucifixes and pictures. The Children's Church marks the new sombre mood by covering their 'Desert Tray' at the end of the service.

SET UP

- The liturgical colour is Purple.
- No candles or bells.
- 'Desert Tray' plus the Jesus candle to hand.
- Leader 1 starts the session with an obvious mobile in his/her pocket or handbag.
- Set up Leader 2 and two kids to play the pickpocket interlude. They'll need a wallet and some mobiles, and should run through the script beforehand. It won't take long.
- Some inflated balloons, one per ten children – and a spare in case of accidents.
- A purple veil to cover the desert (a white cloth will do instead).
- If you have a crucifix or any obvious picture or little statue in the area in which you meet, have another veil, or cloth, to hand to cover it up.

WELCOME *the children and lead them in* **The Sign of the Cross** ✠ **(p. xxxvi).**

THE KYRIE   Lord Jesus, you came to call us back to God,
Lord have mercy
Lord have mercy

Lord Jesus, you fasted in the desert,
Christ have mercy
Christ have mercy

Lord Jesus, you told sinners how much God loved them,
Lord have mercy
Lord have mercy

Ask the children to repeat **The Prayer for Forgiveness** *after you* (**p. xxxvi**).

Leader

Run a brief résumé on Lent – the colour in church and the fact we're getting ready for Easter

We're getting so near Easter now that the church is looking even more serious.
All the statues and pictures in church should be covered up.
We'll make a start here.

Cover any picture or crucifix you have
Bring the 'Desert Tray' forward

Even our desert will need to be covered up – we'll do that at the end.
Let's just look at it.
It's dry, and rocky and lonely – but Jesus is there in the middle.

Place the Jesus candle

Jesus prayed to His Father in the desert, and we'll do the same.

Light the candle and ask the children to repeat after you

OPENING   **God our Father,**
PRAYER   **This Lent, help us to return to you,**
pray to you
and love you

Help us to see you more clearly,
love you more dearly,
and follow you more nearly,
day by day. Amen

BEFORE THE GOSPEL

Thievery

Leader 1   Has anyone here seen the film *Oliver*?

See if anyone has, it doesn't matter if the kids look blank

It's about a little boy who's kidnapped by a gang of pickpockets. What's a pickpocket?

A child may tell you, but carry on explaining anyway …

Yes, a pickpocket is someone who sneaks up behind you

Leader 2 creeps up behind you and steals your mobile
If the kids shout out – look round, but pretend not to see him …

puts his hand in your pocket – and steals your mobile …

Put your hand in your pocket

Hey! My pocket's been picked!
Who did it?

Leader 2   *Coming forward*
Er, sorry about that – I couldn't resist …

Leader 1   I should think not – I need a sit-down – you take over …

Leader 2   Well, kids, as you see I'm good at picking pockets, but I've changed my ways – ever since last week …
I'll show you what happened.

Ad lib the following if you can, doing it off the script is fine however

I was in the park, and I saw this geezer fast asleep on a park bench.

Child 1 brings a chair forward and sits on it

So I crept up and nicked his phone …

He does   Then I sat on a bench.

Pulls a chair forward

And blow me, if some thieving so-and-so didn't creep up behind *me*.

Child 2 creeps up

And steal my wallet!
Anyway, I caught her.

Grabs Child 2's wrist (gently!)

Oi!
And I marched her off to the police.

Leader 1	*As policeman*
	'Allo, 'allo, 'allo?
	What's all this?
Leader 2	*(Very indignant)*
	This thieving little whatnot *(glare at kid, who looks utterly unrepentant)* had the cheek to creep up on ME and steal something from MY pocket. I've never known such wickedness. Lock her up and throw away the key …
To the kids	At which point I was interrupted.
	The bloke whose mobile I'd stolen, woke up
Child 1 does	and joined us.
Child 1	Just a minute – that's the man who stole my mobile!
Policeman	Is that so?
To Leader 2	You've got a cheek, haven't you?
	Standing here accusing this kid when you've done the same thing yourself.
Leader 2	*To the kids*
	And of course the policeman was right.
	It reminded me of today's Gospel.

Settle the children to hear the Gospel, ask one of them to bring it to you

THE GOSPEL   *either St John 12.3–8 or St John 8.2–11*

St John 12.3–8

Start it off with 'Jesus went for dinner to the house of Lazarus and Mary and Martha', *then go from verse 3.*

or

St John 8.2–11

The children may know what adultery means, but the actual sin is not relevant to this session, nor is the barbaric punishment of stoning.

Optional Paraphrase of St John 8.2–11

Some people brought a woman before Jesus who had been caught red-handed.
They said to him, 'Teacher, this woman was caught sinning. The law says we can punish her – what do you say?'
Jesus didn't answer. He just bent down and wrote with His finger in the dust.
But they kept questioning Him so He straightened up and said,
'Let the one among you who has never sinned be the first to punish her.'

Then He bent down and began writing on the ground again.

When they heard that, they went away, one by one, beginning with the oldest, and Jesus was left alone with the woman.

Jesus looked up and said to her, 'Where are they? Has no one condemned you?'

'No one, sir,' she said.

Jesus said, 'Neither do I condemn you. Go your way, and sin no more.'

AFTER THE GOSPEL (for St John 12.3–8)

Leader   So this story is about Mary the sister of Lazarus, pouring a whole bottle of oil over Jesus.

It sounds like an odd thing to do, but in a hot dry country like Palestine it must have felt wonderful.

Then she got ticked off. Who by? (**Judas**)

Yes, Judas said it was a waste of money – he looked all smart-alec and said it should have been given to the poor.

But Jesus knew that Judas didn't care about the poor – all Judas wanted to do was to tick someone off. It's like those horrid kids we meet sometimes who say, '*Umm* – you shouldn't have done that ...'

Do you know, I think that sort of thing really upsets God. It certainly upset Jesus.

Look, here are two sinners.

Bring forward Leader 2 and the girl who picked his pocket

And one of them *(raise Leader 2's hand)*

has the cheek to accuse the other one *(raise her hand)*

of doing wrong.

What do you think God thinks of that?

I bet He thinks, 'Cut it out. You're both as bad as each other – you *both* need forgiveness.'

Leader 2   Yup, that's true. *(He shakes the kid's hand)*

AFTER THE GOSPEL (for St John 8.2–11)

Leader   This is one of the great Gospel stories. Some guys haul a woman up in front of Jesus and tell Him they've caught her sinning.

Jesus doesn't even look up.

But they bang on, they've caught this woman out and want to punish her. They're like those horrid kids we meet sometimes who say, '*Umm* – I'm telling on you ...'

Jesus looks them straight in the face and says, 'OK, so which one of you has never done anything wrong? Stand forward, let's see you ...'

And they all slink away.

Then Jesus turns to the woman – what happened then? (**He forgave her**)

Jesus didn't think much of that woman's accusers.

You know, I think that whole episode distressed Jesus.

Look, here are two sinners.

Bring forward Leader 2 and the girl who picked his pocket

And one of them *(raise Leader 2's hand)*

has the cheek to accuse the other one *(raise her hand)*

of doing something wrong.

What do you think God thinks of that?

I bet He thinks, 'Cut it out. You're both as bad as each other – you *both* need forgiveness.'

Leader 2   Yup, that's true. *(He shakes the kid's hand)*

Leader 1   And perhaps the person whose pocket you picked might feel like forgiving you too.

That kid comes forward and shakes Leader 2's hand

(At this point the alternative Gospels (and the alternative 'After the Gospel') join up. Whichever Gospel you have read, finish the session with the following)

That's what God likes to see – people getting on with each other.

Let's play a game together.

GAME

Group Effort

Either form one huge circle, or split kids and grown-ups into circles of ten each. Everyone holds hands. Lob a balloon into their midst.

The idea is that the group keeps the balloon from touching the ground while still holding hands. If they drop hands, or the balloon touches the ground, they sit down, jump up, hold hands – and start again. If they find that dead easy, add another balloon.

REHEARSAL

Practise your presentation for when you go back into church (see below).

FINAL PRAYER

Leader   We'll finish by saying the Family Prayer of the church.
Our Father ... (see p. xxxvi).

BACK IN CHURCH

Go in with the 'Desert Tray' (with the Jesus candle unlit) and the veil

Child 1	This Lent we have got ready for Easter by following Jesus into the desert.
Child 2	We made our own desert.
Child 3	It's got rocks, and cactuses and even a camel. *(Obviously you adapt this as necessary)*
Leader	But today is the beginning of Passiontide, so we're going to cover the desert up.

Two children hold the veil at each end and solemnly cover the Desert Tray

Script 20 Palm Sunday

St Luke 19.28–40

THEME

This session uses the Palm Sunday Gospel, read at the beginning of the Eucharist, which describes Jesus' Entry into Jerusalem. You will obviously have to fit round whatever your church does on Palm Sunday: the priest will probably bless and distribute palm crosses at the beginning of the service and there might be a procession. This is the beginning of Holy Week and, while the adults hear the whole Passion story in church, the children construct a Passion Cross.

SET UP

- The liturgical colour is Red – make sure there is something red in the hall, even if it's only your jumper.
- Ask your priest to read the script beforehand; it will help the presentation if the clergy know they are about to be presented with a Passion Cross.
- Toy donkey if you've got one.
- Palm crosses.
- Download the photo of the Bessans Cross from the CD-Rom; you and the kids are about to make a cardboard version of this.
- Set up a large table with the materials to make a Passion Cross (see below).
- Materials for a Passion Cross – see template on CD-Rom.
- Thin card, lightweight flower canes, magic tape (the sort of Sellotape that is invisible), scissors, paper, pens for the children.

WELCOME *the children and lead them in* **The Sign of the Cross** ✠ (**p. xxxvi**).

THE KYRIE Lord Jesus,
This week you allowed your enemies to capture you,
Lord have mercy
Lord have mercy

Lord Jesus,
This week you carried the Cross,
Christ have mercy
Christ have mercy

> Lord Jesus,
> This week you died on the Cross for us,
> Lord have mercy
> **Lord have mercy**

Ask the children to repeat **The Prayer for Forgiveness** *after you* (**p. xxxvi**).

OPENING **PRAYER**	Lord Jesus, Today you entered Jerusalem on a donkey As the Jewish children sang your praises. Help us follow their example And sing your praises this morning. **Amen**

BEFORE THE GOSPEL

Leader　　　This is the last Sunday in Lent, and suddenly the colour has changed. Did anyone spot the new colour in church?

Give them a hint – what colour is my jumper? (**Red**)

Red is the colour we use when we remember Christians who've died for their faith. But today we use it to remember Jesus Himself, because today is the start of Holy Week, the last week of Jesus' earthly life. Let's hear how He started it.

Ask a child to bring the Gospel to the front

THE GOSPEL　*St Luke 19.28–40*

AFTER THE GOSPEL

Run through the story with the children

Leader　　　Jesus' disciples brought Him a donkey,

Hold up your donkey if you've got one

and Jesus entered Jerusalem in triumph. His disciples were singing, and people laid down their cloaks in front of Him.
We know from another Gospel that the children climbed up trees and waved palm leaves as Jesus passed.
It's why we've got these palms this morning. *(Hold one up)*
But why is it in the shape of a cross? (**Because Jesus died on the cross**)
Yes. Palm Sunday is the start of Holy Week, by Friday, Jesus will have been arrested and killed on a cross.

The grown-ups are hearing the story of Holy Week in church and we're going to make a cross that will tell the story too.

The Bessans Cross

Show the children the picture of the Bessans Cross, either in a version you have printed out – or on the screen of your laptop

Leader	This is a cross from Bessans, that's a town in France.
	It looks odd, doesn't it?
	There's no Jesus, just lots of things stuck on it – a ladder, some dice, and a cockerel on the top.

Look at it closely

Can anyone guess what these things are?
Look there are some nails …

With a few hints the children will be able to identify some of the objects on the cross

This cross is telling the story of Holy Week.
It's got the nails they used to nail Jesus to the Cross,
and the ladder they used to bring Him down,
it's even got the ear St Peter chopped off – do you remember that bit of the story? *(Probably not – carry on whatever the response)*
We'll go through the story together, and see what sort of things we're going to put on our cross.

Holy Week

Go over to a large table and tell the story of Holy Week, using the pictures from the CD-Rom. Ask the children to find you the pictures as you go through

Leader	Holy Week starts on Palm Sunday with Jesus riding into Jerusalem
CD20.1	on a **donkey**.
	On Monday and Tuesday His disciples prepare for the Passover;
CD20.2	they buy a **lamb**.
	On Wednesday one of His disciples slides off to betray Jesus to the High Priest.*
	Who was that? (**Judas**)
	Quite right. The High Priest gives Judas a **bag of money** with 30
CD20.3	pieces of silver inside.
	On Thursday Jesus has a Passover supper with His disciples – and
CD20.4	He tells them that the **Bread and Wine** are His Body and Blood.

---

* This day used to be called 'Spy Wednesday'; Judas sneaked off to betray Jesus, like a spy.

	Then they go together to the Mount of Olives, where Jesus prays.

CD20.5   Then they go together to the Mount of Olives, where Jesus prays. Judas turns up with a crowd of soldiers – they've got **clubs and swords**.

CD20.6   And Peter draws his **sword**, and cuts off someone's **ear**.
(The man Peter attacked was called Malthus – Jesus healed him.)
Jesus is arrested.
And taken to the High Priest. Peter follows at a distance. Peter is accused of knowing Jesus, but he denies it three times. The third

CD20.7   time he denies Jesus, the **cock crows**.
Very early on Friday morning Jesus is taken to be tried by the Romans.
Pilate, the Roman governor, knows He is innocent, and **washes his**

CD20.8   **hands** of Him.
Then what happens?

The children can probably tell you the rest
Put their narrative in order with the help of the other pictures

Jesus carries His cross.

CD20.9   His **face is wiped** by St Veronica.

CD20.10   He is **stripped**,

CD20.11   and **nailed** to the Cross.

CD20.12   An **inscription** is put above His head

CD20.13   and the soldiers play a **game of dice** for His coat.
Jesus cries out that He is thirsty and someone puts a **sponge** to His

CD20.14   mouth on a **reed**.
Jesus dies on the Cross.

CD20.15   The Centurion pierces His side with a **spear**, to make sure He is dead. And says, 'Truly this was the Son of God!'

CD20.16   Jesus' friends come with a **ladder**, take down His body, and bury Him in a new tomb.

ACTIVITY

Making the Cross

*Make a large card cross, following the template on the CD-Rom – **CD20.17**. Ask two children to colour it green. Once they've done that, stiffen it by taping a couple of light flower canes on its back.*

Meanwhile, the other children are deciding which props to put on the cross. You don't have to use all the ones provided, and the cross will look all the better for being decorated by the children's handiwork. The CD-Rom pictures are merely a guide.

You might feel that some 'real' props would look good – some fake money for the pieces of silver, a couple of real dice, a piece of sponge on a straw, a plasticine ear. (Children are always very struck by the ear ...)

If you need extra props you can add the hand that struck Jesus, the crown of thorns, the purple robe and the lantern the soldiers carried when they arrested Him. Draw the props on to card and cut round them. (If you are in a hurry, neat little rectangles will be fine.) Stick them on the cross.

The donkey and lamb should be at the bottom, the cockerel perched on the top, the inscription in its usual place, Jesus' image on Veronica's handkerchief at the place where the beams of wood cross, and the ladder on the stem.

Try to ensure that each child knows the meaning of his or her object.

Admire the result and practise your presentation (see below).

BEFORE THE FINAL PRAYER

Leave the craft table and gather round the cross, held up by Leader 2

Leader 1   We've got as far as the evening of Friday – but Holy Week doesn't stop there. Good Friday is followed by Holy Saturday, when Jesus lay in His tomb, and then on to Easter Sunday, the day Jesus rose from the dead. That's why our cross is green, to show that Jesus brought life back from the tomb.*

FINAL PRAYER

Ask the children to say the following prayer after you ...

Leader   **We adore you O Christ,**
And we bless you,
Because by your Holy Cross
You have saved the world. Amen

Let's finish by making the Sign of the Cross
✠ In the Name of the Father, and of the Son, and of the Holy Spirit. Amen

---

* The cross in Medieval stained glass is usually coloured green, for the same reason.

BACK IN CHURCH

The children bring in their cross

| Leader | The children have made a cross to tell the story of Holy Week. It starts with a donkey – drawn by *Name*. Why have we got a donkey, *Name*? |
| Child 1 | Because Jesus rode into Jerusalem on a donkey. |

Then go through all the props in order. If there isn't time for every child to speak, acknowledge them as you go through, by saying

This ear was made by …?

Child puts his hand up

Oh yes, of course, by *Name*.

(One of the clergy may like to go through the cross with the children – try to ensure they have read the script beforehand)

Script 21   Rock and Roll

Easter Sunday

St John 20.1–10, St Luke 24.1–12

THEME

There are two possible Gospels for this Sunday; check with your priest as to which you're using. They record the same amazing news – the Empty Tomb.
This Easter we're concentrating on the enormous stone that sealed Jesus' tomb – who moved it? Closely connected is another question: why do we roll Easter Eggs at Easter time?

SET UP

- The liturgical colour is White or Gold.
- The bells and candles are back for the Gospel Procession.
- Dress the table at the front with flowers if you've got the time.
- An Empty Tomb.
- A DIY Tomb and Stone (see template on CD-Rom).
- A hot cross bun.
- Enough hard boiled eggs to give all the kids a chance to roll them. Dyeing the eggs beforehand goes down well.
- You can use solid cream-filled eggs for egg rolling, but you will need about six hard boiled eggs if you want to try egg 'jarping' (see below).
- Two wooden spoons (optional).

THE KYRIE

Leader   Lord Jesus, when you rose from the dead, you defeated evil,
          Lord have mercy
          Lord have mercy

          Lord Jesus, when you rose from the dead, you washed away our sins,
          Christ have mercy
          Christ have mercy

Lord Jesus, when you rose from the dead, you set us free,
Lord have mercy
Lord have mercy

Ask the children to repeat **The Prayer for Forgiveness** *after you* (**p. xxxvi**).

THE EASTER GREETING

Teach the children the Easter Greeting

Leader	Alleluia! Christ is risen!
Children	**He is risen indeed! Alleluia!**

BEFORE THE GOSPEL

Leader   At last, we've got to Easter.
The church is shining in white and gold.
The candles are back, so are the bells, and the Gospel this morning
is so amazing, we're going to hear it right now.

THE GOSPEL PROCESSION

THE GOSPEL   *St John 20.1–10, or St Luke 24.1–12*

AFTER THE GOSPEL

Leader   Hi, well I've brought along something left over from Good Friday.

Produce the hot cross bun

Anyone know what it's called? (**A hot cross bun**)
Well done – but why's it got a cross on it? (**Because Jesus died on the cross**)
Exactly. Jesus died on the Cross on Good Friday.
His friends took Him down and they buried Him in a tomb,

CD21.1   like this …

Show them whatever you're using for a tomb; make sure the entrance is blocked up by the stone

And they rolled a stone across the entrance.
Then what happened?
Who came to the tomb? What did they see?

Encourage the kids to be quite precise – piously answering 'Jesus!' is the wrong answer. Depending on the Gospel you're using, establish that

St Luke's account

> Mary Magdalene (plus Joanna, and Mary the mother of James) came to the tomb, followed by Peter. The women found the tomb empty, then they saw two angels beside them. Peter saw the Empty Tomb and the grave clothes.

St John's account

> Mary Magdalene, followed by Peter and John, came to the tomb. Mary saw the Empty Tomb, as did the two men; Peter peered inside and saw the grave clothes folded up.

Examine the grave clothes, shake them out if you're using a sheet, or unfold the pieces of cloth if you're using a picture. Nope, no Jesus there …

> OK, I think we've worked out what's happened so far.
> What we've got is an Empty Tomb, a great big hole – hey, just a minute …
> What happened to the rock? (**It's been moved/rolled away**)
> Really? Who moved it? *(Take all answers)*
> We don't know – one of the Gospels says an angel moved it. But none of Jesus' friends were around when it happened so we can only guess.
> Nobody knew what was going on that first Easter morning.
> That rock had rolled away, the tomb was empty, people were running about.
> But one thing was very clear indeed – Jesus was not in His tomb.
> Why was that? (**He was risen**)
> Exactly! That's the great news. Jesus was alive.
> Live people don't stay in tombs, they get out. Jesus wasn't going to let a weedy thing like a rock stop Him. That rock is one of the most exciting things about Easter morning. I don't know how it moved – but it did. Jolly quickly.
> Has anyone heard of rock and roll? *(A rhetorical question)*
> Right, well here's a rock – and it rolled …

Roll your stone if you can

> Anyone heard of the Rolling Stones?
> Well, this is the original 'Rolling Stone' …
> I must say what I wanted to do this morning was get a really big boulder and roll it down the aisle. But this place is run by grown-ups, and they wouldn't let me …

Mock dismay – get the other Leaders to respond panto fashion with an 'Ah!'

However, we have got *(produce the hard boiled eggs)* these!
Specially prepared Easter Eggs, boiled nice and hard, so we can roll them …
Anyone want to try?

GAMES

Egg Rolling

Run an egg rolling race along the floor – the children either bowl their egg along, or bat it along with a wooden spoon. If you've got a large number of children you may have to split them into teams and get a representative to bowl the team egg.
Reserve some eggs for the presentation in church.

Egg Jarping

If you've got the time you could also play Egg Jarping. It's very like playing Conkers. Two children face each other, holding a hard boiled egg by the round end, and trying to crack their opponent's egg, using the pointy end. If your egg cracks first, you've lost. The winner then challenges somebody else.*
(This reminds us that Jesus' tomb cracked open on Easter Sunday.)

REHEARSAL

There probably won't be time for kids to roll eggs all the way down the aisle Back in Church, so do some underarm bowling practice. Choose a couple of competent children to bowl eggs across the hall floor. Then practise the presentation below.

MUSIC

Any Easter hymn is suitable, but try to choose one with a swing. Maybe 'Thine be the glory' among the traditional hymns, or 'I danced in the morning' (verses 1, 3 and 5) among the moderns. There's a case for playing Bill Haley's 'Rock around the clock' if you can think up some suitably vigorous movements to accompany your rendering of the word 'Rock!'

---

* In some versions of this game the winner gets to eat the cracked eggs, but today's children are not usually as hungry as earlier generations, who would have been breaking a rigorous Lenten Fast on Easter Sunday. (Of course, small hollow chocolate eggs are another matter…)

FINAL PRAYER	Lord Jesus, When you rose from the dead You filled the hearts of your friends with joy. Your Church is full of happiness today. Help us to share our joy with other people. **Amen**

BACK IN CHURCH

Check that the aisle is clear for egg bowling. If it is, line the children up at the back, behind the egg bowlers. (If the aisle is too full of buggies and people, you'll have to bowl your eggs across the church, at the front.) The Leader goes down the front

Leader   Today we heard about the Empty Tomb and the great rock that had rolled away.
We'd have liked to have rolled a great big rock down the church to show you how amazing this was – but we couldn't find anything big enough. So we're going to make do with eggs.
Roll those eggs, chaps!

The children bowl their eggs down the aisle, one at a time, cheered on by the others

Detachable stone

Black backing paper

Tomb shape

folded cloths tucked inside

Packing box covered in brown paper

Back of hula-hoop covered in grey paper

Detachable stone   folded sheet   rolled napkin

(From CD21.1)

Script 22   Doubting Thomas

Easter 2

St John 20.19–20, 24–29

THEME

Doubting Thomas is one of the most believable saints in the New Testament. We've all met people like him: 'I won't believe that until I see it myself' or 'sounds fishy to me…'

There's no harm in examining the reasons behind our faith, and this session shows the children the difference between sensible belief and blind credulity.

SET UP

- The liturgical colour is White or Gold.
- Magic wand from a toy shop.
- Toy frog or snake or any rubber wriggly (in Leader 2's pocket).
- Prepare three *Sawing the Lady in Half* tricks from the CD-Rom (incredibly easy). Practise the trick, and bring two (unsawn) ladies along to the session.
- Packet of aspirin with dodgy label stuck on (from the CD-Rom). Leader 1 has these in his pocket.
- A Fireman Sam fire helmet, if you've got one – don't worry if you haven't.

WELCOME *the children and lead them in* **The Sign of the Cross** ✠ **(p. xxxvi).**

THE KYRIE   Lord Jesus, when you rose from the dead, you defeated evil,
Lord have mercy
Lord have mercy

Lord Jesus, when you rose from the dead, you washed away our sins,
Christ have mercy
Christ have mercy

Lord Jesus, when you rose from the dead, you set us free,
Lord have mercy
Lord have mercy

Ask the children to repeat **The Prayer for Forgiveness** *after you* (**p. xxxvi**).

THE EASTER GREETING

Leader	It's Easter time, so we're going to say the Easter Greeting. Do you remember how it goes? I say 'Alleluia! Christ is risen!'
	And you say … *(give them a chance to tell you)* **'He is risen indeed! Alleluia!'**

Run this three times, softly, louder, very loud indeed

BEFORE THE GOSPEL

I Don't Believe It!

Leader 1	I'm going to start by doing some magic …

Produce your magic wand

What shall I do?
Turn someone into a frog? *(Or whatever rubber toy Leader 2 has got in her pocket)*

Look speculatively at one of the older children

Leader 2	No, you did that last year. *(Produces a frog (or whatever) from her pocket)* We got into frightful trouble …
Leader 1	OK, well, what's a really neat magic trick?
Leader 2	Sawing a lady in half …
Leader 1	Sawing a lady in half? Easy, no problem at all … Anyone here want to be sawn in half?

If the kids say 'No', fine, you're into the trick
If some brave soul says 'Yes', Leader 2 rushes forward

Leader 2	No! Stop – he's useless. What am I going to say to your mother?
Leader 1	There's a strong feeling of disbelief in this room … However, I *will* saw a lady in half. Here she is. And here is the magic chest I'm going to slide her into …

Hold up the lady and packet you've made from the CD-Rom (**CD22.1**)*, and slide her in*

And here are my scissors …

Apparently cut the lady in half

	Poor lady – perhaps it's just as well I didn't choose one of you …
	And now, I'll just wave my magic wand …
	ABRACADABRA!
	And here she is *(pull her out)*
	joined up again! *(Take a bow)*
Leader 2	How did you do that?
Leader 1	Magic!
Leader 2	I don't believe you.
	What do you think, kids?
	Was it magic – or was it a trick?

(The children usually come down on the side of a trick: it doesn't matter if they don't)

Leader 1	Guys, you've got to believe in me!
Leader 2	Rubbish, it was just a trick. How did you do it?

Leader 1 pulls out the second lady and chest and shows how it's done. Get a child to do the trick

Leader 1	Actually *Name* [Leader 2] is right. Don't ever believe magicians – it's all tricks.
	But what about this?

Belief

Leader 1	Supposing I've got a headache.
	Oh, man! I feel terrible.

Sit on a chair and hold your head. Leader 2 comes forward

Leader 2	Haven't you got any aspirin?
Leader 1	Oh yes. *(Pulls out an aspirin packet)*
Leader 2	I've never seen these before – where did you get them?
Leader 1	From my doctor.
Leader 2	*(Reading the label* **(CD22.2)***)* 'Headache Zonko!?' Sounds fishy to me.
Leader 1	No, it's fine, my doctor is really good. Trust me …
Leader 2	OK, I'll get you some water …

Faith

Leader 1	*(Getting up)* You see, kids, there are a lot of times when you're asked to believe something.
	If you haven't got *proof* that what you're being told is right, you have to decide whether you trust the person who's telling you to believe it.

Show them the aspirin packet

> I must say I wouldn't usually take these pills – but I trust my doctor.
> If you trust someone to tell the truth, it's sensible to believe them.

Fire!

> Let's suppose a fire has broken out, and there you are trapped on your window sill. *Name (any kid)*, would you mind being trapped on a window sill for a moment?

Ask the child to stand on a chair

> OK, the smoke is billowing round you, you can't see the ground – and the kid from next door – the stupid one – shouts out …

Leader 2   JUMP! You can't hurt yourself!

Leader 1   *Restrain the child if they look as if they're going to jump*
> Wait a minute – can you trust that kid?
> Then you hear the fire engine.
> And just below there's someone in a fireman's helmet. He shouts out.

Leader 2   *Leader 2 swaps sides – and puts on a helmet if she's got one*
> JUMP! We've got a safety net fixed up for you.

Leader 1   Do you believe him?
> Yes, you do.
> Jump! *(The kid jumps)*
> In the Gospel today we hear about someone who was asked to believe something – and decided not to. Let's see if he was being sensible.

THE GOSPEL PROCESSION

THE GOSPEL   *St John 20.19–20, 24–29*

AFTER THE GOSPEL

Leader   So Jesus came back from the dead and made Himself known to ten of His friends. But one wasn't there. Who was it? (**Thomas**)
> The others told him they had seen Jesus – but Thomas didn't believe them. Now Thomas was wrong – Jesus *had* come back from the dead – but was he wrong not to believe the others?
> If you had been Thomas, would you have believed them?

Take all answers – it will depend on how old the children are as to how they respond

Establish that Thomas was right in a way – after all, people don't come back from the dead – but his friends didn't usually tell lies either, so he should have believed them (especially as they were so happy)

> Thomas should have believed his friends – but he didn't.
> However, he *did* believe Jesus. The next time Thomas turned up, Jesus came into the room and Thomas could see and touch the Risen Lord.

REHEARSAL

Practise your presentation for when you go back into church (see below).

FINAL PRAYER

Settle the children round a prayer candle

Leader
> Look at the flame.
> Isn't it lovely?
> It would be very difficult to explain what it was to a blind man.
> He'd have to trust us.
> Jesus said to Thomas, 'You believe because you've seen me – blessed are those who have not seen, and yet believe.'
> That's us!
> We haven't actually seen the Risen Jesus, but we trust Him and His friends, so we believe He is alive.

Ask the children to say part of the Creed after you

> **I believe in Jesus Christ**
> **Who suffered, died and was buried.**
> **On the third day He rose again**
> **And ascended into Heaven**
> **And sits on the right hand of the Father.**
> **Amen**

BACK IN CHURCH

Leader	This morning we heard about St Thomas. When his friends told him that Jesus had risen from the dead, Thomas said:
Child 1	I don't believe it!
Child 2	Prove it!
Child 3	Sounds fishy to me.
Leader	But when he saw the Risen Lord, he said:
Everyone	**My Lord and my God!**

Script 23   Jesus Cooks Breakfast

Easter 3

St John 21.1–17

THEME

The wonderful thing about the Risen Jesus is that He did such ordinary things
– went for a walk, ate fish or, in the Gospel today, cooked breakfast. It's a long
story, but the grown-ups and children tell it together and discover how gently
Jesus forgave St Peter for denying Him.

SET UP

- The liturgical colour is White or Gold.
- Pictures from the CD-Rom.
- Black marker pen to write up Peter's denials (see below) and a red marker pen to
  cross them out again. (If you've got a white board, the effect is even better if you
  can wipe out the denials.)
- Write up the crowds' lines (see below).
- Frying pan plus fish – chocolate or cardboard.
- A sheet for use as a fishing net.
- Cast the drama. Peter and Jesus should either be grown-ups or competent older
  kids. Give them a copy of the script.
- Some charcoal – either in a thurible, or some barbecue charcoal in a tin foil dish.
- Box of matches.
- Three cards, with a large NO on one side and a large YES on the other.

WELCOME *the children and lead them in* **The Sign of the Cross** ✠ **(p. xxxvi).**

THE KYRIE   Lord Jesus, when you rose from the dead, you defeated evil,
Lord have mercy
Lord have mercy

Lord Jesus, when you rose from the dead, you washed away our sins,
Christ have mercy
Christ have mercy

Lord Jesus, when you rose from the dead, you set us free,
Lord have mercy
Lord have mercy

Ask the children to repeat **The Prayer for Forgiveness** *after you* (**p. xxxvi**).

THE EASTER GREETING

Leader
It's still Easter time, so we're going to say the Easter Greeting.
Do you remember how it goes? I say,
'Alleluia! Christ is risen!'
And you say ... *(give them a chance to tell you)*
'He is risen indeed! Alleluia!'

Run this three times, softly, louder, very loud indeed

BEFORE THE GOSPEL

Charcoal

Leader 2 goes out of the room to light the charcoal, leave it outside

Leader 1
Easter is a wonderful time – and the best thing about it is that everything is sorted out. Jesus is back from the dead and He puts everything right.
We're going to hear about one of the things He put right today. But to understand the Gospel, we'll have to go back a bit. Back to the night of Jesus' arrest ...

Show them the picture of Peter's Denial, go through the story with their help, and write up each denial on a white board or flip chart

Peter Denies Jesus

After Jesus was arrested, He was taken to the High Priest's house to be tried. St Peter had followed Jesus and the soldiers from a distance, and he got into the courtyard.

CD23.1 A girl at the gate said, 'Aren't you one of that man's disciples?'

CD23.2 'No, I am not' *(write it in the bubble)* said Peter.
It was bitterly cold, so the High Priest's servants made a charcoal fire in the courtyard and everyone huddled round.

CD23.3 Peter got closer to warm himself and somebody else said, 'Surely you're a friend of that man!'

CD23.4 'I don't know the man!' *(write it in the bubble)* said Peter.
By this time everyone was looking at Peter, and another man

said, 'You *were* with Jesus, you've got the same accent.'
And Peter began to swear and said,

CD23.5   'I tell you I don't know Him!' *(Write it in the bubble)*
That was a terrible night, and Peter never forgot how he had denied
Jesus. Today we're going to hear how Jesus forgave him.
We'll tell the story together.

Getting Ready

Leader   I am going to need a John, a James, a Thomas and a Nathaniel.

Choose both boys and girls and bring them to the front

Right, now *Name* is going to be Peter, and *Name* is going to be
Jesus. Jesus will need a frying pan.

Peter joins James and the others. Jesus picks up the frying pan and stands to one side

The rest of you are fish – you need to huddle together.

Get your 'fish' into a shoal

Yup, when fish bunch up like that it's called a shoal.
Can you swim in a shoal?

Help the kids to swim in a shoal – give them directions

Over to the left, not too fast – now forward a bit – now to the right.
Brilliant, stop!
Right, you guys are in a fishing boat and will need to row together.
I'll show you …

Ask the disciples to line up to make a boat, and row along in a line, moving together.
Once they've got that, give Peter the 'net'. The boat stops as he throws it – he never
catches anything and the boat rows on again
Ask the 'fish' to swim up beside the boat, on the right-hand side
Stick up the 'fishes' remarks and get them to shout them out as you cue them in

Fish	You can't catch us!
Fish	You still can't catch us!
Fish	Oh, no!
Everybody	SPLOSH!

The children return to their normal positions for hearing the Gospel, however, as you
read it, cue them in to form up as the boat and shoal and be ready to cue in their lines

THE GOSPEL PROCESSION

THE GOSPEL   *St John 21.1–17*

Narrator	One day, after Jesus had risen from the dead, Simon Peter said,
Peter	'I'm going fishing.'
Narrator	And his friends said, 'We'll go with you.'
	So Peter, James, John, Thomas, Nathaniel and a couple of others got into their fishing boat.

The disciples form up a boat

	And rowed around for a bit.
They do this	And tried to catch fish. They had a terrible time …

The fish swim up in their shoal, and Peter throws his net – he never catches anything

	The fish just laughed at them and said,
Fish	**You can't catch us!**
Narrator	Peter and his friends tried again. *(Off they go …)*
	They still couldn't catch anything and the fish called out,
Fish	**You still can't catch us!**
Narrator	The fish snuck up on the right-hand side of the boat.

The fish move to the right of the boat

	And somebody on the beach called out to them,
Jesus	Children, have you caught anything?
Narrator	The disciples shouted back – what do you think they shouted? (**No!**)
	Quite right – shout back.
The disciples	**No!**
Narrator	So the man on the beach called again.
Jesus	Throw your net out on the right-hand side …
Narrator	The disciples gave the net one more throw.
	In it went.

Peter manages to net some fish

Fish	**Oh, no!**
Narrator	And John looked up and said, 'It is the Lord!'
	And immediately Peter jumped out of the boat.
Everybody	**Splosh!**
Narrator	And waded ashore.

Peter joins Jesus

	The other disciples pulled in the fish, and paddled ashore more carefully. They counted the fish –

Take the net off, do a rapid and improbable count

there were 153 of them. It was a huge catch.

Then they hung around on the beach. They were a bit scared of Jesus – they hadn't quite got used to the idea that He was alive again. But Jesus didn't mind; He called out to them

Jesus   Let's have breakfast …

Ask all the kids to circle Jesus and the frying pan

Narrator   He had cooked their breakfast – what had they got? (**Fish!**)

Once breakfast was over Jesus looked at Peter and said,

Jesus   Simon Peter, son of John, do you love me?

Peter   Yes, Lord, you know I love you.

Jesus   Then feed my sheep.

Narrator   And as Jesus said that, one of Peter's denials was just wiped away.

Wipe off a denial

Then Jesus said again,

Jesus   Simon Peter, son of John, do you love me?

Peter   Yes, Lord, you know I love you.

Jesus   Then, feed my lambs.

Narrator   And as Jesus said that, another of Peter's denials was wiped away.

Wipe off another denial

Narrator   Then Jesus said a third time,

Jesus   Simon Peter, son of John, are you *sure* you love me?

Narrator   Peter was upset that Jesus asked him a third time if he loved Him, and he said,

Peter   Lord, you know everything, you *know* I love you

Jesus   Feed my sheep.

And Peter's third denial was wiped away. Wipe it off

AFTER THE GOSPEL

Leader   So Peter knew that Jesus had forgiven him – and given him a job. When Jesus said, 'Feed my sheep', He meant that Peter should look after Jesus' people, the Church.

Now, how are we going to tell this to the people back in church?

REHEARSAL

Practise your presentation for when you go back into church (see below).

LAST PRAYER

Leader 2 brings the charcoal into the room
Gather the children round it

Leader   Can you smell the charcoal?

Some of you can …

Smells are funny things. Sometimes a smell will bring back a memory faster than a photograph.

Do you remember how Peter stood beside a charcoal fire as he denied Jesus? He must have hated the smell of charcoal after that. But in the story this morning he stood beside another charcoal fire – the one on which Jesus cooked breakfast.

And it was by that fire that Jesus forgave him.

I bet that, for the rest of his life, Peter couldn't smell charcoal, without remembering how the Risen Lord had forgiven him.

Let's pray together

Ask the children to repeat the prayer after you

Lord Jesus,
Friend of sinners,
Thank you for forgiving Peter,
Help us to love you as he did
And do whatever job you send us
This Easter time
And for ever. Amen

BACK IN CHURCH

The children line up down the front – three of them have the No/Yes cards

Leader   Today we heard how St Peter once denied Jesus.

Three people asked him this question,

Child 1   Do you know Jesus?

Leader   And Peter said,

A child holds up a NO card

No!

Then another person asked him,

Child 2   Do you know Jesus?

Leader   And Peter said,

A child holds up a NO card

No!

	Then somebody else asked,
Child 3	Do you know Jesus?
Leader	And Peter said,

A child holds up a NO card

No!
But, when Jesus came back from the dead, He asked Peter three questions.

The person who played Jesus now asks

| **Jesus** | Simon Peter, son of John, do you love me? |
| **Leader** | And Peter said, |

A child reverses the card to read YES

Yes!
Then Jesus said again,

| **Jesus** | Simon Peter, son of John, do you love me? |
| **Leader** | And Peter said, |

Another child reverses the card to read YES

Yes!
Then Jesus said again,

| **Jesus** | Simon Peter, son of John, are you sure you love me? |
| **Leader** | And Peter said, |

The last card is reversed to say YES

Yes!
So Jesus had cancelled Peter's three denials and Peter knew he was really forgiven.

(CD23.5)

Sample cartoon for this script

Script 24   Sheep Stealing

Easter 4

St John 10.27–30

THEME

The children spend a pleasant morning learning to steal sheep. But however adept they become, they'll discover in the Gospel that *nobody* can steal the tiniest lamb from Jesus' flock.

SET UP

- The liturgical colour is White or Gold.
- Several toy lambs, or just one that you throw back across the room to be stolen again.
- The first couple of demonstrations need a line of thin string (fishing reel is ideal) attached to the sheep's front leg.
- Old-fashioned walking stick to serve as a crook.
- If anyone has got a sheepskin, bring it along. But it's not vital.
- Cast a shepherd, and ask Leader 2 to be Mak the sheep stealer: he/she wears a dodgy raincoat, too large – so he/she can hide things under it – with the collar up on the first entrance and a plastic truncheon or similar in one of the pockets.
- Set up the doctored sheep at the front, on one side of the room, the line stretching across to the room – and have a grown-up ready to whizz the sheep across on cue.

WELCOME *the children and lead them in* **The Sign of the Cross** ✠ **(p. xxxvi).**

THE KYRIE   Lord Jesus, when you rose from the dead, you defeated evil,
Lord have mercy
Lord have mercy

Lord Jesus, when you rose from the dead, you washed away our sins,
Christ have mercy
Christ have mercy

Lord Jesus, when you rose from the dead, you set us free,
Lord have mercy
Lord have mercy

Ask the children to repeat **The Prayer for Forgiveness** *after you* (**p. xxxvi**).

THE EASTER GREETING

Leader	It's still Easter time, so we're going to say the Easter Greeting. Do you remember how it goes? I say, 'Alleluia! Christ is risen!'
	And you say … *(give them a chance to tell you)* **'He is risen indeed! Alleluia!'**

Run this three times, softly, louder, very loud indeed

BEFORE THE GOSPEL

Mak the Sheep Stealer

Leader	Today we've got a visitor – here he/she is …

Enter Mak, looking deeply suspicious

Mak	Hi, kids.
Leader	Good to see you – what's your name?
Mak	Mak. *(Hunches his raincoat up and peers round)*
Leader	So, what do you do for a living, Mak?
Mak	Oh, er, I look after sheep …
Leader	I didn't know you had any sheep.
Mak	Ah, well I can't help meself, sheep like me … There's a sheep over there, watch this …

Mak whistles (if you can't whistle, say, 'Oi! Sheep!')
Whizzz! The sheep zips across the room and Mak scoops it up

Leader	Mak! That's sheep stealing! How disgraceful! *(Sidles up)* How else do you steal sheep?

Throw the sheep back, or have another doctored sheep ready

Mak	Sometimes I know its name. *(Looks across at the sheep)* Oi! Come over here, Lamb Chop!

Whizz, the sheep comes across the room again

Leader	Do the sheep always come?

Mak	No, sometimes I have to go to them.
	It's dead easy – you just pretend to be a sheep.

Puts on a sheepskin (if you've got one), sidles across, sits by the sheep, and says

Baa!

If you have someone prepared to operate the sheep, it can look intelligently at Mak and have a brief conversation. It ends, of course, with it being stuffed under the raincoat or sheepskin

Leader	Brilliant! I mean disgraceful ...
	Supposing there's a shepherd in the way?

Places the shepherd, with crook, by the sheep. Mak discards the sheepskin and puts the raincoat back on

Mak	A shepherd?
	Oh, no problem – you just go up ... (Approaches the shepherd)
	'Allo, mate, nice day ...
	Then you pull out a useful little cosh.

Out comes the truncheon. Mak bonks the shepherd on the head – who falls down at once – and scoops up the sheep

Leader	Well, I never thought we'd have a sheep stealer in Children's Church.
	It seems a simple job, though, doesn't it?
	I wonder if you lot would be any good at it?

Sheep Snaffling Game

Set up the classic Sheep Snaffling Game. The shepherd, or a grown-up, sits at the end of the room, his back to the kids and a sheep behind him. The kids creep up cautiously as they try to steal the sheep. The shepherd listens out. If he hears something he points in the direction of the sound and the kid is out. If you've got large numbers you might have to play this in relays

Leader	Well, we started off with one sheep stealer – and we've ended up with *Number (however many children there are in the room)* plus one *(as Mak's still present)*.
	I don't know what Jesus would think of that. Let's find out.

THE GOSPEL PROCESSION

THE GOSPEL   *St John 10.27–30*

AFTER THE GOSPEL

Leader   So is Jesus bothered by sheep stealers? (**No**)
              No, you're quite right.
              He says that nobody, absolutely nobody, will be able to steal His
              sheep from Him.
              What do you think Jesus means by 'His sheep'? Has He got a huge
              flock of sheep in Heaven?

*Take all answers. He may have of course, but what He
means here is His Church*

              We are Jesus' sheep.
              If you ever see an Icon of Jesus the
              Good Shepherd, He always holds His
              sheep like this

*Put the toy sheep on your shoulders, holding its feet
firmly*

              Jesus came all the way down to Earth
              to find us, so He's not going to let
              anyone steal us from Him.

REHEARSAL

Practise your presentation for when you go back into church (see below).

FINAL   We're going to pray part of the Shepherd psalm, number 23.
PRAYER   The response is
              The Lord is my shepherd
              The Lord is my shepherd

              The Lord is my shepherd,
              I shall not want
              The Lord is my shepherd

              He makes me lie down in green pastures;
              He leads me beside still waters;
              The Lord is my shepherd

              He leads me in right paths
              for His name's sake.
              The Lord is my shepherd

Even though I walk through the darkest valley,
I fear no evil;
The Lord is my shepherd

For you are with me;
your rod and your staff –
they comfort me.
The Lord is my shepherd

MUSIC

'The King of love my shepherd is' *(verses 1, 2, 3 and 6), ends the session well.* *

BACK IN CHURCH

Take in the toy sheep, plus a child prepared to operate it. Mak appears in his raincoat again. Sheepskin to hand

Leader	This morning, I am sorry to say, a sheep stealer joined us at Children's Church.

Enter Mak – who places himself on the other side from the sheep

He gave us some useful tips on sheep stealing. How sometimes you just have to whistle *(or call)*

Mak whistles – and the sheep whizzes across

for a sheep to fall into your arms.
Or you can actually pretend to be a sheep …

Mak ambles across as a fake sheep, quick dialogue with the toy, and it's gone …

and steal it that way.

Child 1	We wondered what Jesus would think about this.
Child 2	So we read the Gospel.
Child 3	And we discovered that *nobody* was going to steal Jesus' sheep.
Child 4	Which is a bit of luck for us!

---

* The language is old-fashioned, but children enjoy strange words like 'verdant' for green and the sense is perfectly clear.

Script 25   A New Commandment

Easter 5

St John 13.33–35

THEME

Jesus gives His friends a new commandment, that they should love one another. It's difficult to make this sound as revolutionary as it actually was. The Christians burst on the world with emergency funds, provision for orphans, widows, and care for prisoners. Before this, people's natural kindness had been directed to their extended families – and stopped there. We can't load the children down with relief agencies, but we can show them how Christians go the extra mile by using that popular teaching aid, the Snakes and Ladders game.

SET UP

- The liturgical colour is White or Gold.
- Pictures and game from the CD-Rom.
- A large bouncy die (see page 26).

WELCOME *the children and lead them in* **The Sign of the Cross** ✠ (**p. xxxvi**).

THE KYRIE   Lord Jesus, when you rose from the dead, you defeated evil,
Lord have mercy
Lord have mercy

Lord Jesus, when you rose from the dead, you washed away our sins
Christ have mercy
Christ have mercy

Lord Jesus, when you rose from the dead, you set us free
Lord have mercy
Lord have mercy

Ask the children to repeat **The Prayer for Forgiveness** *after you* (**p. xxxvi**).

THE EASTER GREETING

Leader	It's still Easter time, so we're going to say the Easter Greeting. Do you remember how it goes? I say, 'Alleluia! Christ is risen!'
	And you say … *(give them a chance to tell you)* **'He is risen indeed! Alleluia!'**

Run this three times, softly, louder, very loud indeed

BEFORE THE GOSPEL

Rufus

Leader	We're going to start with hearing the story of Rufus.
CD25.1	He was a Roman – and he had the bad luck to annoy the Roman Emperor. So he was exiled. That means he had to leave Rome and go and live in a very obscure bit of the Roman Empire called Bithynia – miles away from anywhere, with no decent baths, or streets, or any of the things Romans liked best.
	Rufus had to join a crowd of other exiles, and they were pushed across the Empire by soldiers, and had to sleep rough, and hardly had any food and, when they reached their journey's end, they
CD25.2	looked liked this.

Comment on the picture – Rufus is in a dreadful state, unwashed, no shoes, bashed and bruised

	And then something extraordinary happened. A crowd of people appeared from nowhere with bowls of hot water, and bandages, and
CD25.3	food, and cleaned everybody up.
	Rufus couldn't understand it,
	'Why are you doing this?' he said to a man who was giving him some new sandals, 'We're not your family …'
	'Oh, that doesn't matter,' said the man. 'We're Christians, we try and love everybody.'

A New Commandment

Nowadays we expect people to be nice to strangers – especially ones who look as unhappy as Rufus but, before Jesus, people weren't always nice to strangers.

People were usually only kind to their own families. That all changed when Jesus gave His friends a new commandment.

THE GOSPEL PROCESSION

THE GOSPEL   *St John 13.33–35*

AFTER THE GOSPEL

Leader	Did you hear the new commandment? What was it? (**We should love one another**) Quite right – and if you listen carefully, you find it's a special kind of love. Jesus said, 'You must love one another just as I have loved you.' We've got to love each other as *Jesus* loved us. That's difficult. Because we love each other normally about this much. *(Hold your hands open about a foot)* In fact, there're some people we love about this much. *(Hold up your finger and thumb)* But Jesus loved us this much. *(Stretch your hands as far apart as possible)*

Going the Extra Mile

Leader	It's like this.
CD25.4	Here's a family. *(Mum, sister and little brother)* The mother tells this kid *(the sister)* to tidy up her room and, because she loves her mum, she does so. But if she's a Christian, and filled with Jesus' love, she might go further …
CD25.5	and tidy up her little brother's room as well. Let's see how good we'd be at loving people as much as Jesus does.

GAME

Snakes and Ladders

*Depending on numbers, you either gather round a table for the board game, or stick it up on the wall (**CD25.6**). If you go for the latter, divide the children into teams and choose representatives to move the tokens and throw the die.*
The game sends the kids up ladders when they love people, and down snakes when they don't – really-mega acts of love are rewarded with a couple of huge ladders.

REHEARSAL

Practise your presentation for when you go back into church (see below).

FINAL PRAYER

Leader	Easter is such a cheerful time that we keep saying Alleluia – which is Hebrew for 'Hurray'. I'd like you to say alleluia when I give you the signal. Like this,
Cue them in	**Alleluia!**
	Excellent – now I'm going to say an acclamation, watch out for that signal,
Cue	**Alleluia!**
Cue again	**Alleluia!**
	Jesus said, Little children,
Cue	**Alleluia!**
	a new commandment I give you,
Cue	**Alleluia!**
	that you should love one another,
	just as I have loved you.
Cue	**Alleluia!**

Lead the children in a **Glory Be...** **(see p. xxxvii).**

BACK IN CHURCH

Child 1	We've come back to tell you the New Commandment Jesus has given His Church.
Child 2	It's very short, and very important.
Child 3	*(To the other children)* Are you ready? Go!
Everybody	**Love one another!**

(CD25.4)   (CD25.5)

Sample cartoons for this script

Script 26   The Promise of the Holy Spirit

Easter 6

St John 14.23, 25–26

THEME

Today's session is on the Holy Spirit. We can't picture the Spirit, but His many titles give us a clue to His character. In this session we consider the Spirit as the 'Lord and Giver of Life' and (a title the children are bound to approve of) the 'Gift Giver'.

SET UP

- The liturgical colour is White or Gold.
- Plasticine.
- A large sheet of blank paper.
- Marker pens for the children – make sure one of them is red.
- A Bible, with a marker at Genesis 2.7.
- Pictures from the CD-Rom.

For Holy Pass the Parcel

- A collection of cheap religious gifts for the children – tapping 'Sunday School Gifts' into an Internet search engine should bring up a host of Christian yo-yos, mini Christian skateboards, little fluorescent crosses, holy medals, one-decade rosaries, book marks and so on – or go to this site: www.religiouscrafts.co.uk/sunday_school_gifts.asp
- Take each gift and Sellotape it on to a card on which you have written one of the gifts, or fruits, of the Spirit (see below). Template on CD-Rom.
- Create an enormous parcel out of wrapping paper, newspaper and Sellotape – and insert these gifts into its various layers.
- You will need music for this game – either an audio player or someone at the piano.

The gifts of the Spirit are these

Wisdom, understanding, wonder, judgement, knowledge, courage and reverence.*

---

* The list comes from Isaiah 11. The Hebrew translated in your Bible gives only six of these gifts, but the Latin translation has seven. Those *seven* gifts became a standard list for teaching about the Holy Spirit in the middle ages. Since they are all good, we are going to stick with the longer list.

The fruits of the Spirit are these

- Love, joy, peace, patience, kindness, goodness, faithfulness, gentleness and self-control.*

WELCOME *the children and lead them in* **The Sign of the Cross** ✠ **(p. xxxvi).**

BEFORE THE KYRIE

Leader	We're nearly at the end of the Easter Season, and Jesus is getting ready to go back to Heaven – and today He tells His friends He'll send them the Holy Spirit to give them a hand.
	We're going to pray to the Holy Spirit now.

THE KYRIE	Holy Spirit
	You help us to know when we have done wrong
	Lord have mercy
	Lord have mercy
	Holy Spirit
	You help us to say sorry
	Christ have mercy
	Christ have mercy
	Holy Spirit
	You fill us with the love and forgiveness of God
	Lord have mercy
	Lord have mercy

Ask the children to repeat **The Prayer for Forgiveness** *after you* **(p. xxxvi).**

THE EASTER GREETING

Leader	OK, and now we're going to give each other the Easter Greeting. How does it go? You show me ...
	'Alleluia! Christ is risen!
	He is risen indeed! Alleluia!'

Run this three times, softly, louder, very loud indeed

---

* The list comes from Galatians 5.

BEFORE THE GOSPEL

Pictures

Leader   OK, I'd like to start with drawing some pictures.

Stick up a large sheet of paper

Can you draw a picture of God?

(See what comes), establish we can't draw a picture of God Himself – but we can draw pictures of the way He has shown Himself to us

For example, God lived on Earth as Jesus.
Well, we can draw Jesus.
Would anyone like to try? *(Ask a child up to draw, admire the result)*
That's God the Son.
How about God the Father?
He's sometimes called a King in the Bible, that might help.

(See if a child is up to drawing a king)

Super. Now, what about God the Spirit?

Some children will know that He can be represented as a dove or a flame – let them come forward to draw these symbols, and offer the red pen for the tongue of fire. If someone says, 'He's also a wind', put it on hold with an 'Excellent, we're going to talk about that'

Yes – a bird and a flame – the Spirit is difficult isn't He?
Don't let's draw pictures of Him.

Take down the paper, but don't scrunch it up

Let's think about Him instead.

Making Adam

I want to go all the way back to the moment when God created the Earth. In the Bible *(refer to Genesis 2)* it says, 'God took some clay and made a man out of it.'
Can you do that?

Go over to a table, dish out some plasticine and ask the kids to make little men. Make one yourself. When you've finished, lay the figures out in a row and look at them

They look very nice – but they're not exactly hopping about, are they?
I've never seen such a dozy bunch …

To the figurines WAKE UP!

Pick up the Bible again

Let's see what else God did.

Ask a child to read out Genesis 2.7

What did God do to the man He had made? (**He breathed on him**)

Right, let's have a go, when I get to 3, breathe. 1, 2, 3 …

The children breathe on the plasticine

You're not breathing hard enough – try again. 1, 2, 3 …

Nope, it's no good – why can't we do it? (**We're not God**)

You bet. Actually, *(looking at the Bible)* I know this word for 'breath'. In Greek it's Pneuma – what does Pneuma mean? (**Breath, of course**)

Yup, but Pneuma can also mean 'spirit'.

When God breathed on to the man He'd made of clay,

He breathed His Pneuma, His 'Spirit', into Him, and the man became alive.

God called the man Adam.

Well, we still can't draw the Holy Spirit, but now we know something about Him – He's very powerful and can make things come alive.

Let's hear some more.

THE GOSPEL PROCESSION

THE GOSPEL   *St John 14.23, 25–26*

Preface the Gospel with

Before Jesus went back to Heaven, He said to His disciples …

AFTER THE GOSPEL

Leader   Jesus told His friends that He was going home, but that He and His Father would send His friends the Holy Spirit.

And that the Spirit would teach them everything.

How does the Spirit do that?

I can tell you.

He opens up your minds to understand God.

In fact, He gives you the gift of Understanding.

CD26.1   *Put up the present picture from the CD-Rom*

And He helps you work out what's right and wrong.

CD26.2   That's the gift of Judgement. *(Put up picture 2)*

In fact, the Spirit is the 'Gift Giver'.

All Christians get His gifts – and we've got some of them bundled up in this parcel here. Let's find out what He's sent us!

GAME

Pass the Parcel

Gather the children into a circle. Start the music and pass the parcel. When the music stops the child with the parcel can tear some layers off, only to pass it on as the music starts again.
The reluctance of the kids to pass the parcel is a well-known feature of this game but, as the grown-ups are in charge of the music, you can usually ensure that everyone has a fair go. (Have some spare presents ready, in case any kid misses out after all.)
When you've finished, remove the wrapping paper, and keep the children in their circle. Ask them to put their presents in front of them – make sure Leader 2 has one as well.

FINAL PRAYER

Leader	We seem to have done very well. And I see the Spirit has added some yo-yos *(or whatever)* to His more usual gifts. What did you get, *Name? (Leader 2)*

Leader 2 reads out the gift on his/her card, and the children follow suit, going round the circle

Leader	OK, we'll do that again – but this time we're getting ready for what we're going to say in church. So we need to sort ourselves out. The Gifts of the Spirit are these – can you stand up if you've got one of these: wisdom, understanding, wonder, judgement, knowledge, courage, and reverence.

Ask that set of kids to sit together

And the Fruits of the Spirit are these – can you put your hand up if you've got one of these?
love,
joy,

peace,
patience,
kindness,
goodness,
faithfulness,
gentleness,
and self-control.

Make whatever adjustments may be necessary. Small groups may need to ask a child to have both a Gift of the Spirit and a Fruit of the Spirit

REHEARSAL

Practise your presentation for when you go back into church (see below).

FINAL	God the Holy Spirit,
PRAYER	Lord and Giver of Life,
	We thank you for filling our hearts
	With the love of God. **Amen**

BACK IN CHURCH

The children line up with their presents – the Gifts of the Spirit standing on one side, and the Fruits of the Spirit on the other

Leader	In the Gospel today Jesus promised to send the Holy Spirit to the Church.
	We've all received presents this morning – they remind us of the gifts the Spirit pours on the Church.
	The Gifts of the Spirit are these:

Each child says the name of the Gift he/she has received

Wisdom, understanding, wonder, judgement, knowledge, courage and reverence.

Leader	And the Fruits of the Spirit are these:

Each child says the name of the Fruit he/she has received

Love, joy, peace, patience, kindness, goodness, faithfulness, gentleness and self-control.

Leader	Now we know why the Spirit is called:
Everyone	**The Lord and Giver of Life.**

Script 27   Paul and Silas are Shaken but Don't Stir

Easter 7

St John 17.20–22

THEME

Today we hear Jesus' prayer for the Church, both the embryonic Church (with Him in the Upper Room) and the Church as it will be one day, spread throughout the world. Jesus seems to know already that it will be rent by quarrels, but He's confident that the Apostles will do their job and spread the faith. The readings this morning show them doing precisely that. St Stephen witnesses for Christ as the first martyr, and Paul and Silas convert a gaoler by sitting tight in an earthquake. We've gone for the earthquake.

SET UP

- The liturgical colour is White and Gold.
- Teaspoon and cup.
- Cardboard boxes from the local supermarket to make a collapsible gaol (keep them if you can, you'll need them next week for Pentecost).
- Cast Paul, Silas and the gaoler, and ask them to look at their scripts beforehand. Key and plastic sword for the gaoler.
- Somebody who can sing, or play an instrument. If you can't raise a musician, see if there's a hymn the children know (it could be a carol).
- A bundle of paintbrushes (or flower canes). You must be able to snap one of them.

WELCOME *the children and lead them in* **The Sign of the Cross** ✠ **(p. xxxvi).**

THE KYRIE   Lord Jesus, when you rose from the dead, you defeated evil,
Lord have mercy
Lord have mercy

Lord Jesus, when you rose from the dead, you washed away our sins,
Christ have mercy
Christ have mercy

Lord Jesus, when you rose from the dead, you set us free,
Lord have mercy
Lord have mercy

Ask the children to repeat **The Prayer for Forgiveness** *after you* (**p. xxxvi**).

THE EASTER GREETING

Leader   This is the last Sunday that we'll be saying the Easter Greeting.
                Let's do it really well.
                Alleluia! Christ is risen!
                He is risen indeed! Alleluia!

Three times

Leader   Today, we're going to hear the Gospel straight away.

THE GOSPEL PROCESSION

THE GOSPEL· *St John 17.20–22*

Optional Paraphrase

On the night of His arrest, Jesus prayed to God His Father for the disciples. He said,
'Holy Father, I am praying for my friends and for everyone who will one day believe
in me, because of what they have told them. Grant that my friends will stay together
and be one – just as you and I are one – so that the world will know that it was you
who sent me.'

AFTER THE GOSPEL

Leader   We've just heard Jesus pray for the Church.
                It wasn't a very big Church at that moment, but Jesus knew that
                one day it would be enormous, because He was going to send His
                disciples out into the world to preach the Good News.
                Two of Jesus' disciples, Paul and Silas, got as far as Philippi in
                Greece and, one night, they preached the Gospel in a very odd way.
                It happened like this ...

Earthquakes

Narrator   What you have to know about Philippi is that it's in an earthquake
                zone.
                People there were used to earthquakes and, if the spoons in their
                teacups suddenly rattled, like this,

Rattle a teaspoon in a cup

>they'd say, 'Oh that's just a tremor.'
>But if the floor started shaking and there was a ghastly noise –

Leader 2 bangs a chair on the ground

>then they got worried. I'll show you why …

Ask some children to build a tower with the cardboard boxes

Narrator   A bad earthquake can cause a building to jump. If you're lucky, the jump will be straight up …

Leader 2 bangs the chair again; give the tower a cautious jog from the bottom – make sure it stays intact

>So that the building goes straight up in the air, and lands back on its feet.
>But, if you're unlucky, the earthquake will make the building jump skew-whiff.
>In which case the building will

Give the tower a good shake from the bottom

>fall down …

Paul and Silas

>Right, well Paul and Silas turned up in Philippi and annoyed everyone by preaching about Jesus. They were slung into gaol. Let's build them a nice gaol …

The children construct a gaol

>Ah, here they come …

Enter Paul and Silas

>Hi, chaps, we've just got a nice gaol sorted for you.

Paul and Silas look dubiously at the dungeon

Paul   It doesn't look very safe …
Silas   *(Fingering the cardboard)*
Very tacky.

But they go inside

Narrator   They were followed by the gaoler. *(Enter gaoler)*
Gaoler   OK in Cell 13?

Paul and Silas	Yes!
Gaoler	OK, I'll lock you in for the night. *(Turns an imaginary lock)*
Narrator	Then he went home for his supper. Meanwhile, all the other prisoners, the ones who weren't locked in cells, clustered round Cell 13.

Let's gather round. The children circle the prison cell

And all that night Paul talked to them about Jesus, and sang hymns.
What do you think they sang?

See what the children know and sing one verse. Something with a swing works – 'At the Name of Jesus', 'I the Lord of Earth and Sky', even, 'Onward Christian Soldiers'. If you're stuck, choose a carol

Halfway through a hymn, the prisoners noticed that the teaspoons in their prison cups had begun to rattle.

Rattle your teaspoon again

'Oh it's only a tremor,' they said, and sang the second verse.

They get to the end of the second verse ...

Then there was a ghastly noise.

Leader 2 drops a chair suddenly

And the whole building jumped in the air, turned sideways – and landed on Paul and Silas!

Make sure it does ...

The other prisoners went back to bed.
The gaoler rushed over from his house and, seeing the rubble, thought that Paul and Silas had escaped. 'I'm going to get into big trouble for this,' he thought. 'I may as well kill myself now ...'
And he drew his sword. *(He does)*
At which point Paul cried out,

Paul	Stop! We're fine, we stayed put ...
Silas	We knew Jesus would look after us.
Narrator	The gaoler pulled them out and fell on his knees *(which he does)* and said,

Gaoler	You've saved my life – *whom* did you say saved you?
Paul	The Lord Jesus.
Gaoler	Well, come back to my place and tell me about Him.
Narrator	Then the gaoler took Paul and Silas home, gave them a bath and some supper, and listened to everything they had to say about Jesus. The very next morning the gaoler was baptized – and Paul and Silas were released from gaol.
	So Paul and Silas had converted someone by staying together, and trusting in Jesus.
	How good are we at staying together?

GAMES

Any co-operation game works well here. Commando or Chain Tag for example.

Commando

Split the children into two or three teams and tell them their task is to reach the opposite side of the hall (or a given point if the distance is too great).
Each team stands in a line at one side of the hall with their legs spread apart.
The person at the back crawls through all of the pairs of legs and then becomes the person at the front. Once she's reached the front, she calls 'Next', so the person at the back knows when to start. Slowly but surely the line starts to move forward ...

Chain Tag

Ask the children to find a partner. Each pair joins hands and runs round as a unit, joining up with other pairs until the whole room is in a gigantic line. See if they can make a circle, without breaking up, and ask them to sit down.

BEFORE THE FINAL PRAYER

Form a Circle

Leader	I'm going to tell you something about a famous English painter. His name was Turner and one day he was talking to some young painters in London and he said, 'Gentlemen, you must stay together, don't split up. Look at this ...' And he pulled out a paintbrush.
So do you	'If you're by yourself,' he said, 'this can happen to you ...' And he snapped the paintbrush. *(Snap it)* 'But if you're all together ...,' and he showed them a bundle of brushes, 'nobody can hurt you.'

Produce the bundle and try to break them

No, Turner's right, it can't be done.

Jesus wanted Christians to stay together as well. It makes us stronger, as Turner said, but it does something even more important – it helps us to love one another.

Let's pray together the prayer Jesus offered to His Father.

FINAL PRAYER

Ask the children to repeat the petitions after you

> **Holy Father**
> **We pray for the Church.**
> **May it be one,**
> **Just as you and your Son are One,**
> **So the world may believe that**
> **Jesus was the one**
> **You sent into the world. Amen**

REHEARSAL

Practise your presentation for when you go back into church (see below).

BACK IN CHURCH

Line up the children at the front, with Paul, Silas and the gaoler to hand

Leader   Today we heard Jesus pray that His Church would stay together and be one. Then we heard about two Christians, Paul and Silas,

Paul and Silas come forward

who were in prison.

Paul and Silas hold their hands before them as if tied

While they were there, there was a terrible earthquake,

Everybody – kids, Leaders, Paul, Silas and gaoler shake on the spot

and their prison fell down.

Paul and Silas collapse

The doors were open and they could have gone free, but they stayed together and trusted in Jesus. Their gaoler …

Enter gaoler   was so impressed that he asked them to baptize him.

Gaoler kneels

Which just goes to show how impressive it is when Christians …

All the children **Stay together!**

Script 28   Going Home (Ascension Day)

Easter 7 if kept as Ascension Sunday

St Luke 24.50–51, Acts of the Apostles 1.7–12

Ascension Day falls on the 40th day after Easter – a Thursday. However, the Roman Catholic Church in some countries now celebrates this feast on the Sunday following. If that's what you're doing, this is your script. Check with your priest first – it'll either be this or *Script 27*, Easter 7.

THEME

This Ascension Sunday we think about homecoming. The children hear the story of the man who went all the way round the world to go home.* Jesus goes back to His home today and encourages us to set out on a long journey and follow Him.

SET UP

- The liturgical colour is White or Gold.
- A map of the world.
- Pictures from the CD-Rom.
- A prayer candle, as large as possible.

WELCOME *the children and lead them in* **The Sign of the Cross ✠ (p. xxxvi).**

BEFORE THE KYRIE

Leader   This is the day on which we remember that Jesus ascended to Heaven.

Gesture as you do this, so the children register an upward movement

---

* Taken from G. K. Chesterton's novel *Manalive*.

But why did He go?

Jesus had come back from the dead – why didn't He stay with us?

Take all answers – establish that He went home. You may also like to follow any leads the children may give you on Jesus not being locally present. A little girl once told us, 'If Jesus had stayed on Earth, we'd have had to queue up to see Him'

Now that Jesus is in Heaven, we can pray to Him from anywhere, and know that He'll hear us. Let's talk to Him …

THE KYRIE   Jesus, Son of God, you came to Earth to save us from our sins,
Lord have mercy
Lord have mercy

Jesus, Son of God, you went back to Heaven to pray for us to the Father,
Christ have mercy
Christ have mercy

Jesus, Son of God, you have gone home, to prepare a place for us,
Lord have mercy
Lord have mercy.

Ask the children to repeat **The Prayer for Forgiveness** *after you* (**p. xxxvi**).

OPENING   God our Father,
PRAYER   We thank you for the Ascension of your Son, Jesus Christ.
Grant that one day, we too will follow Him to Heaven
Where He lives and reigns with you,
And the Holy Spirit, for ever and ever. **Amen**

The Man Who Went Home

Stick up a map of the world

Leader   Today I'm going to tell you the story of a man who wanted to go home.
He came out of his house one day and said to his wife, 'I've got a house the other side of the world, and I'm going to find it.'
'OK', said his wife, 'keep me posted …'

CD28.1   So off he went.

For the rest of the story, Leader 2 moves the traveller across the world, and sticks on the various people he meets

He crossed the Channel and came to France.

CD28.2   'Bonjour,' said a Frenchman, 'have some wine …'

'Bonjour,' said the traveller, 'I can't stop, I'm going home …'

He went right across Europe until he got to Italy.

CD28.3   'Ciao!' said an Italian.

'Ciao,' said the traveller. 'Love the shades! But I can't stop – I'm going home …'

He went to the end of the Mediterranean and got to the Holy Land.

CD28.4   'Hallo!' said a priest.

'Hallo Father,' said the man, 'I'll come and hear Mass, but I mustn't stop, I've got to get home.'

He travelled right across the Middle East until he got to India.

CD28.5   'Hi,' said an Indian, 'do you fancy a lift?'

'Yes please!' said the man, 'I'm in a terrible hurry, I want to go home …'

The Indian took him to the tip of India and helped him find a boat. The traveller sailed all the way to Australia.

CD28.6   'G' day!' said an Australian. 'Hot, isn't it?'

'Very hot,' said the traveller, 'but I can't let that hold me up – I must get home.'

So he went right across Australia *(land him up in Sydney)* and we seem to have reached the end of our map. What do you think he did then? Fall off the edge?

The kids will tell you the world is a globe – take the map off the wall and fold it round like a cylinder

Oh yes, where do you think he went from here?

Take all answers – but indicate there are some good flights from Sydney to America, so that's what he did. He gets to the West Coast

CD28.7   So the traveller flew across the Pacific, until he landed in America. A cowboy galloped up, 'Hi there!' he said.

'Wow! I always wanted to meet a cowboy!' said the man, and he shook his hand. 'But I'm so homesick, I must go home …'

And he took a train to Canada. 'Nearly home!' he thought, and

CD28.8   rushed off to the airport, nearly knocking over a lumberjack.

'I'm OK,' said the lumberjack.

The traveller boarded an aeroplane and got back to England. He ran for a train, then a bus, and the next thing he knew, he was walking up the garden path to his own house.

'Welcome back!' said his wife.

AFTER THE STORY

Leader   So the man went all the way round the world to go home. I wonder why he did that?

The children may come up with something – it doesn't matter if they look blank

I think it's because he wanted to find his home all over again.
Sometimes you have to leave your home, or your country, for a bit, to realize how much you love them.
Now, one of the reasons Jesus came to Earth was to make us homesick.
You see, although it's very nice living here in England, it's not our real home. He wanted us to start off on a long journey, like that man – and go home.
Hands up if you know where our real home is? *(Clock up the response)*
OK, we'll talk about that after the Gospel.

THE GOSPEL PROCESSION

THE GOSPEL   *St Luke 24.50–51, with a reference to Acts 1.7–12*

Optional Version

Jesus led His disciples out to a place near Bethany, and He lifted up His hands and blessed them. And said to them, 'You will receive power when the Holy Spirit comes upon you, and you will be my witnesses in Jerusalem, and in all Israel, and to the ends of the earth.'

After He said this, He was taken up before their very eyes, and a cloud hid Him from their sight. The disciples stared up into the sky as He went, when suddenly two men in white robes stood beside them.

'Men of Galilee,' they said, 'why are you looking up into the sky? This Jesus, who has been taken from you into Heaven, will come back in the very same way you saw Him go.'

And the disciples went back to Jerusalem full of joy, and went to the Temple every day to thank God.

AFTER THE GOSPEL

Leader   Let's just run through this – where did Jesus go? (**Back to Heaven**)
Yup, back home, to His Father in Heaven.
But, before He left, Jesus said something very interesting. He said, 'I'm going to prepare a place for you ...'

He knew we'd be landing up in Heaven one day, and He wanted us
to feel it was our home too.
Hands up those who knew that Heaven was our home.

Acknowledge the forest of hands

I thought so …
How do we get there?

Some kids will say you go there when you die; indicate you've got to live first

We spend our whole time on Earth travelling to be with our Father
in Heaven.

Move the traveller **(CD28.9)** *along a time line* **(CD28.10)** *as you describe the stages of
human life*

We journey through our childhood, and our teenage years, and we
keep going as grown-ups – and all the time Heaven is getting closer
and closer.
Sometimes the journey is tough; sometimes it's great. But in our
travels, we learn to love God, and do what He wants and, eventually,
He brings us home.

REHEARSAL

Practise your presentation for when you go back into church (see below).

FINAL PRAYER

Gather the children into a prayer circle, put a lit candle in the middle

Leader   In some churches this is the day they put out the Paschal Candle –
the big candle that has been burning since Easter Day.
The candle is a symbol of the risen Jesus, back from the dead.
But today Jesus went back to Heaven and the disciples couldn't see
Him any more. So we put it out …

*Ask a child to snuff out the candle, using a snuffer if possible. Do it carefully – there's
usually a lot of wax on large candles*

The candle's out – but look at the smoke!
Where's it going? (**Up**)

Watch it   It's going up – and disappearing – just like Jesus.
We can't see Jesus any more – but He's still very close to us.
Let's pray to Him now.

Ask the children to repeat the prayers after you

> Lord Jesus,
> After you rose from the dead,
> You ascended to the Father
> And went home.
> Grant that one day
> we will go home too
> And live with you
> And the Father
> And the Holy Spirit. Amen

BACK IN CHURCH

The children come in with the map

Leader	This Sunday we heard about a man who left England to find his home.
	He went to Europe.

A child points that out

	And India.

A child points to India

	And Australia.

Same business …

	What happened then?
Child 1	He went on to America.

A child points to America

	and flew all the way back until
Child 2	He landed up in England again.
Child 3	He'd gone all the way round the world to get home.
Leader	Today, we think Jesus is encouraging us to set out on a long journey to get home. Where is our real home, kids?
Everyone	**With God our Father in Heaven!**
Leader	Yes, in Heaven – and fortunately Jesus has got there before us.

Script 29   Pentecost

St John 20.19–23, Acts 2.1–7

THEME

The Holy Spirit comes in power this morning with the gift of language. We discover how people came to have different languages in the first place, and how the Holy Spirit circumvented that on the day of Pentecost.

SET UP

- The liturgical colour is Red.
- Wear something red, even if it's only a scarf or tie.
- A Bible with a bookmark in Genesis 11.
- The cardboard boxes from last week.
- Set up a table with A4 cards for the children to write on, using coloured marker pens.
- Identify anyone who can speak a foreign language, child or grown-up, and ask them to help you (see below).
- Run through the Tower of Babel script with a sensible kid who will eventually knock the whole thing down (see below).
- Have an unlit prayer candle ready at the start.
- Make a list of the foreign words for 'Peace' and, for the Final Prayer, be prepared to help children with their pronunciation (see below).

Words for Peace

pace – Italian (parchay)
frieden – German (freeden)
paix – French (pay)
paz – Spanish (path – the 'a' sounds like the 'a' in 'maths')
pokój – Polish (pakoy)
shalom – Hebrew (shalom)
pax – Latin (pax)
mir – Russian (mere – as in 'only')

WELCOME *the children and lead them in* **The Sign of the Cross** ✠ **(p. xxxvi).**

Seeing Red

Ask the children if they've noticed the change of colour in church – point out the colour of your scarf or tie ...

Leader   Today we're in Red.

Red is used on special occasions: Palm Sunday, or saint's days when the saint has been martyred, or a day like today, when we think about the Holy Spirit.

We use red for the Holy Spirit, because sometimes He appears on Earth as tongues of fire. Let's light a prayer candle, as we pray to the Holy Spirit.

Ask a child to light the candle for you

THE KYRIE   God our Father, your Spirit fills the whole world,
Lord have mercy
Lord have mercy

Lord Jesus, your Spirit fills our hearts,
Christ have mercy
Christ have mercy

Holy Spirit, inspire us with the love of God,
Lord have mercy
Lord have mercy

*Ask the children to repeat **The Prayer for Forgiveness** after you (**p. xxxvi**).*

OPENING   Almighty God
PRAYER   Today you sent your Spirit on the Church.
May the Holy Spirit breathe on our hearts
And make them glow with love for you
And your Son Jesus Christ. **Amen**

Language

Leader   Today is Pentecost.

It is the day when the Holy Spirit descended on the disciples – and, as always, the Spirit came bearing gifts.

One of the gifts the Spirit gave the disciples was language. Not their language – somebody else's.

Can anyone here speak a foreign language?

Reserve any bilingual child or grown-up for later. See if any of the children can say 'Good morning' in a foreign language. Bouncing off what you get, continue ...

Leader	Well, 'Good morning' in French doesn't sound too difficult. It's 'Bonjour'. Can you say that? *(Practise that a couple of times)*

Do the same sort of thing with German or Spanish greetings ('Guten tag' or 'Buenos dias') if you get them instead

	OK, let's start again.
Make an entry	Bonjour!
Kids	**Bonjour!**
Leader	Fantastic – or, as the French would say, 'fantastique!'
Leader	Now, why do you suppose people speak in all sorts of different languages? *(A rhetorical question)* It's one of those things that people make up stories about. There's a very good story about it in the Bible *(pick up a Bible)* right at the beginning. *(Open the Bible at Genesis 11)* Yup, here it is, the Tower of Babel.

The Tower of Babel

Settle into story-telling mode

Narrator	Once upon a time everybody in the whole world spoke the same language. There weren't so many people around then, and they wandered about over the Earth until they got to the plain of Babylon. It was nice and flat, so somebody said: 'Why don't we make bricks out of clay, and pile them up and make a huge tower?' 'Great idea!' said everyone. And they began to build ...

Ask the kids to start making a tower from the boxes – it can be several boxes thick, but make sure it gets tall enough to necessitate two children standing on chairs to place the top boxes
Keep at least three boxes in reserve
As soon as it's big enough, ask the kids to stay where they are, for the next bit of the story

	The tower got bigger and bigger. 'Wow!' said someone, 'it's going to reach the sky!' At which point God took an interest. He looked down from Heaven and saw the tower and said, 'What a cheek! How dare they build a tower up to the sky – what else are they going to do? I'm going to put a stop to this ...'

And down He came and began to confuse their language.
So instead of somebody on the ground saying,
'Hey, you need another brick!'
The chap on the ground said,

Ask your bilingual person to say this, or something similar, in their second language. If you haven't got a gifted foreign speaker, ask a Leader to have a go at this remark in French or German (it doesn't matter what it sounds like, nobody had ever spoken French or German before)

Either	'Il te faut encore une brique!'
Or	'Du brauchst noch einen Backstein!'
Narrator	'What?' said the chap on the top.
	Then it got worse. As some more bricks were handed up, someone else said, 'Put it there – no! *there*!'
	But it sounded like this –

Your foreign speaker again, or in French or German – or both together of course, we're aiming at maximum confusion

Either	'Mets-la là! Non, pas là, là!'
Or	'Da hinlegen! Nein, nicht da, da!'
Narrator	And the builders at the top looked at each other in bewilderment. 'Does he mean there?' said one.

A box is handed up to the sensible kid you have primed, he/she places it precariously – it mustn't fall yet

'NO!' said the other.
But she said 'No' in German.

Look up at the other child

	Can you say 'No' in German? It's 'Nein' – can you say that?
Child	Nein!
Narrator	Excellent – now louder – he's not listening.
Child	NEIN!
Narrator	'Nine?' said the other guy. 'You want nine more bricks? OK, hand some up.'

Hand up another couple

'Nein!' said the other builder.
'Stop!' said everyone – but it was too late …

Our sensible kid has now added the extra bricks at an impossible angle, they fall and – with his help, and the assistance from the child on the other chair – the whole tower falls to the ground

| Narrator | And that was the end of the tower. People called it the Tower of Babel, because its builders babbled at one another. And from that moment, to this, all the people of the world speak different languages. |

Clear up the tower

Do you think that story is true?

(See what they think)

Well it might be, it was a long time ago.
But *I* think it's a folk tale.
And, like all folk tales, it's got a grain of truth, right in the middle.
This folk tale is telling us that it's a pity people speak in foreign languages – it means they can't do things together.
I don't think God really muddled things up, that's just the story.
He certainly doesn't like people not understanding each other.
So when He sent His Son into our world to put things right, language was one of the things He wanted to sort out as well.
Let's hear about that in the Gospel.

THE GOSPEL PROCESSION

THE GOSPEL   *St John 20.19–23 followed by Acts 2.1–7*

Optional Paraphrase

On the evening of the first Easter Sunday, the disciples were in the Upper Room, behind locked doors. Jesus came and stood among them. He said, 'Peace be with you', and showed them His hands and His side. The disciples were filled with joy when they saw Him and Jesus said again, 'Peace be with you. As the Father sent me, so I am sending you.' And He breathed on them and said, 'Receive the Holy Spirit.'
Then, a few days later, this happened:
On the day of Pentecost, the disciples were altogether in one room, when suddenly they heard the sound of a mighty rushing wind. The noise of it filled the house. Then they saw what looked like flames of fire, flickering over their heads – and everyone began speaking in a foreign language. They rushed out into the street, all speaking different languages, and the foreigners in Jerusalem understood every word they spoke. Everyone was amazed.

AFTER THE GOSPEL

Leader   So, just for a minute, the old confusion lifted, and everyone understood one another. It must have been marvellous.

And, ever since then the Church has discovered that anyone can understand about Jesus, no matter what language they speak.

ACTIVITY

Gather the children round the table

We're going to write a very simple Christian message in lots of languages. It's going to be the first word the Risen Jesus said to His friends, 'Peace.'

Ask the children to write 'peace' in English on one side of the card – as large as possible, you'll be taking this back into church

Now turn over your card, and let's write the word 'peace' in different languages.

Dish out the different words for 'Peace' (see above), adding any extra foreign words the kids or other Leaders may produce. As the child will be asked to pronounce his/her word, take a view on how difficult he/she may find it. 'Pax' is easy to say – you can give that word to several of the smaller children

The foreign words should be written in large colourful letters: some children may want to add the language it's written in as well, so put that in brackets

REHEARSAL

Ask the children to stand in a line with their 'Peace cards' – the foreign word uppermost.

Now ask them to say their word for 'peace', one by one. See how they do, and swap cards if necessary. Ask them to do it again – now holding up their card, with the foreign word showing – as they do so.

Now ask them to say their foreign words all at the same time – on cue.

Then ask them, on cue, to turn all their cards over and say, 'Peace!'

Rehearse the dialogue for the presentation (see below).

FINAL PRAYER

Ask the children to sit down

Leader   The Holy Spirit gave the disciples a really useful gift.
                      It's the sort of thing He does – finding a group of Christians and
                      sending them a gift to help them to do better.
                      One of His gifts is friendship.
                      We'll remember the Holy Spirit, and the other Persons of the Trinity,
                      in our final prayer.

Lead the children in the following

⳨ **The grace of our Lord Jesus Christ**
And the love of God
And the fellowship of the Holy Spirit
Be with us all evermore.
Amen

BACK IN CHURCH

The children line up with their cards

Leader   Everywhere in the whole world, people have a word for 'peace'.
                      Let's hear those words.

The children say their foreign words one by one and hold up their cards

The trouble is, we don't always understand each other, so when we
all talk about peace together, we make a ghastly noise.

The children say all their words for 'peace' at the same time

What was that?

They do it again

But today the Holy Spirit gave the gift of language to the disciples
and, for a moment, everybody heard the Gospel message in their
own tongue. It sounded like this …

The children turn their cards round and say

Peace!

Script 30   The Holy Trinity

Trinity Sunday

St John 16.12–13, 15

THEME

As always, we can only suggest ways of thinking about the Holy Trinity – no comprehensive explanation is possible. This session uses the Rublev Icon of the Trinity – a famous picture and one with satisfying layers of extra meaning, all easily decipherable.

SET UP

- The liturgical colour is White or Gold.
- Pictures from the CD-Rom.
- A paper reproduction of the 'Rublev Icon of the Trinity' – either print the version on the CD-Rom or see if you can get a poster.
- (If you happen to have the image in icon form, it would make an excellent focus for the Final Prayer.)
- Print up several black-and-white copies of the icon on the CD-Rom, one for every child.
- A compass.
- Colouring pens or pencils; you'll need some good blues, greens, yellows and browns.

WELCOME *the children and lead them in* **The Sign of the Cross** ✠ (p. xxxvi).

THE SIGN OF THE CROSS REFRESHER COURSE

Leader	We make the Sign of the Cross every Sunday, and in it we call God three things – can you remember what they are?

Start 'In the Name of …' if they hesitate

(**Father, Son, Holy Spirit**)
We remember the Father – who lives in Heaven.

The Son, Jesus – who came down to our world.
And the Spirit – who lives in our hearts.
The Sign of the Cross helps us remember who's who,
Let's do it slowly.

Start the Sign, touch your head …

The Father is at the top – in Heaven.

Continue, bring your hand down to tummy level …

The Son, Jesus, came down to Earth.

Go on, bring your hand over to your left …

The Spirit lives in our hearts.

Finish over on the right-hand side

And we finish by saying 'Amen'.
There is only one God, but we know Him as three Persons,
Father, Son and Holy Spirit – we call that **the Holy Trinity**.
Today is Trinity Sunday, and we're going to pray to the Trinity in the Kyrie.

THE KYRIE   God our Father, you forgive everybody who says they are sorry,
Lord have mercy
Lord have mercy

Lord Jesus, you came down to tell us how much God loves us,
Christ have mercy
Christ have mercy

Holy Spirit, you fill our hearts with the love of God,
Lord have mercy
Lord have mercy

Ask the children to repeat **The Prayer for Forgiveness** *after you* (**p. xxxvi**).

OPENING PRAYER

Ask the children to repeat the Sanctus after you

Holy Holy Holy
Lord God of Hosts
Heaven and Earth are full of your glory
Hosanna in the highest. Amen

Go straight into the Gospel

THE GOSPEL PROCESSION

THE GOSPEL   *St John 16.12–13, 15*

Leader   *Preface the Gospel by saying*
                      The Gospel is very short today, but all three persons of the Trinity appear in it. Put your hand up if you hear the words 'Jesus' or 'Father' or 'Spirit'.

Optional Paraphrase

Before Jesus went back to Heaven, He said to His disciples,
'I still have many things to say to you, but they'd be too difficult for you to understand right now. When the Spirit comes, He will lead you to the complete truth. Everything He tells you will come from me, and everything that comes from me, comes from my Father, so you'll be able to trust the Spirit when He makes things known to you.'

AFTER THE GOSPEL

Leader   Well done, I think you all got that right. (In fact, the Spirit turned up twice …)
                      There they all were, the Father, the Son and the Holy Spirit.
                      Christians believe in One God.

Write 1 on the flip chart

                      Who is made of Three Persons?

Write 3 on the flip chart – look at it

                      How can someone be one thing and three things?

Fr Dolling

                      Grown-ups get into a complete mess about this – but kids are usually rather good at it. There was one boy who sorted out the Trinity at the age of five.

CD30.1   Here he is, Robert Dolling.
                      Actually, at this age, he was called Rob.
                      One day Rob was sitting having his dinner. There were grown-ups all round him and he heard one of them say to his father, 'I just don't understand the Holy Trinity, how *can* three things be one thing?'
                      Rob looked up and said, 'That's easy!'
                      'Is it, Rob?' said his dad.

CD30.2

'Yes!' said Rob. 'Look here's my plate – it's got meat and potatoes and greens on it; that's three things – but it's only one dinner.'

Rob was right wasn't he? I don't think you'll be surprised to hear that he grew up to become a priest. (He probably realized when he grew up that his explanation wasn't perfect, but it was a good start.) But, you know, I don't think a picture of Rob's dinner is going to help me pray to the Trinity.

The Rublev Trinity

Leader

Let's look at another picture.

CD30.3

Put up the picture of the Rublev Icon of the Trinity

What have we got here?

(Some child might say, 'The Trinity'.) Agree, but ask them to look at the picture itself. What has the artist drawn?

What do the people in the picture look like? (**Angels**)

Quite right, three angels, sitting round a table.

It's a very old picture, but can you see a house in it? (**Yes, top left**)

And a small tree? (**Yes, behind the middle angel**)

There's even a mountain on the right, but it's very difficult to make out *(somebody will see it)*
And what's that on the table?

Take all answers – it's either (**A chalice or a bowl**)

OK, these angels come from a very odd story in the Bible.

Abraham and the Angels

Tell the story, pointing out the details in the icon

Leader   Abraham was sitting outside his tent one day – that's the **house** on the left (the artist didn't want to draw a tent) – when he saw three men standing under an **oak tree**. That's the tree in the middle.
Abraham realized at once there was something strange about the men – and he ran up, bowed to the ground, and said, 'Sir …'
He said 'Sir', not 'Sirs'. Abraham talked to the three men as if they were one person. That's weird.
Anyway, Abraham made them a meal – that's the **bowl** on the table – and as the men talked, he noticed that sometimes the men said, '*We* tell you', and sometimes they said, '*I* tell you'.
Thinking about it afterwards Abraham decided they were **angels**. Which is why they've got wings.
But when Christians read the story, they think,
'That's odd, are the men three people or one?
Could they be the Trinity?'
The man who painted this picture thought they were, and he's left clues, hidden in his picture, as to which angel is which.
Let's see if we can work it out.

Decoding the Rublev Icon

Take the flip chart with the large print-out of the icon, along with the children, over to a table where you've set out their little black and white pictures. Make sure you've got one yourself

Leader   The first thing to notice is that the three figures all fit into a **circle**.

Take a compass and draw a circle round them

That is because the Holy Trinity live in perfect unity with each other. They're sitting in a perfect circle.
Then, if you look closely, you'll see they've all got the **same face**.
Why do you think that is?

(The children may or may not guess – it's because they are all God)

But which is the Father, and which is the Son, and which is the Holy Spirit?

To find out, we have to colour them in.

OK, look at the picture and colour in all the bits of the angels that are in **blue**.

Do this yourself – and keep an eye on what the kids are doing. A small child would be mortified to get it wrong

The Father

In pictures like this, blue is the colour of God.

But there's one figure whose blue is almost hidden – which one is that?

(**The one on the left**)

Yes, His blue is hidden by a shimmering robe. When this picture was new, His cloak would have shone with **gold paint**.

Let's colour it in yellow

When they have done so …

That is God the Father, who cannot be seen by human beings.

He's surrounded by Heavenly light.

Behind Him is Heaven – His House. Do you remember Jesus said, 'In my Father's House there are many rooms, I'm going to prepare a place for you there.'

Now look at the figure on the right.

The Spirit

He's wearing a cloak of **green**, let's colour that in.

When they've finished …

So we've got a figure in blue and green.

Blue is the colour of God, so we can call Him Lord,

and green is the colour of life.

Can anyone remember who is the 'Lord and Giver of Life'?

(**The Holy Spirit**)

Exactly, this is the Spirit.

The Spirit is touching the table – He is the link between Earth and Heaven. He comes to our altars at every Eucharist to make ordinary bread and wine holy.*

---

* The only problem with this icon is the possibility of information overload. If the children ask about the mountain, tell them that people used to go up mountains to find God. They felt that mountains were the link between Heaven and Earth – rather like the Holy Spirit.

The Spirit is leaning towards the middle figure at the table.
Who do you think that is? (**The Son**)
Yes, and to understand Him, we need to colour His clothes. He is
wearing a brown tunic with a yellow stripe.

Once they've finished ...

The Son

In the middle sits the Son.
He is wearing blue – to show He is God – and **brown** – to show He
is man.
Why do you think the artist chose brown? *(Brown represents the*
***mud** of the Earth)*
He's also got a yellow stripe – that should be gold really; it is to
show that Jesus is the King.
Behind Him is a tree. Can anyone guess what that's supposed to
remind us of? (**The wood of the Cross**)
The wood of the Cross – but, hey, it's in leaf. The cross has brought
life to everyone.
And look, the Son is looking straight at His Father. He's taking our
eyes that way too, so we're back where we started; we've come full
circle.

The Holy Trinity

That's what is so wonderful about the Trinity – three different
Persons, but all *(cup your hands to make a circular shape)* in unity
with one another.

*Depending on the time, either let the children finish colouring the picture or suggest
they finish it at home, and gather them round the actual icon to pray. (It is best to
move away from the table at this point: the pencils, etc. are too distracting.)*

FINAL PRAYER

Place a prayer candle before the Rublev Icon

Either say   We'll look at the Holy Trinity together
The Father in Heaven
The Spirit who gives us life
and the Son, God and Man, who tells us to look with Him at the
Father.

And end with   Let's finish our time together, as we began, with the **Sign of the Cross** ✠.

Or use the time to sing

MUSIC

'I believe in God the Father' *or* 'Father in my life I see'.

And then end with

Let's finish our time together, as we began, with the **Sign of the Cross** ✠.

REHEARSAL

If you've got the time, rehearse a presentation with children saying some of the lines (see below) or run the 'Sign of the Cross Refresher Course' (above) with a grown-up leading, and the children doing the actions.

BACK IN CHURCH

Line the kids up down the front

Leader   Today is Trinity Sunday.
               We thought making the Sign of the Cross was a helpful way to think
               about the Holy Trinity: and we're going to do it now, very slowly.

Child 1   The Father is at the top – in Heaven.

The children start the Sign by touching their heads

Child 2   The Son, Jesus, came down to Earth.

The kids bring their hands down to tummy level

Child 3   The Spirit lives in our hearts.

They bring their hands over to their left
Finish over on the right-hand side

Leader   There is only one God, but we know Him as three Persons,
               Father, Son and Holy Spirit – the Holy Trinity.

Everyone   **Amen.**

Script 31   Corpus Christi

The Sunday after Trinity Sunday if kept as the Feast of Corpus Christi

St Luke 9.11–17

The Feast of Corpus Christi traditionally falls on the Thursday after Trinity Sunday. It is, however, celebrated on the Sunday after Trinity Sunday by Roman Catholics in some countries. Anglicans still tend to keep to the traditional day: check with your priest.

THEME

Today we thank God for the gift of the Eucharist. Local customs vary considerably for this feast, so make sure you know what is going on. Your church may have a Procession of the Blessed Sacrament and the children may be called on to scatter rose petals. The Gospel is the Feeding of the Five Thousand and is a useful springboard for discovering the mysterious world of multiplication …

SET UP

- The liturgical colour is White or Gold.
- A basket with a fake bottom made from a tea-towel.
- Two very small fish – make them out of anything: fish-shaped biscuits (if you've got the time) or a couple of fish-shaped cut-outs from a slice of toast (if you haven't).
- Five little rolls; place them and the fish on the tea-towel.

- Small bite-sized chunks of bread placed under the false basket bottom.
- Ask Leader 2 and the person playing Jesus to look at the script beforehand.
- A chess or draught board.
- A calculator.

- A handful of 'grains of wheat' – uncooked popcorn or Puffed Wheat grains will do.
- A handful of uncooked rice.
- An un-consecrated wafer.
- A scroll of paper and some coloured marker pens.

WELCOME *the children and lead them in* **The Sign of the Cross** ✠ **(p. xxxvi)**.

THE KYRIE   God our Father, you are always ready to forgive us,
Lord have mercy
Lord have mercy

Lord Jesus, you taught us to say sorry for our sins,
Christ have mercy
Christ have mercy

Holy Spirit, you help us to repent when we do wrong,
Lord have mercy
Lord have mercy

Ask the children to repeat **The Prayer for Forgiveness** *after you* (**p. xxxvi**).

OPENING   Jesus said
PRAYER   If anyone loves me
They will keep my word.
Help us to love you Lord
And listen to your word this morning. **Amen**

CORPUS CHRISTI

Leader   Today is the feast of Corpus Christi.
It's the day we thank Jesus for giving us His Body and Blood in the
Bread and Wine of the Mass.
Jesus liked giving people food – holy food in the Mass, and ordinary
food for supper. Let's see how He did it in the Gospel.

THE GOSPEL PROCESSION

THE GOSPEL   *St Luke 9.11–17*

Ask one of the other Leaders to hold the basket. Ask the children to stand

Narrator   Jesus was walking through the countryside, on His way to Bethsaida,
when He realized that crowds of people were following Him. He
stopped and talked to them about the Kingdom of God, and healed

anyone who was sick. As the sun began to set, His disciples said to him, 'Tell the people to go away – they need to find food'. But Jesus said to them,

Jesus   *Comes forward and looks round at the kids*
Why don't you give them something to eat?

Narrator   But the disciples said, 'All we've got is … '

Leader 2   *Looks in the basket*
Five small rolls and two fish!
Shows the basket to the kids
That's not enough.

Jesus   *(To the children)* Would you sit down?

Narrator   Then Jesus took the loaves *(he does)*, gave thanks *(he holds them up)*, and shared them out to the people near Him.
Then He did the same with the fish.

Same business. Keep on passing out the bread and fish: make it perfectly obvious that the loaves and fish have run out, but go on dishing out bread to anyone who wants it – from the bottom of the basket, of course

Narrator   Jesus went on handing out bread and fish until everyone had had enough to eat. Five thousand people ate bread and fish for supper. And, at the end of the meal, the disciples filled twelve baskets – like this one – with the scraps left over.

AFTER THE GOSPEL

Leader   How did we do that?

(The children will probably know), show them the basket

Yes, you're quite right, it was a trick.
But how did Jesus do it?
It wasn't a trick, and it wasn't magic either.
It was a miracle.
Miracles aren't magic, they're quite normal – for God. We can't do them, but God can.
God loves making loads of stuff out of hardly anything.
He does it all the time – think of the seeds we put in the ground.

Show the kids your handful of wheat

They're hardly anything, I can hold them in my hand.
But God can multiply them – and turn them into a field of corn.
Now the interesting thing is that there's ordinary multiplication, and there's holy multiplication.

They're both very mysterious.

Multiplication

Leader   Let's start with the ordinary sort.

Gather the children round and pull out the chessboard. Establish what it is – ask if anyone can play chess

How many squares are there on this board? Let's work it out.

Ask the children to count the squares along the top and one of the sides and work it out. Have a calculator handy, this isn't school ... (64)

OK, well centuries ago a Chinaman invented chess, and the Emperor was so grateful he asked him what he'd like as a reward.
'I'd like a grain of rice and a chessboard,' said the man.
'Is that all?' said the Emperor.
'No,' said the man. 'Just put the rice on square 1.'

Put a grain of rice on Square 1

'Right,' he said. The next day he said, 'I'd like you to double the amount of rice I have and put it on square 2.'
'OK,' said the Emperor.

Put two grains of rice on Square 2

'And then go on doubling the amount of rice until you reach the end ...'
'Easy!' said the Emperor.
Let's try that ...

Put down 4, 8, 16 grains of rice – and call a halt

This is getting boring.

Do a swift sum – 16, 32, 64, 128 – by square 8, we'll have to put down 128 grains of rice, and there will be 255 grains on the board

What will it be when we get to Square 20?

Leader 2 does a rapid (and improbable) calculation

Leader 2   524, 288 grains on square 20, and the amount of rice on the board will be over one million ...

Leader 1   We haven't got that much rice!

Leader 2   Neither had the Emperor – if they'd gone on doubling up, the man who invented chess would have ended up with – and this is the longest number I have ever seen ... *(Write it down)*
18,446,744,073,709,551,615 grains

There's 20 numbers in that – that makes it 10 quintillion!
That's more rice than exists in the whole world.

Leader 1   That's serious multiplication. Let's get that number down.

Make a scroll with the number written on it, very large, in brightly coloured marker pens. Roll it up, ready for the presentation

Holy Multiplication

Leader 1   Well, God doesn't need the eight times table.
When He wants to multiply something, He just does.
He multiplies the seed in the ground. He multiplied the five rolls and two fish – and He multiplies this.

Hold up the unconsecrated wafer

Can anyone tell me what this is?

(Children describe the Host in various ways), establish it is the bread the priest blesses at Mass

Actually this is just ordinary bread – the priest hasn't blessed it yet.
But when it is blessed it will become the Body of Christ.
Jesus once held up a piece of bread like this, and said,
'This is my Body, do this in remembrance of me.'
And ever since then Christians have been blessing bread like this, and eating it. It's been multiplied millions of times.

Leader 2   How many millions?

Leader 1   I don't think God is counting.
God just gives and gives, He doesn't count.

REHEARSAL

Practise your presentation for when you go back into church (see below).

BEFORE THE FINAL PRAYER

Bring the children into a circle, and put the basket in the centre

Leader   Our basket is empty.
But when Jesus gives His people food, it never runs out.
His bread is on the altar right now – it's time to go back to church.

FINAL	Lord Jesus Christ,
PRAYER	You are the Bread of Life.
	Thank you for feeding us at the altar
	And thank you for the Mass. **Amen**

Lead the children in a **Glory Be ...** (see p. xxxvii).

BACK IN CHURCH

A Leader brings in the chessboard and the children come down the front with their enormous number

Leader

Holding up the chessboard

> This morning we heard the story of a Chinaman who invented chess. His Emperor asked him what he would like as a reward, and he asked for a grain of rice on one chessboard square, two on the next, four on the next – and so on until they got to square 64.
> How many grains of rice would he have got, kids?

The children unroll the scroll, and one child reels off the number

	18,446,744,073,709,551,615
Leader	We wondered how many times Jesus had given Himself to the faithful in the Holy Sacrament of the altar. One million times?
Child 1	More than that.
Leader 2	Two million?
Child 2	More than that.
Leader 1	We couldn't work it out.
	Name (to a child), why do you think that is?
Child 3	God just gives and gives – He doesn't count.

Script 32   Too Many Fish …

Proper 1, Ordinary Time 5
(Sunday between 3 and 9 February if before Lent)

St Luke 5.1–11

THEME

The theme is vocation. Vocation is God's call to serve Him, and people take it in different ways. Some respond immediately, others try to wriggle out of it. It's odd how often Biblical vocations seem to be mixed up with fish. This session takes a look at two men, both intimately connected with fish, to see how they coped with their vocation. The session ends with the magnetic Fishing Game. Children appear to like a run-through of this game at least once a year.

SET UP

- The liturgical colour is Green.
- Cast Leader 2 as Jonah – he/she will need to have looked at the script beforehand.
- A sheet.
- A pot.
- Six 'lots' – pieces of paper, folded over, with the name 'Jonah' written on all of them.
- Make a large signpost with 'Nineveh' on it.

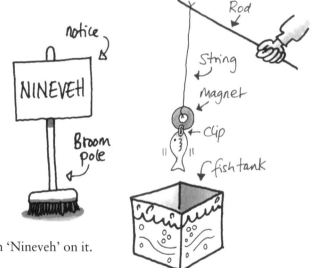

Fishing Game

- Magnetic Fishing Game – either ready-made from a toy shop, or constructed by you.
- Templates for fish and tank provided, you'll need to get at least two magnets (any toy shop or via a website; www.first4magnets.com has a good range).

- Two flower canes and some string.
- Attach paper clips to the pictures of fish and people on the CD-Rom **(CD32.1–2)**; put them in the tank and there you are.

WELCOME *the children and lead them in* **The Sign of the Cross** ✠ **(p. xxxvi)**.

THE KYRIE   Lord, for the times we have forgotten to love you,
Lord have mercy
Lord have mercy

Jesus, for the times we have forgotten to love others,
Christ have mercy
Christ have mercy

Lord, we thank you for never forgetting to love us,
Lord, have mercy
Lord, have mercy

Ask the children to repeat **The Prayer for Forgiveness** *after you* **(p. xxxvi)**.

OPENING   Almighty God
PRAYER   You called your servants Jonah and Peter to do your will.
Help us to hear your voice
And serve you as they did. **Amen**

BEFORE THE GOSPEL

Vocation

Leader   This morning the Gospel is about the way God calls us to serve Him.
God calls all of us to do something for Him.
It can take a bit of time to realize what He wants – and sometimes of course we don't want to do it anyway.
Like this chap ...

Enter Leader 2

The Story of Jonah

Narrator   Hiya, what's your name?
Leader 2   *(Very down in the mouth)* Jonah.
Narrator   Oh right, and what's your job?
Jonah   I'm a prophet, I tell people how much God loves them.
Narrator   Do you like doing that?

Jonah	No, I *don't*. I don't like other people very much.
Narrator	Ah, yes, well, I can see that would be a problem.
Jonah	It's awful – and now God wants me to preach in Nineveh.
Narrator	Nineveh?
Jonah	Yeah, a total dump.
	Well, I'm not going – I'm going to run away.
Narrator	What from God?
Jonah	You bet. I'm going to find a ship and run away to sea.

Exit Jonah

Narrator	*(To the children)* I'm going to need your help with this, I want a ship and some sailors.

Line up some chairs for the ship, and put six kids on board
Set the pot at the front of the boat
Give each of them one of the folded pieces of paper to put in their pocket
Ask another couple to be the whale. (They hold a sheet by one end and envelop Jonah in it at the appropriate moment)
The rest of the kids are the sea. They sit with their arms folded, swaying a little as the sea is calm. Practise the moment when the sea gets rough; the arms (still folded) should move quite violently. Congratulate them when they get it right

Narrator	Back to the story …
	So Jonah boarded a ship, and he thought, 'Great! I'll travel so far that even God won't be able to catch up with me …'
To the kids	Was that a sensible thing to do? (**No!**)
	Well, the ship sailed off, and for a while all was well, the sea was calm, and the ship bobbed along.

The sea sways gently

But suddenly a wind blew up and the waves got bigger …

The sea gets agitated …

To the sea	Stop! You're making me feel seasick … That was brilliant.
	The sailors decided that there was somebody on board who was bringing them bad luck. So they wrote down every man's name on a bit of paper and put them in a pot. *(They do this)*
	And drew 'lots' to find out who the wretch was.

A sailor plunges his hand into the pot and pulls out a lot

Narrator	What does it say?
Sailor	'Jonah'!
Narrator	So they chucked Jonah overboard *(which they do)* and sailed off. Luckily a great fish was passing, which swallowed him up.

The sheet envelops Jonah
Jonah and the fish move towards the flip chart

	Of course poor Jonah didn't think it was lucky at all. He didn't like being in the fish and complained bitterly.
Jonah	*(From inside the whale)* Help! Get me out of here! This place smells of fish!
Narrator	After three days the fish came to land, and spat him out. *(Which it does)* Jonah was very glad to be safe on dry land again, and he thanked God.

Jonah sinks to his knees

| | Then he saw a signpost. |

Put up the Nineveh sign

Jonah	Oh no! Nineveh!
Narrator	And he realized that he *still* had to do the job that God had given him. So, looking very grumpy, Jonah followed the direction on the signpost and went off to preach in Nineveh.
Jonah	*(As he moves off)* Rats!
Narrator	Which all goes to show that when God gives you a job to do, you might as well get on with it. Now, oddly enough, hundreds of years later, another man called Jonah had a son whom God called to serve him. There's no whale in this story – but there are lots of fish. Let's hear it.

THE GOSPEL PROCESSION

THE GOSPEL   *St Luke 5.1–11*

Sit down and tell this as a story

AFTER THE GOSPEL

| Leader | Who was the man Jesus called? (**Peter, Simon Peter**) Yup, Peter, son of Jonah. Did he run away? (**No**) Exactly, Peter was frightened by all the fish Jesus had caught for him, but he didn't run. In fact, he left his boat, and his business, and followed Jesus. Jesus said to him, 'From now on you are not going to catch fish but men!' |

Now it's most unlikely that God is going to call us to leave everything behind like St Peter, but He'd like us to do Peter's work and catch people for Him. We need to practise ...

Fishing Game

Leader   We need a fish pond ... *(Put box on table)*
                And some fish ... *(Throw them in)*
                And some fishing rods ... *(Produce the magnetized rods)*

Give the kids a chance to see how the rods work. You might need to split them into teams if there are too many, with some kids fishing for their team. Once the fish have been caught, say

OK, you're good at catching fish.

Stealthily slide the little people into the 'pool'

But Jesus wanted His disciples to catch ...

Get one kid forward for this – he/she pulls out a little person on the fishing rod ...

People!

REHEARSAL

Practise your presentation for when you go back into church (see below).

FINAL PRAYER

Leader   St Peter heard Jesus' call. Let us ask him to pray for us. Say after me
                Holy Peter,
                Friend of Jesus
                Pray that we too will hear the call of God
                And love Jesus
                As you did. Amen

End with a **Glory Be ...** (see p. xxxvii).

BACK IN CHURCH

The children go in with the fish box which contains a paper fish and a little person. Two kids have magnetized rods
Set it fairly high – on a stool or the top step up to the altar. Two kids flank the box, with rods. A Leader or a child with a nice emphatic delivery reads the script

Script

Child 1   Jesus amazed Peter, James and John,
          by catching loads of ...

One child catches the fish

          Fish! *(Holds it up)*

Child 2   Jesus said to the fishermen,
          'Follow me, and I will make you fishers of ...

The other child catches the person

          People!' *(Holds the little person up)*

Child 3   Jesus was good at catching things – and He wants us to catch things
          too.

Child 4   Not fish, but people.

(CD32.1)

Script 33   Turning the World Upside Down

Proper 2, Ordinary Time 6
(Sunday between 10 and 16 February if before Lent)

St Luke 6.17, 20–23

THEME

The Gospel is from the Sermon on the Plain. Jesus turns everyone's values upside down as He tells them that it is the poor, the hungry and the sad who are blessed by God. (He balances this by a list of 'Woes' – the rich, the full and the cheerful are not so fortunate. They are left out in this children's version.)

SET UP

- The liturgical colour is Green.
- Topsy-Turvy Land pictures from the CD-Rom.
- Three pictures from the CD-Rom – these show the poor, hungry and the mournful. Stick them on pieces of A3 paper – unhappy person on one side, happy on the other. Ensure that as you turn from happy to unhappy person, you have to turn the card upside down **(CD33.6–9)**.
- Map of Great Britain.
- A globe – or a map of the world (not too big).

WELCOME *the children and lead them in* **The Sign of the Cross** ✠ **(p. xxxvi).**

THE KYRIE   Lord Jesus, you came to Earth to find sinners,
Lord have mercy
Lord have mercy

Lord Jesus, you came to Earth to bring us God's forgiveness,
Christ have mercy
Christ have mercy

Lord Jesus, you came to Earth to tell us of the Father's love,
Lord have mercy
Lord have mercy

Ask the children to repeat **The Prayer for Forgiveness** *after you* (**p. xxxvi**).

OPENING	Almighty God,
PRAYER	You sent your Son into the world
	To surprise everybody with His teaching.
	Help us to hear Him
	Love Him
	And follow Him
	Today and always. **Amen**

Topsy-Turvy Land

Leader   Hi everyone – I thought we'd start off by looking at a map.

Stick up the map of the UK, upside down – register the instant uproar

What's up? (**The map's upside down**)

Stand back and look at the map

No it isn't – oh, I see, you think this is a map of the UK?
No, this isn't a map of the UK – this is a country called Topsy-Turvy Land.
Very strange place …
Have you ever been, *Name*? *(Leader 2)*

Leader 2   Yup, it's weird.
I took some pictures.

Up go the pictures, talk them through …

	In Topsy-Turvy Land
CD33.1	Everyone walks on their hands.
CD33.2	*(Parent yelling at a kid picture)*, 'Look at this bedroom! How many times have I told you to leave it in a mess?!'
CD33.3	*(Footballer being interviewed picture)*, 'How did you get on?' 'Terrible, we won again … '
CD33.4	Every meal starts with ice cream.
CD33.5	Kids do the driving, the grown-ups have to sit in the baby seats.
Leader 1	They've got some good games though – stand up and we'll play one.

Opposites

A very simple game. The kids do the opposite of whatever you ask them to do.
If you say 'Sit!' they jump up (and vice versa). 'Turn left' means 'turn right', 'walk two steps forward' means 'walk two steps back', 'stand still' means 'run on the spot' – and so on.

Anyone who moves fractionally the wrong way is out. The last child left in is the winner.

Start quite slowly, to get them used to the idea, then rattle off the commands: don't give them time to think. For a quick kill, saying the 'run' command twice (it means 'stand still' of course) usually gets rid of half the kids in one fell swoop

Leader	Topsy-Turvy Land does my head in …
	But I think Jesus might have liked it.
	He certainly liked turning things on their head.
	We'll hear Him doing just that in the Gospel.

THE GOSPEL PROCESSION

THE GOSPEL   *St Luke 6.17, 20–23*

Whatever version you use, say 'Blesséd' rather than 'Happy'. The unfortunate may not be feeling happy, but they are blessed by God.

AFTER THE GOSPEL

Leader	When Jesus was alive people thought that if you were unhappy or poor it was your fault. You'd probably done something wrong and God didn't like you. Jesus turned this idea upside down.
	Can you remember whom He said were blessed by God?
CD33.6–8	**(The poor, the hungry, people who mourn and the ones everybody hates)**
	God loves all His children, but Jesus said He is particularly close to the unhappy.* That was a new idea and it surprised everyone.

REHEARSAL

Practise your presentation for when you go back into church (see below).

FINAL PRAYER

Gather the children into a circle
Show them the globe, or a small map of the world

Leader	Jesus sent His friends into the whole world, to tell everyone about Him.
	Which is exactly what they did.
	Some people hated it. They said, 'These people are turning the world upside down.' *(Acts 17.6)*

---

* *Why God appears to be so close to the unfortunate is discussed in Script 11, Creative Ideas for Children's Worship, Year A.*

Sometimes it's a good thing to turn the world upside down.

Turn the globe (or map) upside down, and pass it round the circle as you say the last prayer

> Jesus told us that
> The poor and hungry were loved by God.
> That we should laugh if people didn't like us
> And love our enemies
> And do good to those who hate us.
> Lord, help us to turn the world upside down
> As we show the love of God in our lives. **Amen**

BACK IN CHURCH

The children go in with the globe or map and the pictures from the CD-Rom – the unhappy pictures at the front

Leader   Today we heard Jesus talk about people who were unhappy.
              He said that God would bless them.

Child 1   The poor would go to Heaven.

A child turns over the picture of the poor woman **(CD33.6)**

Child 2   The hungry would be filled.

A child turns over the hungry man **(CD33.7)**

Child 3   And the people who cry – will laugh.

A child turns over the weeping man **(CD33.8)**

Leader   In fact, Jesus turned the whole world …

A child turns the globe/map upside down

Everyone   **Upside down!**

(CD33.4)

(CD33.5)

Sample cartoons for this script

Script 34   Crazy Love

Proper 3, Ordinary Time 7
(Sunday between 17 and 23 February if before Lent)

St Luke 6.27–31

THEME

We all know that Jesus wants us to love other people – what we don't always grasp is how much He wants us to love them. So, to shake us out of our vague idea that being nice to others covers it, Jesus reels off a list of impossible commands. Let people rob you; if they take your jacket, give them your shirt (and trousers …). Really love them, be totally crazy about it.

SET UP

- The liturgical colour is Green.
- Six paper books wrapped up as presents.
- A Christmas list (see below).
- Pictures from the CD-Rom.
- Leader 1 should be wearing some easily removable garments – a jacket, a scarf, a cap, a shirt (with a T-shirt underneath) plus some trousers (not that they are coming off …).
- Paper, colouring pens, glue.
- Prayer candle.

Try to use the *New Jerusalem Bible* or the *RSV* for this session; if you haven't got a copy, at least make sure that Leader 2 quotes *St Luke 6.35* using the text as below.

WELCOME *the children and lead them in* **The Sign of the Cross ✠ (p. xxxvi).**

KYRIE	Heavenly Father, You loved us so much, you sent your Son to die for us, Lord have mercy **Lord have mercy**

Lord Jesus
You loved us so much, that you came to Earth to die for us,
Christ have mercy
Christ have mercy

Holy Spirit
You fill our hearts with the love of God,
Lord have mercy
Lord have mercy

Ask the children to repeat **The Prayer for Forgiveness** *after you* (**p. xxxvi**).

OPENING   Heavenly Father
PRAYER   **Help us to listen to the Gospel this morning**
    And learn to love you. Amen

Presents

Leader 1's jacket should be on the back of a chair
He/she starts the session by carrying in the six presents

Leader   Hi – well, it's a bit early for Christmas, but I've done my Christmas
    shopping.
    Here's my list.

Produce list – and tick people off as you go through your presents

    Yup, one for my mum, one for my dad, one for my sister – one for
    my brother, oh I forgot, I'm not talking to him at the moment – shall
    I give him a present?

The children will probably say 'yes'; be generous whatever they say …

    Hey, it's Christmas – why not? *(Tick that off)*
    One for *Name (your priest)*.
    And one extra. Hmm …
    Well, I know Christians should give to the poor so, *look round* – dear
    me, poor old *Name (any grown-up who will play up to you)* looks as
    though she needs a present – here you are, Happy Christmas!
    That's sorted, I've been kind to my family – even my brother who
    doesn't deserve it – I've remembered the vicar and the poor.
    I think I've done rather well …

While you're speaking, Leader 2 sneaks up behind and steals the pile of presents. The
children will almost certainly alert you

Leader 1	Oi! What are you doing! *(Grab Leader 2)*
Leader 2	Sorry, mate, I'm a burglar – I just wanted to do my Christmas burglary early.
	Go on, let me have a couple of these presents …
Leader 1	What! *(Turn to the children)*
	What do you think, kids – shall I give him a present?

See what they think – it usually hinges on how appealing the Leader's acting is – whatever they say, cut it short

	No, I'm not going to – it's not sensible to give a burglar a present.
Leader 2	I bet Jesus would have given me a present.
Leader 1	I bet He wouldn't …
Leader 2	Let's find out.

THE GOSPEL PROCESSION

THE GOSPEL   *St Luke 6.27–31*

AFTER THE GOSPEL

Leader	What an astonishing Gospel!
	Did you hear it? *(Read at random)*
	'If a man steals your jacket, give him your shirt – if someone slaps your cheek, let him slap the other cheek and' – oh rats – 'if someone robs you, don't ask for it back!'
	I just can't see it working …
	Look, here comes *Name* again – thieving away as usual …

Leader 2 calmly steals Leader 1's jacket from the chair

Leader 1	Blimey! He's stolen my jacket! What did Jesus say?

Look in the Gospel

	I thought so. Well, here goes …
	Oi!
Leader 2	Oh no, caught again …
Leader 1	Here – have my cap, and my scarf, and my shirt … *(taking them off)*
Leader 2	Hang on …
Leader 1	And my jeans … *(and is about to take them off)*
Leader 2	Stop! This is getting silly!

Both Leaders sit down and look at the Bible

Leader 1	What can Jesus mean?
Leader 2	*Reading St Luke 6.32 and 35a*

	Ah, listen to this. Jesus said, 'If you only love those who love you – what credit is that to you? Even sinners do that! No, love those that hate you ... ' I think Jesus means we shouldn't make little lists about the people we're going to be nice to ...
Leader 1	*(Produces the Christmas list)* OK. *(And tears it up)* But whom should I be nice to?
Leader 2	What do you think, kids? **(Everyone!)** Jesus wanted us to love everyone – and really love them. Be crazy about it.
Leader 1	Actually, I know a story about a saint who was barmy about loving people.

A Crazy Saint

Leader 1	He was a hermit. **(CD34.1)** And his name was Macarius.
CD34.2	Macarius lived in a hut in the desert. And he hardly had any possessions at all – but one day he came
CD34.3	home to find a couple of burglars stealing his stuff. He stood and watched them for a bit, then he helped them put their
CD34.4	loot on a donkey ...
CD34.5	And pointed out a couple of things they'd missed ... Then he waved goodbye – and the burglars walked off with everything. Macarius really loved people.

ACTIVITY

Ask the children to make their own version of the saint's story for the presentation (see below). Give each child something to draw – the saint, the burglars (they turn up in several pictures), the hut, the stuff the burglars nicked, and the donkey. The CD-Rom illustrations are in black and white and the children can simply colour them in if you're pressed for time. Glue each episode on to an A4 piece of paper, so you can hold them up in church.

REHEARSAL

Practise your presentation for when you go back into church (see below).

BEFORE THE FINAL PRAYER

Light a prayer candle and gather the children round it

Leader	Today Jesus talked to us about love. Not ordinary love, *His* sort of love.

Crazy love – love for people who are unkind, people who cheat, people who are completely ghastly.

Jesus doesn't mind people thinking He's crazy – He's happy to make jokes about this sort of love – just as long as we hear Him, and have a go.

Ask the children to repeat the following prayer after you

Lord Jesus
Thank you for loving us.
Help us to love everyone
As much as you love us,
Even if it does seem slightly crazy.
Amen

BACK IN CHURCH

The children line up down the front, with five of them holding their pictures in sequence

Leader Today we heard about a crazy saint. He was a hermit.

A child holds up **CD34.1**

He lived in a hut in the desert.

A child holds up **CD34.2**

And he hardly had any possessions at all – but one day he came home ...

A child holds up **CD34.3**

to find a couple of burglars stealing his stuff.
He stood and watched them for a bit, then he helped them put their loot ...

A child holds up **CD34.4**

on a donkey ...

A child holds up **CD34.5**

And pointed out a couple of things they'd missed ...
Then he waved goodbye.
I must say he does sound like a nutcase but, after we'd read the Gospel, we thought Jesus would have said,

All the children Well done!

Script 35   **A Plank in the Eye**

Second Sunday before Lent
Ordinary Time 8
(Sunday between 24 and 28 May
if after Trinity Sunday)

St Luke 6.41–42

THEME

One of Jesus' most famous sayings is, 'Why do you notice the splinter in your brother's eye and never notice the plank in your own?' Given Jesus' intense dislike of self-righteousness, it is depressing how often Christians give way to it. This session highlights how important it is to know your own sins, and not waste your time wondering what a fellow sinner is up to. And then, because one doesn't want to bang on too much about sin, we lighten up with the Mini Olympics.

SET UP

- The liturgical colour is Green.
- Pictures from the CD-Rom.
- For the Mini Olympics:
  - marker tape
  - tape measure

Look at the events listed below and decide how many props you'll need. Children may be competing individually or, in large groups, queuing up to take their turn in a team. For three teams you will need

- Three paper plates.
- Three balloons.
- Three wide-topped bottles and 30 pencils.
- Three medals – either gold-covered chocolate coins, or the cheap medals you can get in sports shops.

WELCOME *the children and lead them in* **The Sign of the Cross** ✠ (p. xxxvi).

BEFORE THE KYRIE

Leader   Before we start I'd like us to look back over the week.

Was there anything that went wrong?

And, this is the important bit, was it your fault it went wrong?

I mean, it rained last week *(adapt as necessary)*, but that wasn't your fault, was it?

Perhaps you upset Mum or Dad by leaving your bedroom in a mess? That would be your fault.

We'll all think about that for a moment. *(Pause, think about it yourself)*

Before we say the Kyrie this morning, we're going to confess our sins by saying, three times, that our sins are our own fault.

As we say 'through my fault' we're going to thump our chest like this …

Clench your fist and knock your chest – just enough to make a nice thump sound

That's to show we know whose fault it is.

Can you do that?

Let's try, repeat this prayer after me.

CONFESSION Merciful God

Last week I sinned against you

Through my fault   *(thump)*

Through my fault   *(thump)*

Through my own deliberate fault   *(thump)*

I am very sorry for all my sins

And ask you to forgive me

Through Jesus our Lord. Amen

THE KYRIE   Lord, have mercy

Lord, have mercy

Christ, have mercy

Christ, have mercy

Lord, have mercy

Lord, have mercy

Ask the children to repeat **The Prayer for Forgiveness** *after you* (**p. xxxvi**).

OPENING   We thank you Father
PRAYER   For blotting out our sins
             As though we'd never done them.
             Help us to do better from now on.
             For Jesus' sake. **Amen**

Terrible Tina

As you tell the story, Leader 2 puts up the pictures

Leader	Today we're going to hear the story of …
CD35.1	a dreadful little girl.
	She was called Tina – though sometimes her friends and relations called her Terrible Tina. This wasn't because she was horrible – actually she was rather nice – but because she used to get into such a terrible mess.
CD35.2	She had a little brother called Freddy.
	A quiet child. He spent most his time collecting caterpillars for his mini zoo.
CD35.3	Well, one day Tina went out to play. It had been raining all morning, so she rushed outside and jumped straight in a puddle.
CD35.4	Then she ran off to play football with her friends.
CD35.5	Then she rolled down a hill.
CD35.6	Then she thought she'd help Pete the painter whitewash the garden wall.
CD35.7	Then she oiled her bike.
	And by the time she came home for tea she was looking terrible. As she walked up the garden path, she bumped into Freddie, who had spent the afternoon in the garden.
CD35.8	He'd been looking for caterpillars, and his knees were rather damp.
CD35.9	'Gosh, Freddie!' said Tina. 'Look at your knees!
	You're going to get into big trouble…!'
	And that's the story.
	Do you think Tina was a bit out of order? (**Yes!**)
	Why's that? (**Because she's got much dirtier than her brother**)
	You bet, but it's funny how people can often see what's wrong with other people, and never notice that they're not so good themselves.
	Jesus thought it was odd.
	Let's hear what He said about it.

THE GOSPEL PROCESSION

THE GOSPEL   *St Luke 6.41–42*

AFTER THE GOSPEL

Leader   I think Jesus made His disciples laugh when He said that.
                  Fancy spotting a splinter in someone's eye

Pinch your finger as though you're holding one

                  and never noticing a socking great plank

Hold your arms out wide

                  in your own.
                  Jesus can't bear us telling tales on other people – particularly as He
                  knows we can behave pretty badly all by ourselves.
                  That's why He's so keen on us thumping our own chests when we
                  say sorry.
                  Well, fortunately the whole point about being Christians is that God
                  forgives our sins, and other people's, and we can forget all that and
                  be happy.
                  What shall we do? I think we'll run the Mini Olympics.

The Mini Olympics

Depending on numbers, either let the children compete individually, or in teams.
Run the whole range of events but, if time is a problem, limit the number of events
any individual kid can do. Tape lines to indicate the beginning and end of the track
event, and be ready with a dab of marker tape to show how far the 'discus' or 'shot'
has been thrown.
Take the measurements seriously, and keep a running total of who's winning what on
the flip chart.

Discus	*The children use paper plates*
Shot-put	*The children 'put' a balloon*
Track race	*Each child lines up at the start line, and races to the finish by placing the heel of one foot against the toe of the next. (If they find that too easy, make them do the return journey backwards)*
High jump	*Each child takes a deep breath and whistles. The one who keeps going longest wins*
High dive	*Each child stands on a chair with ten pencils and drops them into an empty bottle on the floor. The one who gets the most wins (let small children kneel on the chair and drop the pencils as they lean against the chair back)*

End with a medal ceremony and then, because of Jesus' well-known indifference to who comes first and last, dish out some consolation prizes – gold-covered chocolate coins for example.

REHEARSAL

Practise your presentation for when you go back into church (see below).

FINAL PRAYER

Gather the athletes round you for a last prayer; there will probably only be time to lead them in **Glory Be ...** (see p. xxxvii).

BACK IN CHURCH

The children come in with a sample discus, shot-put, bottle with pencils in it, and all their medals

Leader	Today we ran the Mini Olympics.
	We threw the discus. *(Kid holds up a paper plate)*
	We shot-put. *(Kid holds up a balloon)*
	We dived pencils into bottles. *(Kid holds up a bottle with pencils)*
	And we won lots of medals. *(The kids brandish these)*
	In fact, we were so busy that we never noticed if people had splinters, or twigs, or even planks in their eyes.
	We think Jesus would approve of that.

Script 36   The Centurion's Servant

Proper 4, Ordinary Time 9
(Sunday between 29 May and 4 June
if after Trinity Sunday)

St Luke 7.1–10

THEME

This is one of the few Gospel stories which shows the Roman occupation of Palestine in a good light. The Roman officer in charge of Capernaum has built a synagogue for the locals. He's liked by the Jewish elders and, in his dealings with Jesus, acts with scrupulous courtesy.

What stands out in this passage is the respect he has for Jesus' authority. Presumably the Centurion didn't think through the implications of his belief that Jesus could order a natural force, like illness, to retreat, but we can. Only God has authority over evil and disease.

SET UP

- The liturgical colour is Green.
- Small mats, hula hoops – anything the children can use to jump round the room. (Double spreads of newspaper are OK, though they tend to slip.)
- Pictures from the CD-Rom.
- If you've got a plastic Roman helmet for the Centurion, it will look good in the presentation.

WELCOME *the children and lead them in* **The Sign of the Cross** ✠ **(p. xxxvi).**

THE KYRIE   Lord Jesus, we are sorry for the times we forgot you last week
Lord have mercy
Lord have mercy

Lord Jesus, we come to you for forgiveness
Christ have mercy
Christ have mercy

Lord Jesus, you have only to say the word and we shall be forgiven
Lord have mercy
Lord have mercy

Ask the children to repeat **The Prayer for Forgiveness** *after you* (**p. xxxvi**).

OPENING **PRAYER**	Almighty God, You said the Word And all Creation came to life. You said, let there be light And there was light You said, let the sun and the moon shine in the sky And they did. Help us to hear your Word And obey it Now and for ever. **Amen**

BEFORE THE GOSPEL

Jumping

Spread your mats, hoops or whatever you've got round the room

Leader	Right, I want to think about jumping. Can you jump? Let's see you jump up … Yup, brilliant. Sometimes we can't help jumping, especially if we hear a loud noise.

Leader 2 bangs a door, preferably behind you. Jump round

Like that.
But quite often we just jump for fun.
Let's see if you can jump round the room on these mats.

Line the children up

OK, jump!

After the first circuit

Hmm, I think we made that too easy.

Spread the mats out a bit

Now, let's see how you do.
Jump!
OK, come over here and sit down.

The kids come down the front and sit

Orders

Leader   Have you noticed how I've been ordering you about? Sit down, jump up – nothing but orders.
And now there's all these mats to clear up.
Who shall I order to clear them up?

Look in the direction of Leader 2, or any spare grown-up

Shall I try *Name*?
I better be quite polite, he/she's bigger *(or older or tougher)* than me.
Hi, would you mind clearing up the mats?

He/she does so

It's nice to give orders, isn't it?
Are there any things you don't like being told to do?

See what they say, it's usually homework and having to go to bed. Use the kids' answers as a springboard to the next question – for example:

Who tells you not to talk with your mouth full? (**Mum or Dad**)
Who tells you not to talk in the classroom? (**Teacher**)
Yup, they're the sort of people you have to obey, aren't they?
But there are some people you can ignore.
Look, here's a kid being told to jump – which person has she absolutely got to obey?

Put up pictures **CD36.1**, **CD36.2**, **CD36.3** *– they'll choose* **CD36.3**, *the Fireman, who is saying 'Jump!'*

Quite right, it's daft to jump off a cliff,
you don't have to jump into a swimming pool if you don't want to,
but if a Fireman says jump, you jump. He knows what he's talking about.
We get to know the people who've got a right to give orders. We say, 'they've got authority'.
Well today the Gospel story is about a man who spent his life giving orders; he was a Roman soldier.

THE GOSPEL PROCESSION

THE GOSPEL   *St Luke 7.1–10*

Tell the Gospel as conversationally as you can; it's full of dialogue.

AFTER THE GOSPEL

Leader	*(Run through the story)* The Centurion sends some people to Jesus. What did he want Jesus to do? (**Cure his servant**)
	But Jesus doesn't get as far as the house – the Centurion stops Him. Why was that? *(A rhetorical question probably)*
	The centurion didn't think he was worthy to have Jesus as a visitor.
CD36.4	Let's look at the Centurion.
	Here he is – covered in armour, red cloak, check out the sword.
	He was the man in charge, he gave orders all the time …
CD36.5	And here's Jesus.
	Just a wandering teacher, young, dusty, one of the natives.
	But the Centurion knew Jesus had more authority than him.
	Let's think about that authority.
	If you're ill, a doctor comes along and gives *you* orders.
	'Stick out your tongue, take this medicine …'
	But the doctor doesn't give orders to the illness. She doesn't say, 'Measles! Leave that kid alone!' 'Tonsils! Get better at once!'
	There's only one Person who can *order* a disease to leave someone alone – who is that? (**God**)
	Yup, God just has to speak, and things happen.
	The Centurion knew that Jesus only had to say the word and his servant would get better. So, whom did he think Jesus was? (**God**)
	He must have done, mustn't he?
	That's why Jesus said He'd never seen faith like his.
	And of course He cured the centurion's servant at once.

REHEARSAL

Cast one child as the Roman Centurion, another as Jesus, and another as the sick servant. Practise your presentation for when you go back into church (see below).

FINAL PRAYER

Leader	We're going to use Psalm 29 for our last prayer, it's about the way the power of God's Word makes things happen.
	The response to the Psalm is:

Let us worship the Lord
Let us worship the Lord

Worship the Lord with holy worship.
It is He that commands the waters
Let us worship the Lord

God's voice echoes over the oceans
And makes the lightning flash.
Let us worship the Lord

The voice of the Lord is a glorious voice
It makes the mountains jump and the deserts shake
Let us worship the Lord

The Lord's voice shakes the oaks
And strips the leaves from the trees
While everyone in His Temple shouts, 'Holy, Holy, Holy!'
Let us worship the Lord

MUSIC

The traditional hymn 'At the Name of Jesus', verses 1, 2 and 5, wraps up the session well.

BACK IN CHURCH

Line up the children, the Centurion one end, Jesus the other, the rest, including the servant, in the middle

Leader	Today we heard about a Centurion. He was a Roman soldier and when he gave orders, people jumped to it. If he said:
Centurion	Run! *(The kids run on the spot)*
Leader	People ran. And if he said:
Centurion	Stop! *(The kids stop)*
Leader	People stopped. But one day he asked for help from a man who just had to hear about a sick servant … *(The servant clutches her tummy)* And could say the word that would make her better.
Jesus	Be cured! *(The servant straightens up)*
Leader	Who was that man, kids?
All the children	Jesus!
Leader	Quite right, it was Jesus. The Centurion knew that Jesus had more authority than he.

Script 37   Families

Proper 5, Ordinary Time 10
(Sunday between 5 and 11 June if after Trinity Sunday)

St Luke 7.11–17

THEME

The challenge is to present this Gospel seriously without being too harrowing about loss and death, especially if there are children in your group from one-parent families, or who have experienced a family death. Jesus encounters a funeral procession of a widow's only son. He feels compassion for the woman, and brings the boy back to life. He acts promptly and decisively, something we pick up in a demo after the gospel.

SET UP

- The liturgical colour is Green.
- Marker pen for the flip chart.
- Sellotape.
- The children are going to make a chain of paper men so you will need paper, pens and child-friendly scissors.
- Make a chain before the session, to get the size of the paper right – and remind yourself how it's done. Template on CD-Rom **(CD37.1)**.
- Have one family chain of just three people ready.
- Cast Leader 2 as Jesus for the demo after the Gospel.
- Ask a family in church if they'd be prepared to stand up together at the end.

WELCOME *the children and lead them in* **The Sign of the Cross** ✠ **(p. xxxvi).**

THE KYRIE   Lord Jesus, we are sorry for the times we forgot you last week,
Lord have mercy
Lord have mercy

Lord Jesus, we are sorry for the times we were unkind,
Christ have mercy
Christ have mercy

Lord Jesus, we thank you for forgiving us when we do wrong,
Lord have mercy
Lord have mercy

Ask the children to repeat **The Prayer for Forgiveness** *after you* (**p. xxxvi**).

OPENING	Lord God
PRAYER	Father of all,
	We thank you for the love of our families
	and the people who care for us.
	Help us to pass on that love
	to any lonely person we meet,
	for your Son's sake. **Amen**

BEFORE THE GOSPEL

Families

Leader   This Sunday I'd like to talk about families.
What sort of people do you get in a family? *(Start the ball rolling)*
For example, I've got a mum and a brother …

Write up the family members that come in, mums, dads, siblings – push them a bit – anyone got a grandad? Or an auntie?

OK, that's a good list.
Now I'd like us to make some families …

Paper Families

Gather the children round and show them how to make a chain of paper men. Dish out the materials and get them to make some. Have grown-ups on hand to help the little ones.
Once they're done, ask the kids to give them faces, and label them 'Mum' or 'Dad' or 'Sister'. They might not have time to label them all – that's fine.
Make a chain of about six little men yourself.
Keep the session moving and, at the end, gather the kids round and go through some of the chains they've made.

Leader   OK, now I've got a line here – I've got a mum and a dad and two
sisters and a grandma and an uncle.

Show them – the uncle should be next to the dad

| | Now supposing the uncle leaves the family to be a soldier. |

Cut him out   What does the family do?

Well, they join hands again *(Sellotape the rest together)* and wait for him to come back.

But supposing he dies?

Well, I think the family prays for him and carries on.

The Widow of Nain

Leader   Today we're going to hear about a very small family.

Here it is.

Hold up a chain with just three people on it

Just a mum, a dad and a son.

No uncles, no grandads …

Well, dad died. *(Cut him off)*

And the mother became a widow, but she still had her son.

Two people are a perfectly good family.

But then the son died too. *(Cut him off)*

This doesn't happen very often – but it meant that the widow *(hold her up)* was left all alone. No family at all.

This happened in Jesus' time, and it was very serious.

Because in those days women weren't allowed to keep family money.

If a widow was left all alone, she'd have to beg to stay alive.

Fortunately she met Jesus, and we're going to hear about that now.

THE GOSPEL PROCESSION

THE GOSPEL   *St Luke 7.11–17*

Whatever translation you use, make sure you use the phrase, 'When Jesus saw her, He had compassion on her and said …' at verse 13.

AFTER THE GOSPEL

Run through the story; emphasize the widow had lost her husband and her only son. She was really alone – and then highlight Jesus' reaction

Leader   Jesus had *compassion* on her.

If you have 'compassion' you feel someone's sorrow as though it's your own – deep in your heart.

That's what Jesus felt – and He moved fast.

Let's get that bit of the story right.

Jesus Acts Fast – demo

Leader   *Line up three chairs*
                   OK, this is going to be the bier.

Or the coffin – it depends what translation you've been using

                   Now, I need someone to be the dead son.
                   Thanks. *(To the volunteer)*
                   You lie down on the chairs.
                   And I need a widow – you stand behind his head.
                   I need the people who carried the son – two at his head and two at
                   his feet.
                   And a procession – that's the rest of you, just behind the widow.
                   And now Jesus – that can be *Name.*
                   Right, you're all walking to the burial ground –
                   I think you can just walk on the spot –
                   and you're very sorry, so look sad.

Suggest they cross their arms and shake their heads

                   The widow is crying – perhaps you put your hands to your eyes.
                   OK, so everyone was walking out of the city to the burial ground,
                   when Jesus arrived.
                   Watch what He does. *(Enter Leader 2)*
Jesus (Leader 2)   Stop! *(Everyone stops walking)*
Leader 1   He put His hand on the bier and grasped it.

Leader 2 holds the chairs firmly

                   Then He said,
Jesus (Leader 2)   'Young man, I say to you arise!'
Leader 1   The young man sat up at once. *(He does)*
                   And Jesus handed him back to his mother.

*Leader 2 takes the boy by the hand, helps him to his feet, and presents him to the
widow*

                   Brilliant! Sit down, everyone.
                   Let's think about that.
                   Jesus stopped everything. He grasped the bier, He ordered the young
                   man to get up, and then He gave him back to his mother.
                   It took about 30 seconds.
                   You see, when you feel compassion, you don't just feel sorry – you
                   do something.
                   And Jesus did something only He could do,
                   He brought the young man back to life.

Sellotape a little man back to the paper 'widow'

> She had a family again.

REHEARSAL

For once you don't need one! (See below.)

FINAL	Lord God
PRAYER	We thank you for sending your Son Jesus into the world
	and for the miracle He performed when He met the poor widow.
	Help us to move as fast as Jesus when we see someone in trouble,
	For His sake. **Amen**

Glory Be ... (see p. xxxvii).

BACK IN CHURCH

Line the children up at the front

Leader   Today we heard how Jesus saw a widow and her dead son, and had compassion on them. It made us realize how much God loves families.
Here in Children's Church we only see a bit of a family each week – it would be nice to see the whole lot.
Name, can you find your family?

Choose a child whose family is obviously present. The kid runs off; ask the entire family to stand up. Ad lib as necessary – it might be politic to notice a new baby, or a grandparent

How about *Name*? *(Run it again)*

To the other kids

And the rest of you – can you see someone you know?
Wave to them ...
Are they waving back? *(They should be by now)*
So the church is full of families this morning – and every one of them is greatly loved by God.

Script 38 Jesus and the Unwelcome Guest

Proper 6, Ordinary Time 11
(Sunday between 12 and 18 June
if after Trinity Sunday)

St Luke 7.36–50

THEME

Jesus has a meal with Simon the Pharisee. While they are eating, a woman comes in and weeps over His feet (Jesus is reclining at table in the Roman fashion). For Jesus' fellow guests it's very embarrassing and, to make matters worse, the woman is a notorious sinner. The good people at table with Jesus are appalled, but He treats the unwelcome guest seriously. He is moved by her penitence and capacity for love, and forgives her sins. This session offers a dramatic re-telling of the story.

SET UP

- The liturgical colour is Green.
- A fake cheque for £100.
- Token food for a feast, anything you've got – pitta bread, grapes, fruit juice.
- An alb for Jesus.
- Simon should look rich – sunglasses, rings on his fingers, anything flashy.
- Aromatic oil in a nice-looking pot (try the aromatherapy section at the chemist's).

Set Up Simon's House

If you have got a separate room or space that you can set aside for Simon's house, use it. Most people will have to opt for the far end of the room.

- *Place as many cushions as you can in a large circle and put the food in the middle.*
- *Cast Jesus, Simon and the woman. They should look at their scripts beforehand – though the Narrator does most of the work.*
- *A couple of saucers.*
- *Print up the presentation (see below) without all the parentheses.*

WELCOME *the children and lead them in* **The Sign of the Cross** ✠ (**p. xxxvi**).

THE KYRIE	Lord Jesus, you came to earth to tell us how much God loved us,
	Lord have mercy
	Lord have mercy
	Lord Jesus, you came to earth to help us,
	Christ have mercy
	Christ have mercy
	Lord Jesus, you came to earth to forgive us,
	Lord have mercy
	Lord have mercy

Ask the children to repeat **The Prayer for Forgiveness** *after you* (**p. xxxvi**).

OPENING	Lord Jesus
PRAYER	You welcome all people into your presence
	Young and old,
	Girls and boys
	Saints and sinners.
	Thank you for bringing us here this morning,
	Help us to hear you
	And love you. **Amen**

Leader 1	Good morning, everyone. I'm going to start with one of the shortest stories Jesus ever told.
	He said that once there was a man who lent a friend of his 10p.

Give 10p to a child

	And he lent another friend £100.
To Leader 2	Will you take a cheque?
Leader 2	No problem!
Leader 1	Then when the day came to pay back the money he said to the friend who'd got 10p – don't worry, keep it!
	And to the other friend, don't worry about the £100 – you can keep that as well.
	Now of course both friends thanked him very much – but which one do you think was really, really grateful? (**Leader 2**)
	Let's see.
To the kid	OK, you can keep the 10p.
Child	Thanks!

Leader 1	*(To Leader 2)* Don't worry about the £100, you hang on to it.
Leader 2	Wow! Thanks, what a star! *(Shakes Leader 1 vigorously by the hand)*
	Fantastic! *(And so on – go over the top ...)*
Leader 1	Yup, I think she's really grateful.
	I'd like you to remember that as we hear the Gospel.

Simon, Jesus and the woman get ready

THE GOSPEL PROCESSION

THE GOSPEL   *St Luke 7.36–50*

Scan the text and look up

Leader	It's the story of Simon and the Unwelcome Guest.
	Ah, here is Simon ... *(Introduce Simon)*
	You can see he's dead rich.
	And where's the Unwelcome Guest? Oh, she's slipping out ...

The woman picks up the pot of oil and moves to the door of the room
Rifle through the Gospel

> Jesus must be in here somewhere – yes, here He is.

Enter Jesus, in alb

	OK, we're ready.
Narrator	One day a rich man called Simon the Pharisee asked Jesus to dinner. He said he had a lot of guests coming, and they wanted to hear Jesus speak.
	So Jesus went along to Simon's house and knocked at the door.

Jesus raps something, like a table, and ad libs a greeting with Simon

Jesus	Hello, are you Simon the Pharisee?
Simon	I am indeed – oh hallo, Jesus – welcome to my house.
Narrator	Then the rest of the guests arrived – that's us!

Lead the children to Simon's house and ask a kid to knock at the door. Simon shakes hands with his guests and welcomes them in

Narrator	Simon had produced a wonderful feast, and everybody ate lying on cushions, propped on one elbow – like this ...

Lie on a cushion
If the food is out of reach, designate a couple of slaves to go round with grapes, or bits of bread. Give the children time to enjoy this bit of the show

Narrator	Now there was a woman* in that town whom everybody knew was a great sinner and, when she heard Jesus was going to Simon's house, she bought a pot and filled it with precious ointment. Then she knocked at the door. *(The woman does so)*
Simon	Come in!
	Oh no! Not *her*! What's she doing here?
Narrator	But the woman took no notice of Simon; she came in and stood behind Jesus …

She stands by his feet – and mimes the following actions

> And began to cry.
> She bathed His feet with her tears,
> and dried them with her hair.
> Then she kissed Him

She kisses her fingers and presses them on Jesus' forehead

> and poured her precious ointment on Him.

(Keep the top on the pot …)

> Simon watched this and said to himself …

Simon	Jesus can't know how bad that woman is, otherwise He wouldn't let her touch Him.
Narrator	But Jesus said … *(Jesus can read this from his script)*
Jesus	Simon, do you see this woman?
	When I came to your house you didn't bathe my feet – but she has washed them with her tears.

---

* Annoyingly, she doesn't have a name.

	You didn't greet me with a kiss or pour ointment on me – but she has both kissed and anointed me.
	She has done all this because she loves me. Can you guess why she loves me?
Simon	No, Jesus, I can't.
Jesus	Because she is a sinner. She has many sins, and I have forgiven them all. When you have been forgiven for many things, you can't help loving the person who forgives you.
Narrator	And Jesus said to the woman,
Jesus	Your sins are forgiven, go in peace.
Narrator	Then everybody finished their supper.

When the children have eaten everything they can find, ask them to stow the cushions and come back to the body of the room

AFTER THE GOSPEL

Leader	That was really well done, thanks.
	Now, why do you think that woman loved Jesus so much?
	(Because He had forgiven her)
	Yes, He'd forgiven all her sins.
	She felt like *Name* did when I let her off that £100.
	People who know they are sinful have a very special friendship with God.
	And they're very grateful when He forgives them.

REHEARSAL

Practise your presentation for when you go back into church (see below).

Anointing

Leader	OK, the other thing about this story is the ointment the woman used.
	Can I see it? *(The woman passes over the pot. Open it up)*
	It smells good.

Pour the oil into two saucers – let some of the children smell it

	You use oil like this to anoint people.
	Babies are anointed when they are baptized and, in Great Britain, kings and queens are anointed when they're crowned.
	For the Jews an anointed person was very special, set apart.
	They knew that one day God would send them a Saviour – the 'Messiah'. That's Hebrew for 'The Anointed One'.

The Greek word for 'Messiah' is 'Christ'.
Which means, if you think about it, that a '*Christ*ian', a 'Messiah' person, is anointed too.
This oil *(hold it up)* reminds us that were anointed when we were baptized, and that God has called us to be 'Christians'.

FINAL PRAYER

Leader   Anyone who likes can be anointed now.

Make sure some grown-ups come up at once
Anoint the children by making the Sign of the Cross on their foreheads with the oil
Line them up as you would for Communion and say, as you anoint each one,

Remember, *Name*, that you are a Christian.

Ask the children to repeat the final prayer after you

Lord Jesus Christ,
We thank you for our baptism
And for calling us to be Christians.
Help us to show your love in the world
So that other people will learn to love you too.
Amen

BACK IN CHURCH

The children go down to the front. Leaders 1 and 2, and the kid who got 10p, stand in the middle of the line

Child 1   Today we watched *Name (Leader 1)* lend 10p to *Name (child)* and £100 to *Name (Leader 2)*.

Leader 1 dishes out the money again

Child 2   Then he said they didn't have to pay him back.
Name (child) thanked him.

The child gives Leader 1 a handshake and sits down

But *Name (Leader 2)* was really pleased – we thought she wouldn't ever stop thanking him …

Leader 2 puts on an impressive display of gratitude

Child 3   Jesus said it was the same with sinners.
A sinner who had been forgiven for lots of sins would really love God.

Script 39   The Gadarene Swine

Proper 7 (Church of England)
(Sunday between 19 and 25 June
if after Trinity Sunday)

St Luke 8.26–39

This is one of those Sundays when Roman Catholics and Anglicans in the Church of England read different Gospels during Mass. Roman Catholics should use *Script 40* (Peter Gets It Right), while English Anglicans use this one.

THEME

This Gospel was made for Sunday School: children love it, especially the moment when the pigs jump off the cliff. For adults, it reads strangely – presumably Jesus re-routed the psychic disturbance crackling round the maniac into the nearby herd. From the children's point of view, however, it's quite straightforward. The maniac needed a cure and Jesus gave him one, with dramatic results.

SET UP
- The liturgical colour is Green.
- Enough flowers to make a bunch.
- A child prepared to come to church in a football top.
- Pictures from the CD-Rom – but go through the collective nouns they illustrate. If you can make the point with toys, particularly toy Roman soldiers, it'll look more interesting.
- Props for the play – an alb for Jesus if possible, and some crooks, or walking sticks, for the swineherds.
- Ask the person playing Jesus to look through the script before the session.
- If you've got a step or shallow platform the children can leap off without hurting themselves, so much the better.
- See if it's OK to do a short play for your presentation.
- A prayer candle – one that can stand safely on its own base.

WELCOME *the children and lead them in* **The Sign of the Cross** ✠ **(p. xxxvi).**

THE KYRIE	Lord, you always forgive those who say they are sorry,
	Lord, have mercy
	Lord, have mercy

Jesus, we are sorry for the times we have been unkind,
Christ, have mercy
Christ, have mercy

Lord, we thank you for always loving and forgiving us,
Lord, have mercy
Lord, have mercy

Ask the children to repeat **The Prayer for Forgiveness** *after you* (**p. xxxvi**).

OPENING	Lord God
PRAYER	Our Heavenly Father
	We thank you for bringing us together this Sunday.
	Help us to hear the Gospel
	and learn to love your Son, Jesus Christ,
	who came into the world to save and heal us. **Amen**

BEFORE THE GOSPEL

Collective Nouns

Leader	OK, I'd like to start by thinking about the words we use to
	describe things when we put them in a group.
	We've got some flowers here ... *(hold up a couple)*
	and if I put them all together ... *(do so)*
	they become a ...? (**Bunch**)

Ask any footballer present to come forward

Or we might have one footballer – like *Name*.
But if he/she joins up with some others ...

See if any other kids would like to join him/her

	we've got a ...? (**Team**)
CD39.1	It's the same with animals.
	One lamb is just a lamb.
CD39.2	But lots of lambs are a ...? (**Flock**)
CD39.3	And in England, one soldier is just a soldier.
CD39.4	But lots are ...? (**A Regiment**)
	Back in Roman times soldiers weren't put together in regiments.
CD39.5	You might get one Roman.

	He's just a soldier.
CD39.6	But a lot of them were called ...? (**A Legion**)
	'Legion' – we'll hear that word again as we listen to the Gospel.

THE GOSPEL PROCESSION

THE GOSPEL   *St Luke 8.26–39*

Optional Paraphrase

One day Jesus crossed the lake to the country of Gadarea. This was a Gentile country where the people kept pigs. In fact, there was a large herd of them feeding on the hillside, looked after by their swineherds.

As Jesus got out of the boat, a maniac rushed up to Him. He was completely mad, he wore no clothes, and was so strong that he could rip up chains and knock over anyone who tried to catch him. People thought he had an evil spirit.

The maniac fell down in front of Jesus, and Jesus said to the evil spirit inside him, 'Come out of this man, you evil spirit – what's your name?'

The evil spirit said, 'Legion!'

(He said that because there seemed to be hundreds of evil spirits inside the man.) Then he said, 'Don't just throw us out – let us go into those pigs over there ...'

Jesus wanted the man to be cured immediately, so He threw out the evil spirits – who went straight into the pigs. And the next minute, the pigs got together, rushed down the hill – and jumped into the sea.

The swineherds were terrified and ran off to tell their neighbours. Very shortly afterwards they came back, with a crowd at their heels, but all they saw was Jesus, and the man, sitting quietly together.

Then Jesus went back to His boat, and the man He had cured went back to Gadarea, telling everyone what Jesus had done for him.

Madness

Leader	Nobody really knows why people go mad.
	In Jesus' day, people thought that mad people had evil spirits inside them and, in this story, the maniac was so completely mad that everyone thought he had a *legion* of evil spirits inside him.
	We don't know what Jesus thought about madness, but He obviously didn't like it and He cured it, very quickly.

ACTIVITY

A Re-enactment of the Gadarene Swine

Leader	OK, now the grown-ups will have heard this story in church. They probably won't know what to make of it, so we're going to help them.
	We're going to tell this story again – together ...
(Casting)	We'll need a Jesus, some swineherds, a maniac – and loads of pigs.

Do some casting

The Narrator should be a Leader, especially if you're going to do this Back in Church.

Run a few pig auditions – what noise do pigs make? Let's hear that. (**Oink oink**)

Practise cueing in the 'oinks' with an emphatic hand movement and 'killing' the sound with a finger across the throat.

Get the maniac down to a mere T-shirt and jeans and dress Jesus in an alb.

The Narrator has a script (and reads from the lectern when you do this in church). The pigs bunch up, looked after by a couple of swineherds (with crooks or old-fashioned walking sticks).

Practise the maniac's mad moment. He/she might not want to roar, but flapping the arms about, or trying to head butt Jesus, will do just as well.

Another grown-up has a script and helps to cue the kids in.

The Gadarene Swine

Narrator	One day Jesus crossed the lake to the country of Gadarea.

Enter Jesus, rowing ...

This was a Gentile country and the people there kept pigs.

Enter pigs, upright but oinking: herdsmen keep them together with a non-tactile use of the sticks. They cross the room/platform/playing area and settle down on all fours to graze

Narrator	As Jesus got out of the boat, a maniac rushed up to Him.

Maniac rushes up, flapping his arms, and circling Jesus. Eventually he stands still, twitching a bit

The maniac was very strong, nobody had been able to catch him, or tie him up. People thought he had an evil spirit.

Jesus calmed him down.

Jesus puts his hands on the maniac's shoulders; the maniac goes still

	And said,
Jesus	'Come out of this man, you evil spirit – what is your name?'
Narrator	And the maniac said,

Maniac	'Legion.'
Narrator	He said that, because he felt as if he had hundreds of evil spirits inside him.
	Then the evil spirit inside the man spoke to Jesus.

The maniac kneels

He asked Jesus not to throw him out into the countryside, but to let him and the other evil spirits enter the herd of pigs that were grazing nearby.

Well, Jesus wanted the man cured immediately so He threw the spirit out.

Jesus puts his hands on the maniac's head

Narrator	And something happened to the pigs – because the next moment they got up
They do	And rushed down a steep bank, straight into the sea.

An impressive pig leap moment, 'oinking' as they go

The swineherds were terrified and ran away.

Exit swineherds

But the man thanked Jesus.

He shakes Jesus' hand

And he went round the entire countryside telling everybody what Jesus had done for him.

Steps forward with arms open wide
Everybody gets into a line and bows (to indicate the play is over)

FINAL PRAYER

Gather the children round a prayer candle

Let's sit very still and look at the flame.
How quiet it is.
How beautiful.
Think about the poor man with the evil spirit.
Thank goodness Jesus cured him.
I don't know much about evil spirits – but Jesus does.
He can always get rid of them.

Let's think about a good Spirit instead.
The Holy Spirit.
He's in this room now.

In our minds and in our hearts.
Helping us to pray.

Either say, or sing, 'Be still for the presence of the Lord', together.
If you say it, you may have to ask the children to repeat the words after you.

Be still for the presence of the Lord
The Holy One is here
Come bow before Him now
With reverence and fear
In Him no sin is found
We stand on holy ground
Be still for the presence of the Lord
The Holy One is here. Amen

BACK IN CHURCH

Re-enact the story of the Gadarene Swine (see above).

(CD39.1)

Sample cartoons for this script   (CD39.3)   (CD39.5)

Script 40   Peter Gets It Right

Ordinary Time 12 (Roman Catholic)
(Sunday between 19 and 25 June
if after Trinity Sunday)

St Luke 9.18–20

This is one of the Sundays when Roman Catholics and Anglicans read different Gospels. Most English Anglicans will be hearing about the Gadarene Swine (*Script 39*), while Catholics will be hearing this one. Check with your priest if you are unsure.

THEME

Jesus asks His disciples who they think He is, and St Peter is inspired to say He is the Christ. The Gospel accounts make it sound as if Peter blurted this out impulsively but, whether his rational mind was working or not, his heart knew the truth – and was open to the prompting of the Holy Spirit.

SET UP

- The liturgical colour is Green.
- A clear jar full of marbles (or little rubber balls or jelly babies). Count how many you put in and remember the number.
- A 'Feely Bag' – a capacious bag into which a child can insert its arm.
- Various objects which you can place in the bag (one by one) and invite children to feel and identify. For example: a lemon, a spoon, a padlock, a small teddy, some macaroni, a bar of soap, a sponge, a toothbrush – anything that catches your eye round the house. Add some very easy objects for the little ones – a ball or an apple.
- Print up the Rock Quiz from the CD-Rom.
- Sellotape, or something to stick the jigsaw pieces on to their backing paper with (see below).
- Picture or icon of St Peter – his statue outside St Peter's is on the CD-Rom **(CD40.2)**.
- Leader 1 should make sure he/she has some breakfast this morning – if only to give conviction to the section on *Guessing*.

THE KYRIE   Lord, you always forgive those who say they are sorry,
Lord, have mercy
Lord, have mercy

Jesus, we are sorry for the times we have been unkind.
Christ, have mercy
Christ, have mercy

Lord, we thank you for always loving and forgiving us.
Lord, have mercy
Lord, have mercy

WELCOME *the children and lead them in* **The Sign of the Cross** ✠ **(p. xxxvi).**

Ask the children to repeat **The Prayer for Forgiveness** *after you* (**p. xxxvi**).

OPENING   Lord God
PRAYER   You sent your Son
Jesus Christ into the world
to save us from our sins.
Help us to know Him
and love Him,
As our Saviour. **Amen**

BEFORE THE GOSPEL

Guessing

Leader 1   This morning I'd like to think about guessing.
I used to do a lot of guessing when I went to school, especially when
I hadn't done my homework.
Sometimes we take a guess when we haven't got a clue what the right
answer is. Can anyone guess what I had for breakfast this morning?

*See what they come up with and react accordingly. You could prime Leader 2 to
suggest something deeply unlikely – like roast beef and Yorkshire pudding*

Sometimes we take a guess when we've got a chance of getting it
right. Like this …

*Produce the jar of marbles. Ask the kids to guess how many marbles are in the jar –
they can hold the jar if they like, but don't let them settle down to count the contents.
Write each child's guess down; the winner is the child whose total came nearest to the
actual amount*

And sometimes we guess, when we're pretty sure we know the
answer …

Produce the Feely Bag. Offer it to various children – making sure the little ones get something easy

	If we know somebody well, we can make very good guesses indeed.
To Leader 2	Can you guess what my favourite TV programme is?

Or 'Where I'm going on holiday?' Anything that Leader 2 is bound to get right

In the Gospel today we're going to hear how St Peter once made a brilliant guess. Let's hear it.

THE GOSPEL PROCESSION

THE GOSPEL   *St Luke 9.18–20*

AFTER THE GOSPEL

Go through the Gospel with the children

Leader   Jesus asked His disciples who the crowds thought He was.
And they said, 'Oh people are saying you're John the Baptist come back to life – or one of the prophets.'
Then Jesus said, 'What about you? Who do you think I am?'
And Peter said … What *did* Peter say?

Read that bit of the Gospel again if they can't remember

(**You are the Christ**)
Exactly – Jesus was the Christ.
The Christ was the Saviour God was going to send into the world.
In a way, Peter guessed that.
But it was a good guess.
He knew Jesus so well that he realized who Jesus really was.
Jesus was very impressed with Peter's answer.
He could see that Peter had rock-solid faith – so he called Peter a 'Rock'; something firm on which He could build His Church.

CD40.1   I've got a quiz here, let's see if we're as good as St Peter at getting the answers right.
Every right answer is a little rock *(hold one up)* and altogether the rocks should make up a good firm foundation for Jesus' Church.

ACTIVITY

Play the Rock Quiz. Instructions on the CD-Rom.

REHEARSAL

Practise your presentation for when you go back into church (see below).

FINAL PRAYER

Gather the children round an image of St Peter, talk about it

Leader	What's he holding? (**Keys**) Yes, Jesus said He would give Peter the keys to the Gates of Heaven.

Look at Peter's face

Jesus knew that face very well – Peter was one of His best friends.
Let's ask St Peter for his prayers.
The response is, **Pray for us.**

Holy Peter, Friend of Jesus,
Pray for us

Holy Peter, Rock on which the Church was built,
Pray for us

Holy Peter, Holder of the keys to Heaven,
Pray for us

Lord Jesus
Hear the prayers of your friend St Peter
As he prays for us
And the Church built on his faith. **Amen**

BACK IN CHURCH

The children come in with their completed Rock Quiz

Leader	Today we heard how Jesus asked His disciples who they thought He was. Most of them weren't too sure but St Peter said:
Child 1	'You are the Christ!'
Child 2	Jesus said that Peter would be the Rock on which He would build His Church.
Leader	So we ran a Rock Quiz, and every right answer built up a rock …

The children hold up their completed Rocks

	and the Rock reminded us of
Everyone	**St Peter!**

Script 41   St Francis Takes His Clothes Off

Proper 8, Ordinary Time 13
(Sunday between 26 June and 2 July)

St Luke 9.57–62

THEME

We have a difficult Gospel this morning and one that comes from the heart of a different culture. In the Middle East to this day no young man makes a major decision without consulting his family, knowing full well that he'd be in dead trouble if he proposed anything too radical. The chap who tells Jesus that he 'wants to say goodbye to his father' is quite aware that the old man would probably keep him at home.* Jesus hasn't got time for this; He knows that things are reaching a crisis and warns His disciples of tough times ahead. The children are probably too young to fully comprehend the issues here. Instead we introduce them to the challenge of the Gospel by offering them a story about that very radical young man, St Francis.

SET UP

- The liturgical colour is Green.
- A table.
- Some brightly coloured cloth (a duvet cover perhaps).
- A small pile of sheets.
- Pocket Bible, with various texts inserted between its pages (see below).
- 'Francis' wears some snazzy clothes, a leather jacket perhaps, a flashy tie (anything eye-catching). In his pockets he has the Bible (above), a wallet and a mobile.
- Cast St Francis, the dad, the beggar and the bishop. Run through the script beforehand, it's very easy.
- Pictures from the CD-Rom, print as large as possible.
- Marker pens.

---

  * Similarly, the man who wants to 'bury his father' isn't asking for permission to attend his funeral. He is proposing to put off following Jesus until his father has died and he *could* bury him.

Optional

- A paper mitre for the bishop – template on the CD-Rom **(CD41.1)**.
- An image of St Francis if you've got one.

WELCOME *the children and lead them in* **The Sign of the Cross** ✠ **(p. xxxvi).**

KYRIE	God our Father, you forgive everybody who says they are sorry,
	Lord have mercy
	Lord have mercy
	Lord Jesus, you came to Earth to tell us how much God loves us
	Christ have mercy
	Christ have mercy
	Holy Spirit, you fill our hearts with the love of God
	Lord have mercy
	Lord have mercy

Ask the children to repeat **The Prayer for Forgiveness** *after you* **(p. xxxvi).**

OPENING PRAYER	Father of us all
	You call your children to leave everything behind
	to follow your Son.
	Help us to hear your voice
	And give us the courage to follow Jesus
	Wherever He may lead,
	We ask this in His Name. **Amen**
Leader	OK, it's quite a tough Gospel this morning, let's hear it straight away.

Straight into …

THE GOSPEL PROCESSION

THE GOSPEL   *St Luke 9.57–62*

Leader	*Introduce the Gospel by saying,*
	As Jesus was making His last journey to Jerusalem, He met some people on the road who wanted to follow Him, and this is what He said to them …

AFTER THE GOSPEL

Leader   *Go through the text again – make the point that the men are*
                making excuses
                Jesus was very firm with these chaps.
                I think that's because He knew that life was about to get very
                dangerous, so He said to the people who wanted to follow Him,
                'OK, but there'll be nowhere to sleep – and you've got to come *now*
                – tomorrow is too late.'
                Some Christians have been quite worried by this Gospel – but there's
                one who wasn't.
                His name was Francis, and he was always up for anything Jesus
                asked of him.
                Let's hear about him.

St Francis Takes His Clothes Off

*One of the Leaders narrates this story and cues in Francis' dad, the beggar and the
bishop. Francis wears his flashy clothes, and has a Bible, a mobile and a wallet in his
pocket*

Narrator   Right, this is St Francis.
Enter Francis   Wow, love the jacket! Do you like clothes, Francis?

*Francis does a cool dude act; he loves his clothes and points out his tie, hat, anything
he's wearing*

                St Francis lived in Assisi with his very rich family. His dad was a
                cloth merchant, and on market days Francis and his dad would set
                up a stall in the market.

*Francis and his dad bring forward the table and pile it with the sheets and the brightly
coloured cloth*

                Now Francis may have been a rich kid, but he didn't just think about
                clothes.
                He went to church, and read the Bible,
                and took being a Christian very seriously.
                One day he was helping his father at the market when a beggar came
                up to them.

Enter beggar – in just a T-shirt (as long as the hall isn't too cold)

                He was shivering with cold.

The beggar shivers

                And Francis remembered something Jesus had said in the Bible,

Francis pulls out his Bible and reads out Text 1

Francis	'I was naked and you clothed me.'
Narrator	So he told his father they ought to help the poor man.

Francis and Dad ad lib a bit of dialogue

Francis	Dad, we ought to give this poor man something to wear
Dad	Forget it, son! I'm not giving my stuff away.
Francis	But Jesus said …
Dad	I'm not interested in Jesus!
Narrator	And Francis' dad was so fed up that he cleared off to have a drink and left Francis alone with the cloth. Francis thought, 'What shall I do? I know, if I sign a cloth with the Cross, it will belong to God, and then I can give it to the beggar …'
	So he picked up a piece of cloth,

He picks up the brightly coloured one

	made the Sign of the Cross over it,
He does so	and gave it to the beggar.

The beggar wraps it round him, shakes hands with Francis, and runs off

At which point, his dad came back, very pleased with himself. He'd found a customer for one of his best bits of cloth, the nicely coloured one.

Dad reappears, and looks for the cloth. He can't believe it's not there and begins to hunt through the sheets

Francis had to tell him what he had done – and his father went completely berserk.

Dad waves his hands about

In fact, he wanted to have his son arrested for stealing cloth.

Dad	*(To the kids)* Oi! Is there a policeman anywhere round here?
Narrator	OK! said Francis, so you want to arrest me, do you?
	Well, I have just remembered another bit of the Bible …

Francis pulls out his Bible again, riffles through, and finds Text 2

Francis	Jesus said, 'Give up everything you've got and follow me!'
	So I'm going to give everything up – right now!
Narrator	And there, in the market place, Francis threw down his wallet, his mobile,

He slaps these down on the table

then he began to take off his fine clothes …

his jacket, his hat, his tie ...

Francis takes these off; he should get down to a T-shirt

	And he was just about to take off his trousers when ...
Enter bishop	a bishop arrived.
	He saw what was happening, grabbed a sheet from the market stall, and quickly wrapped Francis up.

Bishop wraps Francis in a sheet

Then the bishop stood between the two angry men.

Bishop stands in the middle, keeping them apart

He put his hand on the father's shoulder.
And told him to calm down. *(He does)*
And he shook his head at Francis. *(Which he does)*
And told him he had no right to give away cloth that didn't belong to him.
Francis listened to the bishop and hung his head.

Francis looks penitent

He was sorry he'd annoyed his father – but he couldn't go back to being a rich young dude.
So he went away, and found something that looked like a sack, and put it on. He fastened it with a rope round his waist and, for the rest of his life, he lived a life of poverty.

To the actors	Thanks, guys. *(Encourage a round of applause)*

St Francis' Wardrobe

Leader	So, let's think about Francis, before and after.
Stick up **CD41.2**	
	What do you think he wore before he had the row with his dad?

Ask the kids to draw Francis' trendy clothes. (There's a variety of pictures round the margin of the picture to give them a clue)

	And what did he wear afterwards?
Add **CD41.3**	*Get someone to draw in Francis' 'habit'. Admire the result*
	Have you ever seen anyone looking like this?

*Take all answers, the children may well say a 'monk'. Establish this is what friars wear**

---

* Friars are not monks. Whether you want to distinguish between a friar (such as a Franciscan) and a monk (such as a Benedictine) is up to you. The difference is that monks stay put while friars move about the place. To be honest, they do look quite similar.

For the rest of his life Francis looked like this *(hold up* **CD41.3***)*, and he slept rough and begged for his food – and it all sounds very uncomfortable, but some people thought, 'Yup, that's a good way to follow Jesus', and they copied him.

Francis's followers are named after him; they are called Franciscans.

REHEARSAL

Practise your presentation for when you go back into church (see below).

BEFORE THE FINAL PRAYER

Gather the children round an image of St Francis, or a prayer candle

Leader   Let's think for a moment about the nice clothes we're wearing.

Look round and admire anything that catches your eye – a kid's stripy socks, or a smart jumper

                Then think of St Francis in his sack.

Address another Leader

                Do you fancy being a Franciscan, *Name*?

The other Leader should agree it's an amazing way to follow Jesus, but add that perhaps it isn't for him/her

Leader   Yup, I feel the same.
                Actually, we don't have to feel bad about our clothes. Jesus doesn't usually ask us to give everything up – but He'd like us to be ready to give things up if we have to.
                I wonder if we can?
                What happens if a football game, or a really good TV programme happens at the same time as Mass?
                It's difficult isn't it?
                So this Gospel is about Jesus saying,
                'Listen, following me can be tough – I want you to know that.'
                Fortunately He also said:

(Have 'Francis' read out Text 3 from his Bible)

Francis   Jesus said,
                'In this world you'll probably run into danger – but don't be frightened, I have conquered the world.' *(St John 16.33)*

FINAL **PRAYER**	We're going to end by asking St Francis for his prayers. The response to the prayer is Pray for us **Pray for us**

Holy Francis
Friend of Jesus
Pray for us

Holy Francis
Lover of poverty
Pray for us

Holy Francis
Soldier of Christ
Pray for us

Almighty God
We thank you for the example of St Francis,
Help us to be as brave as him,
and follow your Son, Jesus Christ. **Amen**

BACK IN CHURCH

Take in the two pictures

Child 1   Today we hear about a rich kid.

Hold up **CD41.2**

Child 2   He wore cool clothes.
Child 3   And his name was Francis.
Child 4   Then one day, he gave up everything for Jesus.
               Even his clothes.

Hold up **CD41.3**

Leader   We thought about this and decided that, though God doesn't ask
              everyone to be like St Francis, He'd like us to be ready to give up
              things – even our designer labels – if we have to.
              So we asked St Francis for his prayers.

Script 42   Trusting in God

Proper 9, Ordinary Time 14
(Sunday between 3 and 9 July)

St Luke 10.1, 3–4, 7–9

THEME

Jesus sends out 72 of His disciples on their first preaching tour. They are to take nothing with them – no money, no spare sandals, nothing but their trust in God. It's a testing Gospel but, even nowadays, missionaries have discovered that God will send them food and help when they least expect it. The session centres round the story of a contemporary Catholic mission in Mozambique.

SET UP

- The liturgical colour is Green.
- Print up the pictures from the CD-Rom.
- A simple lunch in a plastic box – two sandwiches and an apple for example – stowed in a satchel or small rucksack.

WELCOME *the children and lead them in* **The Sign of the Cross** ✠ **(p. xxxvi).**

THE KYRIE   Lord, for the times we have forgotten to love you,
Lord have mercy
Lord have mercy

Jesus, for the times we have forgotten to love others,
Christ have mercy
Christ have mercy

Lord, we thank you for never forgetting to love us,
Lord, have mercy
Lord, have mercy

Ask the children to repeat **The Prayer for Forgiveness** *after you* **(p. xxxvi).**

OPENING   God our Father,
PRAYER   We thank you for giving us everything we need,
           Sun and rain,
           Food and drink,
           Arms and legs,
           People to love us,
           And friends to play with.
           We thank you especially for bringing us together this morning,
           To worship you and learn about your Son,
           Jesus Christ. **Amen**

BEFORE THE GOSPEL

Trust

Leader   Has anyone here ever acted in a play? Hands up …

Ask a couple of children about their stage experience

           Well, I was in a play the other day – and I had a terrible time …
           I was supposed to faint on stage – like this

Start a faint – hands to head, stagger a bit

           But before I hit the floor, another character was going to catch me
           like this …

*Leader 2 comes forward. Leader 1 apparently faints and Leader 2 catches him/her
before they crash to the floor*

           We rehearsed it and rehearsed it and, when it came to the show,
           I got ready to faint *(hand to head)*
           and old *Name (Leader 2)* there wandered off *(he does)* – and …

*Disaster – Leader 1 (apparently) crashes to the floor. Make sure you fall without
hurting yourself*

           I shan't be trusting *Name* again.

Run a Trust Game. The easiest – and most popular – is the Deadly Swamps Game.

The Deadly Swamps Game

*Set up some chairs in the middle of the room as an obstacle course. The chairs are the
deadly swamps. Your task is to get Leader 2 across in a fog. Blindfold Leader 2 and
direct her across the room by telling her to go three steps to the left and so on. (Don't
take too long.) If she inadvertently knocks a chair, make a ghastly sucking noise –
'Blimey, that was close' – but make sure nothing fatal happens.*

Leader 1   Could any of you do that?

Let the children guide some other victims across. Give each kid a chance to call out an instruction as there probably won't be time for everyone to have a complete turn. Collisions are not deemed fatal; just yell 'Stop!' if a kid bangs into something. Review the game

It's great to trust your mates. It helps in plays, and in games – and in anything we want to do together.

When Jesus sent His friends off to tell people the Good News about Him, He sent them off in twos. That way, they could learn to trust each other.

He wanted them to trust Someone else as well.

Let's hear who that was …

THE GOSPEL PROCESSION

THE GOSPEL   *St Luke 10.1, 3–4, 7–9*

AFTER THE GOSPEL

Leader   So Jesus sends 72 disciples off to preach and gives them strict instructions about their journey. He says they're not to take a rucksack, or spare shoes, or any money – nothing!

How did He expect them to eat?

The children may tell you – He expected people to give them food – if they don't, read out verses 5 and 7 again

Jesus expected His friends would be given food by the people they met. But they couldn't be sure.

Whom could they trust? *(A rhetorical question)*

(God)

They'd have to trust that God would send them the people and the food they needed.

That was pretty difficult.

When I was a kid, I had to trust people to give me food – whom do you think I trusted? (**Mum or Dad**)

Yup, every morning I'd look in my satchel …

Pull out the bag with your lunch pack in it

> and there would be my lunch.

Open up the lunch pack

> Fantastic – sandwiches!
> Well, Jesus' disciples didn't have a satchel or a lunch pack.
> But they did have God.
> Do you think it would work?
> Actually it does. There were some friends of Jesus who went off to Mozambique only five years ago, who had to rely on God to encourage people to send them food. Let me tell you about them.

Christmas in Mozambique

Leader 1 goes into story-telling mode – while Leader 2 is ready with the pictures

> Mozambique is a country in Africa. The people there have suffered from wars and drought and famine – they've had a terrible time.
> So Christians from all over the world have gone over to give them medical aid, and set up churches, and help them get going again. Three Christians went from Acton – their names were Rosie, Fergal and Eamon.
> Rosie was there to run the medical centre, and Eamon and Fergal were priests. They ran the church and tried to get some farms started up. But the people only had porridge to eat – and they didn't have any to spare. So Rosie, Eamon and Fergal had to trust God for their food.
> So God encouraged the people of Acton to send them food packages. Let's see what they sent.

List off the foodstuffs as **CD42.1–CD42.6** *go up*

CD42.1	Ah, pasta,
CD42.2	corned beef,
CD42.3	tins of fruit,
CD42.4	chocolate,
CD42.5	biscuits
CD42.6	and pots of jam.

> Well, the children in Mozambique knew that all this nice stuff used to end up with Rosie and her friends, so they hung round their front door, and Rosie gave them *(peel off the pictures of these foodstuffs)* the tins of fruit, and the chocolate, the biscuits and the jam.
> And for six months Rosie and the two priests lived on pasta and corned beef. And not very much of it either.

CD42.7   Eventually Christmas came round and, on Christmas Eve, they sat down to eat supper. Fergal came in with a big saucepan and held it up. 'Merry Christmas, everyone!' he said, and poured their supper into a bowl. It was pasta and corned beef.

Everyone burst into tears …

At which point there was a knock at the door. Eamon answered it and there, beaming on the doorstep, were two Dutch Protestant

CD42.8   missionaries.

'Merry Christmas!' they said – and came in with a huge box.

They went straight to the table and tipped out everything that was inside.

CD42.9   Christmas cake,

CD42.10   dried figs,

CD42.11   tinned chicken,

CD42.12   and a bottle of Dutch gin.

It was the most fantastic Christmas Rosie, Eamon and Fergal had ever had.

How did that happen?

I think God had seen His three friends trusting Him for their food – and giving most of it away – and He sent them two more friends, the Dutch missionaries, to give them a Christmas present.

That's what happens when you trust in God.

It's a bit scary sometimes, but you get the most wonderful surprises.

REHEARSAL

Practise your presentation for when you go back into church (see below).

FINAL   Jesus wants us to trust God, and trust each other.

PRAYER   One way to do that is to pray for each other and ask the saints for their prayers.

We're going to do that now.

Ask the children to repeat after you

Lord God
Help us to trust you
And trust each other
So that together
we can build your Kingdom on Earth. Amen

And knowing there is one saint in Heaven who we can always trust to pray for us, let us ask for the prayers of Our Lady, the Virgin Mary.

Finish with the **Hail Mary ... (p. xxxvii).**

MUSIC

The modern hymn 'Father in my life I see ...' is all about trust, it works very well as a round (which is itself a form of co-operation).

BACK IN CHURCH

The children form up in pairs

Child 1	Today we read the Gospel and realized that God wanted us to trust Him.
Child 2	And trust each other ...
Child 3	So we decided to practise trusting each other.
Child 4	And so we got our Leaders to show us how you caught someone on stage ...

Leaders 1 and 2 demonstrate their famous stage fall

Two possible endings

If it's successful

Leader 1   And we realized how marvellous it was to trust your mates.

And if it's a disaster

Leader 2   We're still working on it ...

Sample cartoons for this script

Script 43   The Good Samaritan

Proper 10, Ordinary Time 15
(Sunday between 10 and 16 July)

St Luke 10.30–37

THEME

Today we hear one of Jesus' greatest stories; the only trouble is – we all know the ending. The surprise has gone. Jesus' original audience would never have guessed that a *Samaritan* was going to do the right thing. Nowadays it's difficult to think up a substitute for the unpopular Samaritan. However, though it's un-PC to say so, we're surrounded by people guaranteed to cause a groan the moment they're mentioned. In one parish, where the children were solid QPR fans, we had an Arsenal supporter play the Samaritan. Perhaps there are some irritating stereotypes in your locality that you can show in a good light – the Good Banker for example, or the Virtuous Yuppie? This script introduces the Good Hoodie.

SET UP

- The liturgical colour is Green.
- Pictures from the CD-Rom.
- Props for the Samaritan story:
  - mobile phone
  - sweatshirt with hood
  - football scarf
  - empty lager tin
  - plastic cudgel/truncheon
  - a black server's cassock for the child playing the priest.
- Cast children to play the characters in the parable:
  - the traveller
  - the mugger
  - the priest
  - the kid from Children's Church
- Mix up the genders. (They don't have to learn anything in advance.)

- Ask a Leader or teenager to be the Hoodie: he should read it in advance (the role needs a certain swagger), and he should start the session with his hood down.

WELCOME *the children and lead them in* **The Sign of the Cross** ✠ **(p. xxxvi).**

THE KYRIE   Lord, for the times we have forgotten to love you,
Lord have mercy
Lord have mercy

Jesus, for the times we have forgotten to love others
Christ have mercy
Christ have mercy

Lord, we thank you for never forgetting to love us
Lord, have mercy
Lord, have mercy

Ask the children to repeat **The Prayer for Forgiveness** *after you* **(p. xxxvi).**

OPENING   Heavenly Father
PRAYER   You want us to love other people as much as ourselves.
Help us to try to do this
Even when it's difficult,
through your Son, Jesus Christ. **Amen**

Neighbours

Leader   OK, we're going to hear one of Jesus' great stories today.
It's called 'the Good Samaritan'.
So the first thing we've got to do is find out what a Samaritan is.

If some children put up their hands – ask them to put their knowledge on hold for a moment

    Samaritans lived in Palestine, just like the Jews, and were very easy to spot. Look …
CD43.1   This is a Samaritan.
CD43.2   And this is a Jew.
Can anyone spot the difference? *(The pictures are identical)*
Yup, they look the same – only a Samaritan or a Jew would know the difference.
Samaritans were the same race as the Jews; they spoke the same language and wore the same clothes.

BUT, as far as the Jews were concerned, the Samaritans had funny accents, they prayed differently, they lived just down the road – they were really irritating.

It's easy to get annoyed with people.

Use a local example, the next village, or perhaps you live near a border – what about those jokes we make about the English/Welsh/Scots? It might be another football team, or another school. Keep it light, unless of course the children want to talk about more serious forms of aggravation – they'll tell you at once how wrong it is to be racist or unkind

Why do we get annoyed with other people?

Probably because they're different from us – it makes us feel uncomfortable.

Jesus knows how difficult it is to get on with people and He told a story about it in the Gospel.

BEFORE THE GOSPEL

Leader	First we have to meet the man Jesus told the story to ...
CD43.3	It's this bloke.

He was very religious, knew the Bible by heart, and he said to Jesus, 'Teacher, what must I do to get to Heaven?'

Jesus answered, 'You know your Bible, what does it say?'

And the man said, 'I must love God with all my heart and I must love my neighbour as myself.'

'Excellent!' said Jesus. 'That's your answer!'

But the man wanted to show how clever he was, so he asked another question,

'Oh yes?' he said. 'And who is my neighbour?'

Actually that's a good question, who is our neighbour?

Take all answers but don't comment

Well, Jesus wanted the man to work out who his neighbour was all by himself. So He told him a story.

We're going to tell that story now – with a couple of changes.

One Leader narrates and the other plucks children out of the group to play the parts as needed. The Hoodie keeps his hood down, until needed, and puts the lager tin in his pocket

The Good Hoodie

Narrator   Once upon a time a man went on a journey all the way from
              Jerusalem *(indicate one side of the hall)*
              to Jericho.

Indicate the other, and get a kid walking across the hall

              But on the way, a robber *(hand the cudgel to a child)*
              snuck up behind him *(he/she does)*
              and mugged him. Bop!
              The traveller fell to the ground.
              The robber took some money from his pockets and sneaked off.

The kid mimes this

              And the poor traveller found he was so hurt he couldn't move. He
              made an awful lot of noise –
              (To traveller) What do you say when you're hurt?
Traveller   *(Or any of the other children)* Ow! Ow!
Narrator   Fortunately a priest came along.

Ask a kid to put on the cassock and send him/her over to the traveller

Narrator   'O good!' thought the traveller. 'A priest, he'll help me!'
              But the priest gave him one look – and stepped over him …
              He/she does so
              'Ouch!' said the traveller.
              Then a kid from Children's Church turned up.

Ask another child to walk over

              'Great!' thought the traveller. 'She goes to Children's Church –
              she'll give me a hand …'
              But the kid took one look, and jumped over him.
              The child does
              'Hey!' said the traveller.
              Then a third person turned up.

Hoodie gets up, hood over face, scarf round neck, lager tin in hand

              'Oh no!' said the traveller.
              The Hoodie was drinking lager and staggering about, and chanting.

Up comes the Hoodie, doing some sort of football chant (England! England!)

              And the traveller wished he could run away, but he was too
              bashed up.
              The Hoodie saw him and came across.
              'Oi!' he said. 'What's the matter with you???'

The Hoodie now mirrors whatever you say – with what flourishes he thinks are appropriate. One Hoodie I knew placed a large foot on the traveller, to stop him crawling away …

> He took off his scarf and bandaged the traveller's head.
> He helped him to his feet.
> He even gave him some of his lager …
> And then he phoned up the nearest pub on his mobile.
> 'Hiya,' he said, 'I've got a geezer here who needs looking after, I'll just bring him in …'
> And he helped him all the way to a pub.

The Hoodie directs the traveller to a chair and sits him down

> Then he made sure he was OK – and gave him some money for a cup of tea.

Leader Now then …

Bring the Hoodie, the priest and the Children's Church kid forward

> Which of these three was the neighbour to the poor traveller?

(The children always get this right)

> Brilliant, it was the man who was kind to the traveller.
> Let's see if the man in the Gospel got it right too.

THE GOSPEL PROCESSION

THE GOSPEL   *St Luke 10.30–37*

Start off by referring back to **CD43.3** *– the man who questioned Jesus and asked, 'Who is my neighbour?'*

Leader Jesus told him this story …

AFTER THE GOSPEL

Leader Who was the neighbour in that story? (**The Samaritan**)
So the man got it right.
And the point is this, the Samaritan probably knew the traveller was Jewish, but he didn't care. He could see the man needed help – so he was a good neighbour to him.
Jesus wants us to be good neighbours, just like that Samaritan.

REHEARSAL

Practise your presentation for when you go back into church (see below).

FINAL PRAYER

Ask the children to put their hands together

> God is the father of everyone in the world
> and He wants all His children to love one another.
> Let's say the Family Prayer of the Church.
> **Our Father … (see p. xxxvi).**

MUSIC

The Hymn 'Brother, sister, let me serve you' *works well here.*

BACK IN CHURCH

The children come down the front – the cast of 'The Good Hoodie' standing in a line beside the Leader. The Hoodie has a lager tin, but his hood is down

Leader   Today we heard about a traveller

The traveller steps forward

> who was mugged.

The robber gives him a bop, the traveller collapses

> Fortunately a priest

The kid in a black cassock steps forward

> and a nice kid from Children's Church

He/she steps forward

> saw him – but they didn't help him.

They shake their heads, fold their arms – anything negative – and stand back

> Then a really dodgy character arrived

The Hoodie puts up his hood

> and he helped the traveller to his feet *(he does)*
> and looked after him.

The Hoodie hands over his lager tin
To the other kids

> So, who was a neighbour to the traveller?

The children point to the Hoodie
The Hoodie pulls down his hood and says:

Hoodie   Jesus called the Hoodie a Samaritan. But He meant the same thing. It doesn't matter how unlikely the person is – your neighbour is the person who is kind to you. And Jesus asked us to be Good Samaritans to other people.

Script 44   Mary and Martha

Proper 11, Ordinary Time 16
(Sunday between 17 and 23 July)

St Luke 10.38–42

THEME

Women owe a great debt of gratitude to St Martha. If she hadn't tried to micro-manage St Mary, Jesus might never have endorsed a woman's right to learn so publicly. (And it would have taken even longer for women to be allowed to read, write and study.) Older children sometimes like to unpack this Gospel and options are provided for you to think about the story more thoroughly, if they show an interest.

SET UP

- The liturgical colour is Green.
- Saucepan and wooden spoon.
- The 12 Apostles, Mary, and Martha puppets from the CD-Rom.

WELCOME *the children and lead them in* **The Sign of the Cross** ✠ **(p. xxxvi).**

THE KYRIE   Lord, for the times we have forgotten to love you,
Lord have mercy
Lord have mercy

Jesus, for the times we have forgotten to love others,
Christ have mercy
Christ have mercy

Lord, we thank you for never forgetting to love us,
Lord, have mercy
Lord, have mercy

Ask the children to repeat **The Prayer for Forgiveness** *after you* **(p. xxxvi).**

OPENING PRAYER	Almighty God Thank you for the gifts you give us. Thank you for our hands and our brains. Help us to use your gifts And be eager to serve you, In mind and body, Today and for ever. **Amen**

BEFORE THE GOSPEL

Invisible Women

Leader
CD44.1–12

Before we hear the Gospel today, I'd like us to think about Jesus' 12 friends. Can anyone remember their names?

Have the 12 Apostle pictures to hand and put up each one as his name is called out; with a few heavy hints, the children can usually remember most of them. The pictures show:

> Peter, John,
> James the Great,
> Andrew, Philip,
> Thomas,
> Bartholomew,
> Matthew,
> James the Less,
> Simon the Zealot,
> Judas *not* Iscariot (sometimes called Thaddeus)
> and Judas Iscariot.

Leader

Brilliant – so here are the 12 disciples, the friends of Jesus.

Look at the pictures and react

Just a minute, do you notice anything about the disciples? There's something similar about them ...

See what the kids think – they're all cartoons, all wearing stripy clothes, anything – keep pushing until they get it: they're all men.

What about women? Did Jesus know any?

See who the children remember; His mother Mary, obviously, and Mary Magdalene. They don't usually get further than that

For Older Children

Leader   Let's try it another way: can we think of any woman, with or without
                a name, who turns up in a Gospel story?*

Give a few hints – did Jesus ever heal a woman, or talk to one? Keep it brief

For Everyone

Leader   There're not many, are there?
                That's probably because, when Jesus was alive, it wasn't thought
                proper to notice women. Women were around of course, but nobody
                mentioned them.
                Except Jesus.
                Jesus thought women, and men, and children, were all equally
                interesting, and He noticed everyone.
                There're two women in the Gospel today – we're going to hear
                about them now.

THE GOSPEL PROCESSION

THE GOSPEL   *St Luke 10.38–42*

AFTER THE GOSPEL

Go through the Gospel

Leader   That's an interesting story. Let's set it up.
                We're in the home of Mary and Martha and Jesus comes to tea …
                We need a Jesus *(cast a child and sit him down at the front)*
CD44.1–44.12 and His disciples. *(Hand out the Apostle puppets **CD44.13**)*

*Give the Judas Iscariot puppet to a sensible kid. He was certainly there, so make sure
he joins the circle round Jesus, but the puppet will have to be placed on one side for
the Final Prayer*

Leader   OK, disciples are like students. Jesus was their teacher and, in those
                days, if you were being taught, you sat at your teacher's feet. So you
                guys sit round Jesus. *(The children sit on the floor round 'Jesus')*

---

* For reference only (don't reel these off), among the women mentioned in the Gospels there are:
the Samaritan woman by the well, the woman with the ointment, the woman who touched Jesus, the
woman bent double, Jairus' daughter, the women (Mary Magdalene, Joanna, the wife of Herod's steward, and Susanna) who ministered to Jesus, the woman caught in adultery, the women who brought their
children to be blessed by Jesus, the Syro-Phoenician woman, Mary and Martha, St Elizabeth the mother
of St John the Baptist, Anna in the Temple, Mary the mother of James and Joses, Salome the mother of
James and John, Mary's sister, Mary the wife of Cleophas, and the mother of Zebedee's children.

CD44.14–15   Then there were the two women – what were their names?
(**Mary and Martha**)
OK, I need a Martha. *(Hand the saucepan and spoon to Leader 2)*
What was Martha doing?

Leader 2 makes a meal of stirring up stuff in a saucepan and worrying about the food

Yup, she was bustling about.
And what about Mary – *(to a child)* could you be Mary?
What was she doing? (**Sitting at Jesus' feet**)
Yes, being a student, with the men. *(Ask Mary to sit at Jesus' feet)*
Then what happened?

Leader 2 (**Martha**) *(Moves in quickly and ad libs on these lines)*
I'll tell you exactly what happened! Here I am, working my fingers
to the bone, 13 people to feed, and where's Mary – look at her, just
sitting around listening to Jesus. I told Him to send her straight back
to the kitchen!

Leader 1   What did Jesus say?

Go behind the child playing Jesus and say his lines for him

He said that Martha was making too much fuss, and Mary was fine
where she was.
Do you think that was fair? (**See what they say**)
Well, let's think about it. If Jesus came to tea with us here, right
now, what would we do?

*See what they say; make sure a grown-up is ready to say, 'I'd get some nice things for
Him to eat' in case a child doesn't*

Martha   *(Ad lib)* I'll tell you what I'd do – I'd clean this place up, and get out
some nice crockery, and bake a cake, and cut some sandwiches …

Leader 1   That's all fine – but while you're stirring Jesus' tea and giving Him
more cake – would you have time to listen to Him?

Raise 'Mary' up and present her to the kids

You see Mary realized this was a once in a lifetime opportunity to sit
and listen to Jesus – so she did.
And Jesus thought she was right.

For Older Children

Leader   Jesus also thought it was right for Mary to sit and learn with the
men.
That was pretty amazing – can you guess why?

They may get it – because women weren't educated, girls didn't go to school

> Ever since Jesus welcomed Mary as a disciple, Christians have known that it's OK for women to learn to read and write and study.

For Everyone

Leader   So today Jesus acquired a new disciple.

Give the Mary puppet to the child playing Mary

> And you'll be pleased to know that Martha and Jesus stayed friends – and that Martha became a saint.

Give Leader 2 the Martha puppet

REHEARSAL

Practise your presentation for when you go back into church (see below).

FINAL PRAYER

Gather the children, with 11 Apostle puppets (Judas has been quietly put aside) and the Mary and Martha puppets, round a prayer candle

Leader   Today we've heard about the men and women who were Jesus' friends. Let's see them.

The children hold up their puppets

> They're in Heaven now, and sit round Jesus – just like us, sitting round this candle. We'll pray to Jesus together.

Ask the children to repeat this prayer after you

> **Lord Jesus**
> **Thank you for calling us to be your friends.**
> **Help us to serve you**
> **As faithfully as …**

Ask the children to say their puppet's Apostle name one by one. Add Mary and Martha. (Small groups will have to double up on puppets)

> **And bring us, with them, to Heaven,**
> **To live with you for ever. Amen**

BACK IN CHURCH

The children and Leader 2 line up with their puppets (Judas has rejoined the 12); Mary and Martha to one side

Leader 1   This morning we heard how Jesus sat and taught His disciples. All 12 of them sat at His feet. There were ...

The children say their Apostle names, and hold up their puppet as they speak

While He was speaking, a woman joined the disciples. Her name was ...

Child   *(With Mary puppet)* Mary!

She joins the disciples

Leader 1   And one woman got rather cross about it. Her name was ...
Leader 2   *(Not joining the group)* Martha!
Leader 1   Fortunately Martha and Jesus stayed friends.
(To Leader 2) So I guess you made it up with Mary?
Leader 2   Actually I did. *(Go over and shake hands with Mary)*
And I became a saint! *(Hold up the Martha puppet – it has a very obvious halo on it)*

(CD44.14)   (CD44.15)

Sample cartoons for this script

Script 45   Learning to Pray

Proper 12, Ordinary Time 17
(Sunday between 24 and 30 July)

St Luke 11.5–8, 11, 13, plus St Matthew 7.9

THEME

Various sayings of Jesus are included in the Gospel today, including His great legacy to the Church, the Lord's Prayer. Jesus' teaching on prayer seems to be a response to the anxieties the disciples had about praying – does God even listen to us? And how do we pray?

SET UP

- The liturgical colour is Green.
- Pictures from the CD-Rom.
- The Our Father cards (**see p. xxiv**).
- Three bread rolls wrapped in a napkin.
- A sleeping bag.
- Leader 2 and two reliable children to help you act out the Gospel. They'll need to see the script beforehand.

WELCOME *the children and lead them in* **The Sign of the Cross** ✠ **(p. xxxvi)**.

THE KYRIE   Lord, for the times we have forgotten to pray to you
Lord have mercy
Lord have mercy

Jesus, for the times we have forgotten to pray for others
Christ have mercy
Christ have mercy

Lord, we thank you for listening to us and forgiving us our sins
Lord, have mercy
Lord, have mercy

Ask the children to repeat **The Prayer for Forgiveness** *after you* **(p. xxxvi)**.

OPENING
PRAYER

God our Father,
Hear the prayers of your children
gathered together this morning.
Help us to hear you
And love you
And pray to you
Through Jesus, your Son. **Amen**

BEFORE THE GOSPEL

Swimming

Leader

Can anyone here swim? Hands up ... *(React suitably)*
Anyone learning to swim?
Yup, quite a few.
Anyone just like splashing about?
So do I ...

CD45.1

Well, I've got a picture here of a little boy who can't swim.
There he is, standing at the edge of the pool, looking nervous.

CD45.2

And he's thinking *(thought balloon)*,
'Who's going to teach me?'

CD45.3

And *(another thought balloon)* 'Will I float?'
Can you think of something that might help him?

See what they think. Establish that he needs inflatable arm bands or a rubber ring

CD45.4

OK, here he is with inflatable arm bands ...
Oh dear, he's still looking worried ...

CD45.5

What's he thinking now? *(Thought balloon)* 'Will it work?'
Do arm bands work?
Of course they do, but a very little kid might not know that.

Praying

Jesus' disciples were a bit like that kid.
Not about swimming – but about praying.

CD45.6

Here's a picture of one of them.

CD45.7–CD45.8 He's thinking, 'Does God listen?'
and 'Will God know how to help me?'
Do you think those are sensible questions?

Throw it open

They probably are quite sensible if you don't know much about
prayer.
Jesus answered His disciples by telling them a story.

The Large Family

Leader   We're going to act out His story. It's about a father with a large
                  family.
                  He had (*take a rapid survey of the children in the room*)
                  about *Number* children. Good Heavens, that's how many we've
                  got! And they all lived together in one enormous room.
                  So when they went to bed, they lay down together on the floor.
                  Dad slept on one side of the room, with all the kids between him and
                  the door.

Arrange the kids to sleep in a row right across the hall, make sure they squash up
Leader 2 is the Father and settles down on the side of the room farthest from the door
(with the three bread rolls beside him)

                  Now the trouble with this arrangement is that if dad ever needed to
                  open the door, he'd have to climb over all the kids to get to it. But,
                  hey, why should he want to open the door in the middle of the night?
                  OK, jump up and be ready to get back in position when I tell you.

The children who are going to help you with the Gospel come down the front.
Lay a sleeping bag on the floor for one of them

THE GOSPEL PROCESSION

THE GOSPEL   *St Luke 11.5–8, 11, 13, with an added verse from* **St Matthew 7.9**

Leader   Jesus' disciples asked Him to tell them about prayer. And He told
                  them a story. It went something like this …
                  One night a villager

Introduce **Child 1**

                  went to bed,

The child lies on top of the sleeping bag

                  and was woken up by a knock on the door.

Child 2 *raps a table or something hard*

                  It was a friend of hers.

Child 1 *gets up and shakes* **Child 2** *warmly by the hand*

                  The friend had been on a long journey and had just got back:
                  he was starving hungry.

Child 2 *clutches his tum*

The villager was horrified. There was no food in the house, and the whole village was fast asleep. What could she do?

Well, she sat her friend down …

Set a chair for **Child 2**, *who sits down*

and ran across to the house next door – the house with all the children in it …

To the children   That's you! Stretch out across the room and pretend to be fast asleep.

Leader 2 and the kids get into position
Child 1 *runs to the door of the room*

And then she knocked at the door …

The child stands outside and knocks
Leader 2 *(Stirring)*

Eh? What was that?

Leader 1   And she knocked again …

The kid outside knocks

Leader 2   Who's there?

Child outside   Wake up! I want to borrow some food for a guest …

Leader 2   You're kidding, it's midnight! The door's locked, the kids are all in bed. I'm not getting up!

Leader 1   But she went on knocking.

The kid knocks again

Leader 2   Go away!

Leader 1   That didn't stop her, she just knocked harder …

The kid bangs at the door

And eventually that bad-tempered father found he *had* to get up – just to stop the noise …

Leader 2 gets up, picks up the bread, and makes his way across the children, saying things like, 'Sorry, son', 'Was that your arm?', and 'OK, go back to sleep' as he does so
He hands over the bread – and then has to go all the way back again – rather less carefully this time …

Leader 1   Right, get up everyone and come and sit around me.

AFTER THE GOSPEL

Leader   So you see, the bad-tempered dad ended up giving his neighbour
              some bread just because she kept on asking.
              Well, God isn't bad-tempered, so just think how quickly He will
              answer us when we pray to Him.
              But Jesus' disciples were still a bit unsure about praying so, to help
              them, Jesus taught them the Our Father. That's a prayer we all know
              – let's see how quickly we can put it together.

ACTIVITY

*Lay out the scrambled Our Father cards and ask the children to put them together in
record time. Circle round the completed prayer.*

FINAL PRAYER

Leader   The 'Our Father' is one of the treasures of the Church.
              Some Christians stand when they say this prayer – and put their
              hands out like this …

              Can you do that?

The children stand in a circle with their hands in the prayer gesture

              Actually, it's such a marvellous prayer, we can do all sorts of things
              with our hands and arms when we pray it.
              Watch me …

*Go through the pro-active 'Our Father' with the kids. The children watch you and
imitate the mime as they say the prayer*

Our Father who art in Heaven	*look up*
Hallowed be your Name	*arms up in prayer gesture*
Your Kingdom come	*cue in the Kingdom with an emphatic index finger*

Your will be done on Earth	*point down*
As it is in Heaven	*point up*
Give us this day our daily bread	*hands together in prayer*
And forgive us our trespasses	*knock chest three times*
As we forgive those who trespass against us	*shake hands with the people round you*
And lead us not into temptation	*fold arms*
But deliver us from evil	*shake your heads (no way!)*
For thine is the Kingdom, the power and the glory	*arms up in prayer*
For ever and ever.	*hands together in prayer*
Amen!	*punch the air with your fist*

REHEARSAL

Practise your presentation for when you go back into church (see below).

BACK IN CHURCH

The children line up at the front

Child 1	Today Jesus taught His friends the Lord's Prayer.
Child 2	It's the greatest prayer the Church knows.
Leader	We like to pray it with everything we've got – our arms and heads and fists ...

The children pray the pro-active Lord's Prayer

Script 46   The Rich Fool

Proper 13, Ordinary Time 18
(Sunday between 31 July and 6 August)

St Luke 12.16–21

THEME

Jesus tells the story of the Rich Fool – the farmer who stores up his riches, and sits on them. Apart from the greed, it is the selfishness of the Fool that Jesus emphasizes (the Fool says nothing but 'I' and 'me' throughout the whole story). Rich Fools abound in the world's literature: sometimes they are misers and sometimes – like the story re-told here – they're dragons …

SET UP

- The liturgical colour is Green.
- Pictures from the CD-Rom.
- A pile of the pirate coins you can buy from party suppliers – or a large quantity of actual coins: about 60 in all.
- Leader 1 starts with some real cash in her pocket.
- Leader 2 has as much of the toy coinage as possible in his pockets.
- The rest is in a bag.

WELCOME *the children and lead them in* **The Sign of the Cross** ✠ **(p. xxxvi)**.

THE KYRIE   Lord Jesus, for the times we have forgotten you,
Lord have mercy
Lord have mercy

Lord Jesus, for the times we have forgotten to be kind to others,
Christ have mercy
Christ have mercy

Lord Jesus, we thank you for never forgetting us,
Lord, have mercy
Lord, have mercy

Ask the children to repeat **The Prayer for Forgiveness** *after you* (**p. xxxvi**).

OPENING PRAYER	*Ask the children to repeat this after you*
	God our Creator,
	We thank you for the gifts you have given us,
	For the food we eat
	The books we read
	And the toys we play with.
	Help us to use them properly
	And share them with other people,
	Through Jesus Christ our Lord. Amen

Money

Leader 1   We're going to start with a game today. It's about money.

Jingle the coins in your pocket

I've got loads of the stuff ...

(Pull out the coins and count them) 50, 60, 85p!

Leader 2   85p! That's peanuts!
If you want to see money – look at this ...

Pulls out money from every pocket he possesses and stacks it up

Leader 1   How did you get so much money?
Leader 2   I saved it.
Leader 1   Can we borrow it for a game?
Leader 2   *(Reluctantly)* I suppose so. I'll want it all back ...
Leader 1   No problem. OK, kids, we're going to run a Treasure Race.

Treasure Race

Split the kids into teams and have one-half of each team at each end of the room. The first runners cup their hands and have them filled up with pirate gold – just a little too much.

The child has to walk or run to the other end of the room and hand the coins over without dropping them. The child at the other end takes the coins and goes back again, to give to the next child in the line.

If they drop a coin en route, they have to wait for a member of their team to sprint up, pick the coin up, and put it back in their hands. Then they carry on.

Start with the little ones, and give them a few coins so they complete the course quite easily. As the older children come forward, add more coins to the pile.

You might want to limit the distance they race, to keep the game snappy. Monitor the spillages – nobody gets to the end without all their coins.
The first team to cover the distance – and get all the coins back to base, wins.

Leader 1	*Handing the coins back to Leader 2*
	Here you are – I'm glad you've got them back.
To the children	Well, I liked the game – but I thought all that money was a bit of a bother. I can see why purses were invented.
	I'm going to tell you the story of somebody who had loads of money. More than *Name (Leader 2)*, but he didn't do anything sensible with it – like run races – he sat on it …

Leader 1 tells the story, Leader 2 puts up pictures

Fafner the Dragon*

CD46.1	His name was Fafner …
	And, as you can see, he was a giant.
CD46.2	He had a brother, Fasolt. Another giant.
CD46.3	And the pair of them quarrelled over a pile of treasure.
CD46.4	And Fafner picked up his club, killed his brother …
	and grabbed the treasure. He dragged it off to his cave.
	Now all giants are *shape changers*, and Fafner, as he looked at the treasure, thought, 'I'd better change my shape, so I can guard this treasure, and stop some other person turning up and killing me.'
	Can you guess what shape he changed into …?
CD46.5	*(This picture is in several pieces, put it up bit by bit, starting with the tail)*
	(A dragon!)
	Yes, Fafner changed himself into a dragon.
	And he sat in his cave, on his treasure, for years and years.
	He never spent it, he never went out, and all the time, in his heart of hearts, he knew that one day a young hero would appear from
CD46.6	nowhere.
	He even knew his name, Siegfried.
	And he guessed that Siegfried would have a bright sword, and there'd be a fight – which he'd lose – and Siegfried would walk off with the treasure. Which is exactly what happened.
	Do you think Fafner was happy? *(See what they think)*
	Fafner *thought* he was happy – he counted his treasure every day –

---

* Fafner appears, as a giant and a dragon, in Wagner's *Ring Cycle* – as does Siegfried, the hero who eventually kills him.

but, deep inside, he knew Siegfried was coming.
He was actually very unhappy.

Leader   Jesus told a story like that once. Not about a dragon, but about a stupid farmer. We'll hear it now.

THE GOSPEL PROCESSION

THE GOSPEL   *St Luke 12.16–21*

AFTER THE GOSPEL

Leader   Let's work out what happened.
A farmer had a very good harvest, so he built huge barns, and stowed his grain away in them and thought,
'Great! I can stop working and eat, drink and be merry.'
And God said to him, 'You fool!'
Why did God say that?

(See what they think – children often pick up the fact that the farmer was just about to die, and some notice that he didn't intend to share his goods)

Well, to start with, you can't assume you're going to live for ever – and actually that farmer only had a day to live.
Can you take money to Heaven with you? (**No**)
What do you take to Heaven? (**Just yourself**)
Yup, so money isn't much use up there.
Also do you notice how the farmer talked about his wealth?
'*I'm* going to build new barns,' he said, or, '*I'm* going to have a good time …'
It was all about him, he wasn't going to share his goods.
God was not impressed.

REHEARSAL

Practise your presentation for when you go back into church (see below).

BEFORE THE FINAL PRAYER

Ask the children to sit round a prayer candle

Leader   After Jesus told this story, He said to His friends,
'Don't worry about food or drink or clothes.
God knows what you need, He'll make sure you get these things.'
God sends food to all His creatures – even the ravens.
Let's think about that as we say some of Psalm 147 together.

The response to the psalm is:
Give thanks to the Lord
Give thanks to the Lord

Great is our Lord, and great is His power,
His wisdom is infinite
Give thanks to the Lord

He makes grass to grow upon the mountains,
and plants for us to use.
Give thanks to the Lord

He gives fodder to the cattle,
and feeds the young ravens that call upon Him.
Give thanks to the Lord

The Lord's delight is in them that fear Him
and put their trust in His mercy.
Give thanks to the Lord

BACK IN CHURCH

Bring in a couple of kids with pirate coins piled up in their hands

Leader 1   Today we thought about money.
                   We ran a relay race, holding loads of money in our hands – like this …

The two kids race each other across the front (make sure they do it with the utmost difficulty …)

                   You can see what a nuisance the money is when we're clinging on to it.
                   Let's take the money away.

Leader 2 relieves them of it

Leader 1   OK, guys, run back!

They do – very free and fast

                   There's no doubt at all, money can be a problem.
                   We think that's what Jesus was saying to us today in the Gospel.

Script 47   A Summer Panto

Proper 14, Ordinary Time 19
(Sunday between 7 and 13 August)

St Luke 12.32–34

THEME

Treasure is a constant theme in the Gospels. Jesus obviously realized its appeal as He thought of new ways to describe the Kingdom of God. In this session we follow the adventures of Jim Hawkins, in a panto re-run of *Treasure Island*, only to discover that there's treasure and there's treasure…

SET UP

- The liturgical colour is Green.
- Pirate gear – anything you've got. Scarves to make pirate headdresses are easy, plus a trip to a party supplier or toy shop if you've got time. Two essential props are a truncheon – to dispose of Long John – and a chest of 'treasure', a box of bling in fact.
- A beer mug.
- Parrot puppet and treasure map from the CD-Rom.
- Make a Black Spot – a huge black spot drawn on a piece of A4 paper.
- An image of the Infant Jesus – the Bambino from the crib set would be ideal – placed in a box. (A small plastic statue of the Sacred Heart is just as effective.)
- The box with treasure in it should be hidden at one end of the room; the box with the image of Jesus at the other.
- Place a piece of paper with a large red X on the treasure chest.
- Cast Jim and Long John; ask them to look at the script beforehand.
- A child can be primed just before the session to be the Parrot.

WELCOME *the children and lead them in* **The Sign of the Cross** ✠ **(p. xxxvi).**

THE KYRIE   Lord Jesus, we are sorry for the times we have been unkind,
Lord have mercy
Lord have mercy

Lord Jesus, we are sorry for the times we have forgotten to pray,
Christ have mercy
Christ have mercy

Lord Jesus, we thank you for never forgetting us,
Lord, have mercy
Lord, have mercy

Ask the children to repeat **The Prayer for Forgiveness** *after you* (**p. xxxvi**).

OPENING PRAYER	Almighty God Your Son said 'Ask and it shall be given, Knock and the door shall be opened, Seek and you shall find.' Help us to seek and find Jesus here this morning. **Amen**
Leader	*Looking very cheerful* Has anyone here ever been to a pantomime?

Most kids have – make sure a grown-up is ready to answer if you don't get a response

Which one was it? (**Cinderella, Mother Goose, Aladdin ...** etc)
When do pantomimes usually happen? (**Christmas**)
(React) Christmas? You're kidding!
But I've got one ready for this morning.

Produce some props

I've got some pirate hats and a parrot and everything ...
What shall we do?

Whatever the kids say, make sure the grown-ups insist we run the panto

OK – let's have a summer panto, this one is called 'Treasure Island'

Treasure Island

Narrator	Treasure Island is a story about a young lad called Jim. Here he is ... *(enter Jim)*
Jim	Hi, kids!
Narrator	What do you do, Jim?
Jim	I work in a pub, it's called the Old Ship.
Narrator	Oh, that pub.
To the kids	The customers there are a funny lot. Look, here's one now ...

Enter Long John

He's got a …

Long John puts on the list of things that follow as you say them – adapt as necessary. (He also has a treasure map in his pocket)

… cutlass.
And an eye patch.
And an ear-ring.
And a scarf on his head.
And a black hat.
And one of his hands is missing – so he has a …
Can you guess? (**A hook!**)
Do you know what he is? (**A pirate!**)
Yup, a pirate! His name is Long John Saliva …

Jim	*(Doing a double take)* Long John Saliva?
Narrator	Yes, Long John Saliva – he was the spitting image of his father.
	Well, Jim thought Long John was fantastic, he hung round him asking him questions all the time.
Jim	*(Handing over a mug of beer)* Where's your pirate-ship, Long John?
Long John	Arh! My pirate-ship. She's a'quivering at the bottom of the Thames. *(Or whatever your local river is)*
Jim	Quivering at the bottom of the Thames?
Long John	Yup, she's a nervous wreck …
Narrator	And Long John was so pleased with his joke (he's the only one who is …) that he sat down with his beer …

Pull up a chair for Long John

and went to sleep in the sun.
While he sat there sleeping, a small pirate …

To the kids Anyone want to be a small pirate?

Give the volunteer a pirate scarf and the Black Spot

A small pirate crept up to Long John and placed this on Long John's jacket …

The small pirate creeps up and places the Black Spot

Then he snuck away with an evil laugh.

He does so

Long John woke up and saw …
What is it?

The Black Spot – most children know all about this from The Pirates of the Caribbean

He was horrified – and called Jim over.

Long John	*Ad libs to this effect*
	Jim Lad, I'm done for – some of my old mates have found out where I am.
	I cheated them of their treasure and they're out to kill me.
CD47.1	Now if anything happens, I want you to have this –

Pulls treasure map out of his pocket

	you're a nice lad, and deserve a break …
Narrator	And that very night – a band of pirates – who wants to be a pirate?

Dish out some hats and the truncheon

> A band of pirates crept up on Long John as he was sleeping, and one of them clonked him on the head.

Long John dies horribly

> Leaving Jim with the bit of paper Long John had pulled out of his pocket.

Jim shows it to the kids

Jim	What is it? (**A treasure map**)
	Treasure! Wow! I'm off!
	I've never liked this old pub, I'm going to find that treasure and be happy for the rest of my life!
Narrator	At which point, a voice squawked

Enter Parrot

Parrot	I'll help you, Jim!
Jim	Who said that? (**A parrot!**)
CD47.2–3	Where?

Run the 'Look behind you' gag …
Eventually Jim and the Parrot decide to find the treasure together

Narrator	So Jim and the Parrot went off to find Long John's treasure.
	Does anyone want to go with them?

Jim leads the kids round the room, apparently following the treasure map
Jim can ad lib this: three steps to the east; swim the river; four steps North – anything
that will eventually land them up at the treasure chest. Jim finds it

Jim	Here it is! Look! 'X' marks the spot! *(Hold up the X)*
Narrator	So Jim found the treasure …
	Jim looks glum
	Aren't you pleased, Jim?
Jim	Well, I enjoyed looking for it, and it's nice to have a bit of money, but, I don't know …

It's not as great as I thought it would be.
I mean it's just treasure, it's no big deal …

Parrot　　*Looking over Jim's shoulder at the treasure map*
Turn over!

Jim turns round, turns his hat round, turns round anything that comes to hand and eventually realizes that the Parrot means the map

Jim　　Oh, there's a bit more – it says 'Follow your heart' …

Jim puts his hand on his chest

Follow my heart?
Well my heart says – 'go home!'
Narrator　　So Jim went home and,
still following his heart, he went to church and there he found a box.

Jim finds the box with the Bambino in it

It didn't look very exciting, but when Jim opened it, he said,
Jim　　Ah, now this really *is* treasure …

And he holds up Baby Jesus

Narrator　　Jesus talks about treasure in the Gospel today.
Let's get rid of this pirate stuff and be ready to greet the Gospel.

THE GOSPEL PROCESSION

THE GOSPEL　　*St Luke 12.32–34*

AFTER THE GOSPEL

Bring the treasure chest down to the front and run the bling through your fingers

Leader　　What does Jesus think about treasure?

Take what comes – establish that Jesus is not bothered with ordinary treasure

Jesus wants us to find our treasure in Heaven.
He said, 'Where your treasure is, there your heart will be also.'

REHEARSAL

Practise your presentation for when you go back into church (see below).

FINAL PRAYER

Leader   *Bring the Bambino forward*
            We started this morning by asking God to help us find Jesus His Son.
            And we found this statue of Him.

Hold up the Bambino

            Let's pray our Opening Prayer again,
            and ask God to help us find Jesus in the coming week.

            Almighty God
            Your Son said
            'Ask and it shall be given,
            Knock and the door shall be opened,
            Seek and you shall find.'
            Help us to seek and find Jesus in the week ahead
            And for the rest of our lives. **Amen**

Don some pirate hats and take the crew into church

BACK IN CHURCH

The children line up at the front,
Jim has the Parrot next to him,
one child has the treasure chest,
another has the Bambino

Child 1   Today we did a pantomime.
Child 2   We were all pirates.
Child 3   And we went off with our friend Jim and his Parrot …

Jim and the Parrot wave

            to find some treasure.
Child 4   But the treasure turned out to be just money.

Another child holds up some bling

Leader   So we went on a bit further, and we found Baby Jesus in a manger.

A child holds up the Bambino

            Jim thought that was the best treasure of all – and so do we!

Script 48 Fire!

Proper 15, Ordinary Time 20
(Sunday between 14 and 20 August)

St Luke 12.49

THEME

Today's Gospel makes uncomfortable reading: Jesus foresees His baptism of fire, and the disruption the Gospel will bring. As the children are almost certainly too young to handle that, this session confines itself to the opening verse, 'I have come to bring fire to the earth'. Fire, real and metaphorical, flickers through the whole Bible, beautiful – and dangerous.

Fire

- Most people find fire fascinating (as long as it's contained) and the session begins with the children looking at some flames. How you do that will depend on your circumstances: four possible fire demonstrations are given below.

Self-lighting candle

- The simplest option is a candle in a candlestick (use an ordinary long candle, a votive light is too small).
- A box of long matches.

Charcoal fire

- Some charcoal.
- A thurible from the vestry, if your church uses incense.
- *Or* A foil tray and some barbecue charcoal.
- In either case you will need a box of long matches.
- Appoint a grown-up to douse the charcoal afterwards. It stays hot a long time …

Blue fire

- Slice of solid fruit cake on a plate.
- Cup of very cheap brandy.

- Ladle.
- Box of long matches.
- Access to a kitchen as the brandy must be warmed up before it can be set alight.

Brazier

- A brazier (if available and the weather is dry) is the best option of all.
- Set up the brazier outside and stack it with
  - crumpled newspaper,
  - firelighters,
  - kindling (from the local garage). Don't add coals – they stay alight too long.
- Box of long matches.
- Somebody on hand to douse the brazier and make sure it's standing away from anything it could set light to. (Fires retain their heat and self-igniting properties long after they appear to be out.)

SET UP

- The liturgical colour is Green.
- Pictures from the CD-Rom.
- Bible with a bookmark at Exodus 3.
- Black and red marker pens.
- Pens and paper for the children.
- Child-friendly scissors.
- Sellotape.
- Whatever props you need for your fire demonstration (see above).

WELCOME *the children and lead them in* **The Sign of the Cross** ✠ (p. xxxvi).

THE KYRIE   Lord Jesus, we are sorry for the times we have been unkind,
Lord have mercy
Lord have mercy

Lord Jesus, we are sorry for the times we have forgotten to pray,
Christ have mercy
Christ have mercy

Lord Jesus, we thank you for never ceasing to hear us and forgive,
Lord, have mercy
Lord, have mercy

Ask the children to repeat **The Prayer for Forgiveness** *after you* (p. xxxvi).

OPENING	Lord Jesus,
PRAYER	We thank you for bringing us here this morning.
	As we listen to the Gospel
	Enflame our hearts with love for you. **Amen**

Leader   *Quote the last line of the prayer:*
'Enflame our hearts with love for you.'
Who knows what 'enflame' means? (**Set on fire, set alight**)

Put your hand on your chest

'Set our hearts alight …'
That sounds a bit odd. Does God want to set our hearts alight like a firework and shoot us off somewhere?
Or does He just want to warm our hearts?
Let's read the Gospel and find out.

THE GOSPEL PROCESSION

THE GOSPEL   *St Luke 12.49*

'Jesus said to His disciples, "I have come to bring fire to the Earth, and how I wish it were blazing already!"'

AFTER THE GOSPEL

Leader   Gosh, Jesus wants to start a blaze. Perhaps we'd better think about fire.

Choose one (or more) of the fire demonstrations below:

Self-lighting candle

Set the unlit candle in its candlestick in front of the children
Light a match and, as you do so, say,

One of the odd things about fire is you can take a flame, like this, and make another flame from it – the same size and colour …

Light the candle – keep the match burning

Watch this …

Blow the candle out, give it a second, then place the lit match in the candle's smoke stream. The candle will relight

Isn't that odd? Shall I do it again …?

Do so, or let an older child have a go

What colour is the flame? (**Yellow**)

Sharp-eyed children may discern some blue at the base

Charcoal fire

Bring the thurible or foil tray over

Leader   Fire is very odd, sometimes it doesn't burst into flame, it just smoulders …
Look at this.

Put a match flame to the pieces of charcoal, and ask the kids to watch out for the sparks which tell you that the charcoal has caught

OK, no flame – but there's fire in the heart of this charcoal.
Let's give it some oxygen …

Swing the thurible or blow on the barbecue charcoal – show the kids how the charcoal goes red to start with, then white

White means it's very hot – you could warm your hands at this.
Can you feel the heat?

Ask the kids to warm their hands cautiously at the charcoal

God loves to think that our hearts are as warm as this, and filled with His love.

Brazier

Take the children outside to look at the stacked brazier
Ask them to stand well back and watch as Leader 2 puts a match to the firelighters. As the first flames burn the newspaper, gauge the direction of the wind and move the children to the safe side. Tell them what you're doing so they keep a watchful eye on the wind as well

Leader   We start with newspaper because that burns easily,
now we're going to put on some wood.

Leader 2 throws a small amount of kindling on

Tell me when the wood is alight.

The children will stare, fascinated. Let the wood flare up and die down a bit

Do we need some more? (**YES**)

If the wood really has died down, allow an older child to throw some kindling on

Fire's very interesting, isn't it? You can't help wanting to feed it …

Chuck on a bit of wood

or poke it …

If there's a stick nearby, give the fire a poke

What colour is it? (**Red and yellow**)

It's all right while it's in this brazier – but fire is not much fun if it gets out. It can burn people and houses and whole forests. That's why we've got that bucket of water.

OK, *Name* is going to put the fire out as we go back …

Blue fire

Before you start this demonstration, Leader 2 will have to pour some brandy in a ladle; go into the kitchen and warm it over a low gas flame

Light a candle and ask the children to look at the flame

What colour is it? (**Yellow**)

And why is fire so dangerous? (**It can burn you**)

Yes, that's why we're so careful when we light things.

But there's one sort of fire we use at Christmas that's not very good at burning …

Has anyone seen a Christmas pudding alight?

(See what they say)

It's a bit like this …

Bring forward the slab of fruit cake

Clear a path for Leader 2 and call:

Are you ready?

In he/she comes with the warm brandy. Pour it over the fruit cake and set light to it.

Let the children enjoy the blue flames dancing over the surface

What colour are the flames? (**Blue**)

Yes – that's because we're burning brandy.

And look! The cake isn't burning at all!

It's odd, isn't it?

Sum up

Leader   So, what sort of words describe fire?

Write them up – hot, yellow, red, blue, dangerous, mysterious, beautiful, scary, interesting. Stand back and look at the words

Yes – some of these words could be used to describe God …

Which ones do you think? *(Circle the words the kids suggest)*

God and fire seem to get on. He uses it sometimes to talk to people.

There's a story right at the beginning of the Bible – when the Jews didn't know very much about God. So He used fire to attract their attention.
Here it is … *(Open your Bible at Exodus 3)*

Leader 1 tells the story using this script, but keep the Bible open
Leader 2 puts up the pictures

Moses

Leader 1	One day, a very long time ago,
CD48.1	a shepherd was looking after his sheep.
	He was deeply fed up …
	Can anyone fill in this picture to make him look unhappy?

Give a child a black marker pen to draw in an unhappy mouth

Yup, he looks really fed up. That's because he was a Jew living in Egypt. Lots of other Jews were in Egypt too – and the Egyptians treated them as slaves.
So the shepherd sat on the grass, watching the sheep, and wishing he was somewhere else, when suddenly he saw something strange …

CD48.2   It was a bush,
on fire …

Draw in some flames with a red marker pen

But not burning up.
'That's weird,' said the shepherd, and went to see what was happening.

CD48.3   'Moses!' said a Voice. *(Speech balloon)*
'That's me!' said the shepherd.
'Come closer,' said the Voice, 'take off your shoes – this is holy ground.'

CD48.4   Moses took off his shoes and came closer.
'I am the God of your father and your grandfather,' said the Voice. 'And I want you to lead my people out of Egypt to another country that I will show you.'
'Oh,' said Moses, and he thought for a moment. 'The trouble is,' he said, 'I don't think anyone is likely to listen to me. Who shall I say you are? Lord God, have you got a Name?'
'I am who I am,' said the Voice. 'If anyone says to you, "Who told
CD48.5   you to lead me?" tell them that I Am sent you.' *(Speech bubble)*
CD48.6   So Moses led the Jews out of Egypt.

It took for ever ...
But God showed Moses the way by sending a cloud of smoke to guide them by day, and a pillar of

CD48.7   fire by night.

Pick up the Bible, riffle through ...

The Holy Spirit

Leader   Well, God went on speaking to His people. Until eventually He came down to Earth to speak as a Man.
                What was His name then? (**Jesus**)
                Quite right. And when Jesus went back to Heaven, He told His disciples that He'd send God the Holy Spirit to help them.
                God the Holy Spirit doesn't look like a human being – can anyone remember what He decided to look like when He came?

CD48.8   *He came as fire and wind*
                Look at the picture with them, point out the tongues of flame

                That fire didn't burn; it was the Holy Spirit, lighting on everyone's head and filling their hearts with the love of God.

ACTIVITY

Ask the children to draw the flame of God (template on the CD-Rom – but they will be quite capable of drawing and colouring their own flame).
Cut out the flames and stick them to the kids' chests. Make sure you have a flame yourself.

REHEARSAL

Practise your presentation for when you go back into church (see below).

BEFORE THE FINAL PRAYER

Gather the children in a circle

Leader   You all look great!
                You remind me of a man called Richard Rolles who – ages ago – felt the fire of God in his chest. It must have been like *Name*'s fire *(choose a kid's picture with a brightly coloured flame)* because Richard felt so warm he thought he *was* on fire, and *(slap your chest vigorously)* slapped his jacket to put himself out.
                Then Richard realized he was wrong – the warmth was in his heart.

| FINAL
PRAYER | Let's pray to God the Holy Spirit
Ask the children to repeat after you:
Come Holy Spirit,
Fill the hearts of your faithful people
And kindle in them the fire of your love. Amen |

MUSIC

Charles Wesley's hymn 'Holy Spirit, Truth Divine' *is a good one to finish the session, especially if it's sung to its pleasant old-fashioned tune.*

BACK IN CHURCH

The children line up at the front

Child 1	Today Jesus told us that He'd come to bring fire to the Earth.
Child 2	We've been thinking about fire all morning.
Leader	We've lit candles and charcoal, we've burnt brandy and poured it over cake, we've had a bonfire in a brazier *(adapt as necessary)*, and we've made flames of fire and stuck them on our chests. Why have we done that?
Everyone	**To show the fire of God is in our hearts.**

(CD48.2)

(CD48.1)

Sample cartoons for this script

Script 49   The Woman Who Was Bent Double

Proper 16
(Sunday between 21 and 27 August)

St Luke 13.10–17

This Sunday Anglicans and Roman Catholics have different Gospel readings. Check with your priest first but, on the whole, Anglicans will be using this script, while Catholics will be using *Script 50*, The Narrow Gate.

THEME

Jesus heals a woman who has been crippled for 18 years and annoys the leader of the synagogue. The cure takes place on the Sabbath and, technically, healing counts as 'work'. 'You could have been healed any day of the week,' the leader grumbles. 'Why turn up on the Sabbath?' Jesus makes short work of him, and reminds us of the danger of being so bound up in the minutiae of church life that we forget the law of charity. This morning the children are encouraged to forget the rules and see the miracle from the woman's point of view. (Which was, emphatically, Jesus' starting point as well.)

SET UP

- The liturgical colour is Green.
- Set up an indoor obstacle course (see below).

WELCOME *the children and lead them in* **The Sign of the Cross** ✠ **(p. xxxvi).**

THE KYRIE   Lord Jesus, for the times we have been unkind,
Lord have mercy
Lord have mercy

Lord Jesus, for the times we have forgotten to pray,
Christ have mercy
Christ have mercy

Lord Jesus, thank you for never ceasing to hear us and forgive,

Lord, have mercy
Lord, have mercy

Ask the children to repeat **The Prayer for Forgiveness** *after you* (**p. xxxvi**).

OPENING PRAYER	Lord God
	Your Son, Jesus Christ, felt the unhappiness of the sick
	And reached out to heal them.
	May we be like Him
	And do our best to be kind
	To the sick, the lonely and the unloved
	For His Name's sake. **Amen**

Leader   OK, we're going to kick off this morning with some obstacles.

GAMES

Indoor Obstacle Course

Several obstacle games are suggested below (don't do them all).
Run the course in sections. Set up one set of obstacles, let the children loose on them, then set up the next. The children run the sections of the course in one go or play in teams – depending on numbers.

Chair Climb

The classic obstacle course, and one that needs no preliminary set-up, is a row of chairs over and under which the children are asked to climb.
(Increase the difficulty after the first run by giving them things like bean bags or hymn books to hold as they climb over the chairs, and putting large hats on their heads as they climb under. If a hat falls off, the child is out.)

Underground

Make a tunnel for the kids to crawl through by draping a sheet or blanket over a line of chairs.

Shoe Box Slalom

Line up a series of shoe boxes and run a relay race in which the children zigzag between the boxes.

Tightrope

Stretch a skipping rope across the floor and ask the kids to walk across it as if it were a tightrope.

Course

Lily Pads

Set out a series of hula hoops or squares of newspaper (taped down) for the children to leap across the room on.

Tummy Crawl

The children slither on their tums under a piece of string tied between two chair legs.

Box Race

If you've got large packing boxes left over from a move, knock the tops and bottoms out, line them up – leaving a space between each one – and get the kids to crawl through.

IN →   OUT

Finish

The last two games should be a crawling game. One of the Leaders should have a go.

Clear away the last obstacles and ask the children to sit down

Leader   What did you think of that? Which was the most difficult?

Take all answers

> I thought the one where we crawled under the string *(or whatever you did)* was the worst – I was really glad to straighten up.
> Well, it's good fun to run an obstacle course, but it's another matter if your life is one continual obstacle.
> We're going to hear about a woman who ran an obstacle race every day of her life.
> She was bent double – like this…

Leader 2 bends double

Bending Double

Leader 1	Imagine walking round like this. What can you see, *Name*?
Leader 2	Not much – the floor and my feet

Leader 1 moves towards her

	Oh, and your feet too …
Leader 1	Can you see what I'm writing on the flip chart?

Write up 'Good morning'

Leader 2 tries it and finds that the only way to see anything above her is to turn sideways and hang her head upside down

	Do you want to straighten up?
Leader 2	Yes please!
Leader 1	Would someone else like to bend double for me?

Choose a sensible child and circle the other children round him. Make sure the doubled-up kid really is doubled up – turn him round a couple of times, and ask him to identify the other kids from their shoes. (This only works in small groups where the children know each other.)
Congratulate him, however well he does

Leader	Well done for having a go. *(If he was on the whole unsuccessful)*
Or	Brilliant, but wouldn't it be awful to spend your whole life only knowing people by their shoes? *(If he's managed to name the others)*

If the group is too large for this to work, ask the doubled-up kid to make his way to the door and find the door handle and the light switch

Leader	Yup, well done! *(Whatever happens)*
	Right, everyone stand up. Now, let's all bend over.

Bend with them

Gosh, supposing this was all you saw. Just your own feet.
OK, straighten up!
What would be really difficult for somebody who was bent over?
Could she drive? (**No**)
Could she cross the road? (**It would be difficult**)
What about the supermarket? (**Difficult, she couldn't see the shelves**)
Could she come to church? (**Yes, but she'd have to get there**)
OK, well the lady we're thinking about today had been bent double for 18 years. She lived at the time of Jesus, so there were no cars

or supermarkets – but there were plenty of people, sheep and dogs to bump into. Still, she could just about get to the synagogue, and that's where Jesus met her.

Now as we listen to this Gospel we're going to hear it as she did – bent double. So the moment the Gospel Procession begins I want you to bend over. Listen carefully and only straighten up when the woman does. If it gets difficult to keep bent, put your hands on your knees.

THE GOSPEL PROCESSION *(The kids in the Procession do not bend over)*

THE GOSPEL   *St Luke 13.10–17*

Optional Paraphrase

Jesus was teaching in the synagogue on the Sabbath when a woman turned up. She was bent double and quite unable to stand up straight. When Jesus saw her, He called her over and said, 'Woman, you are free from your illness.' Then He laid His hands on her and immediately she stood up straight!

The children straighten up

The woman praised God, but the leader of the synagogue was annoyed because Jesus had cured somebody on the Sabbath.

Look up and add the following:

Jews are not supposed to work on the Sabbath, and healing counts as work.

Back to the Gospel

The leader said to the people around, 'You've got six days to work in – come and get cured on those days. Not the Sabbath!'

But Jesus said, 'Oh really? Don't you untie your ox and donkey on the Sabbath day? What about a human being? Shouldn't this woman, a daughter of Abraham, who's been crippled for 18 long years, also be untied on the Sabbath?'

That put the leader of the synagogue to shame, while everybody else rejoiced at the wonderful things Jesus was doing.

AFTER THE GOSPEL

Leader   You can imagine how super it was for the woman to stand up straight at last.

And who was the first person she saw? (**Jesus**)

Everybody was delighted, except ... Who? (**The synagogue leader**)
Yup, the man who ran the synagogue. He was cross that Jesus had broken the rules and healed someone on the Sabbath.
Think about that for a moment.
Supposing the vicar turned up late for church one Sunday. And said, 'Sorry I'm late. Old Mrs so and so was dying and I had to rush off to pray with her.'
Can you imagine anyone saying, 'That's disgraceful! It's Sunday! You should have been here in church!'
And if anyone did moan, I bet the vicar would say, 'Just a minute! Getting here on time on a Sunday is important – but not as important as a dying person!'
Well, that's how Jesus felt. He knew how that woman felt. He couldn't bear to see her crippled for one moment longer – so He freed her.
The Sabbath was important, but not as important as a human being.

REHEARSAL

Practise your presentation for when you go back into church (see below).

FINAL PRAYER

Ask the children to sit down

Leader   When Jesus saw the lady bent double, He had compassion on her. Compassion is a way of loving somebody so much that we feel their unhappiness as though it were our own.
We're going to ask God to help us feel compassion and we'll use a prayer written by Mother Teresa of Calcutta, a saint whose life was full of compassion.

Ask the children to repeat this after you

Lord, open our eyes
that we may see you in our brothers and sisters.
Lord, open our ears
that we may hear the cries of the unhappy.
Lord, open our hearts
that we may love each other as you love us. Amen

BACK IN CHURCH

The children line up down the front, and bend double on cue. The two child readers flank them and stay upright

Child 1	In the Gospel today, we heard about a lady who was bent double. She looked like this …

The children bend double

Child 2	She couldn't see anyone's face.
Child 1	She couldn't see where she was going.
Child 2	Even so, she found Jesus, and He said, 'Woman, you are free!'
Child 1	So she stood up.

The children straighten up

Child 2	And the first thing she saw was …
Everyone	**Jesus!**

Script 50   The Narrow Gate

Ordinary Time 21
(Sunday between 21 and 27 August)

St Luke 13.22–24

This Sunday Anglicans and Roman Catholics have different Gospel readings. Check with your priest first but, on the whole, Catholics will be using this script (*Script 50*) while Anglicans will be using *Script 49*, The Woman Who Was Bent Double.

THEME

This is an alarming Gospel. Heaven is entered through a narrow gate – and not everyone will get through. This session is resolutely upbeat. Why has God made the gate so narrow? And what does He want us to do to get through?

SET UP

- The liturgical colour is Green.
- Photo from the CD-Rom.
- A large bundle of wrapping paper that looks as if it's Pass the Parcel. (It isn't – so don't bother to put any presents inside.)
- Audio player plus CD or piano player.
- A camera.
- Ask Leader 2 to come with too many clothes – coat, scarf, hat, sunglasses – plus some personal belongings. Ideal ones would be a mobile phone, photo of someone they're fond of, picture of pet, driving licence, passport and something that represents a hobby. These props should be stowed in the pockets of the coat, or held under the coat if they're too bulky. (Leader 2 should be the slimmest of the adult helpers.)

WELCOME *the children and lead them in* **The Sign of the Cross** ✠ (p. xxxvi).

THE KYRIE   Lord Jesus, for the times we have been unkind,
Lord have mercy
Lord have mercy

Lord Jesus, for the times we have forgotten to pray,
Christ have mercy
Christ have mercy

Lord Jesus, thank you for never ceasing to hear us and forgive,
Lord, have mercy
Lord, have mercy

Ask the children to repeat **The Prayer for Forgiveness** *after you* (**p. xxxvi**).

OPENING PRAYER   Jesus said
Anyone who loves me will keep my word
And my Father will love them.
Help us to love you, Lord,
And keep your word. **Amen**

BEFORE THE GOSPEL

Set up the music for a game of Pass the Parcel. Leader 2 retires to put on all his/her clothes.

Getting Rid of Things

Leader   We're going to play a game.

Hold up the parcel

Can anyone guess what it is? (**Pass the Parcel**)
Yes, you're right – except we're going to play it with some different rules.

Gather the children in a circle, and sit down with them

When the music starts, we pass the parcel round the circle, like this …

Throw it to the child next to you

and when the music stops – this is the different bit – anyone caught with the parcel is out!

Play the game until only one child is left with the parcel: you'll find the parcel is passed round at the speed of light

Brilliant! You were all fast in getting rid of that parcel. Sometimes it's a good idea to get rid of other things …

Photo Session

Leader 1	For example, the other day, I thought I'd take a nice picture of *Name* (Leader 2).
	I set up a chair and little table *(do so)* and I got my camera ready – and she turned up looking like this ...

Enter Leader 2, scarf across her face, hat down – she is hidden beneath her clothes. She sits down

Leader 1	I can't take a picture of you looking like that!
Leader 2	I want a picture of me in my best clothes.
Leader 1	Yes, but we've got to see your face.
Leader 2	Oh – oh, all right.

Removes scarf and hat, but keeps the collar up on her coat and sits hunched up

Leader 1	I'm still not seeing much of you!
Leader 2	Well, I'm not taking off my cool shades – but this can go.
Removes coat	I want this photo to show the sort of person I am.
	I've got to be shown holding my mobile – and I want this picture of my Mum on a table beside me, oh and my driving licence – have you seen the super car I've got? And a picture of Tibby ...

Pulling out all these things

Leader 1	Stop! It's too much.
Leader 2	... and my football *(or whatever the hobby is)* and my passport ...
Leader 1	What do you want the passport for?
Leader 2	To show that I'm British.
Leader 1	I think you need to get rid of some of these things.
Leader 2	Oh no!
Leader 1	*(To the children)* What shall we do?
	Can we help *Name* get rid of a few things for this photo?
	It doesn't all have to go ...

See what they say – don't comment ... get rid of anything they suggest and take the photo

Leader 1	OK, that's going to be an interesting photo.

The Narrow Gate

Leader	So, we had to get rid of the parcel, and *Name* had to get rid of some things for a photo. There are times when other things have to go as well.
	Has anyone ever been through a turnstile for a football match?

See if there are any takers

CD50.1

The turnstiles look like this.
Show the image on the CD-Rom
Really narrow.
The people who put them up want to make sure only one person gets through at a time.*
I wonder how narrow that is? Let's find out …

Set up two chairs back to back, with enough space for two children to get through. An adult braces each chair
Line up the children, let them squeeze in, in pairs, and slowly narrow the gap. The space that only allows one kid through is quite astonishingly small

Leader 1   Supposing *Name (Leader 2)*
                wants to get through?

Leader 2 approaches with all her extra clothes on, and she can't make it through
Takes all the clobber off and she just gets through (cheat if necessary – she must make it …)

Leader 1   Phew, she just did it!
                Now, why are we so interested in getting rid of things and narrow gates?
                It's because of today's Gospel – which we're just about to hear …

THE GOSPEL PROCESSION

THE GOSPEL   *St Luke 13.22–24*

AFTER THE GOSPEL

Leader   Jesus tells us that the gate to Heaven is very narrow.
                I wonder why that is?

(A rhetorical question – unless someone is bursting to tell you)

                I think it's because God wants you, and only you, to get in.
                He's not interested in your clothes, or your mobile, or all the stuff you've got.
                I think He'd feel OK about *Name* bringing in her photos and the football …

---

* Presumably so six people don't get in on one ticket.

Can you get through our gate with those, *Name*?

She tries it and can – by dint of holding them above her head probably

God is interested in what you love and what you're good at. Because that's you – it's your heart, and your talents.
But you can get rid of all the other stuff.

REHEARSAL

Practise your presentation for when you go back into church (see below).

FINAL PRAYER

Settle the children to pray

Leader   God loves us just as we are.
That's because He made us, and He wants to see what He made coming through that gate – not a load of extra stuff.

Lord God,
You made us
And love us.
Help us to come back to you
The way you want us to be.
Just as we are... **Amen**

MUSIC

The modern hymn 'Abba, Abba, Father, you are the potter' ends the session well, especially if the children are clever enough to sing it as a round.

BACK IN CHURCH

Set up two chairs back to back as you did for the Narrow Gate and line up the kids

Child 1   Today Jesus told us that the gate of Heaven is very narrow.

Child 2   We thought that might be to make sure only one person came in at a time.

Child 3   So we thought we'd discover how narrow that is ...

Run a fast version of the Narrow Gate activity, and end with a very narrow gap indeed

Leader   We realized that to get through that Narrow Gate, we had to leave loads of stuff behind – extra clothes, luggage, everything. Only *we* could get through. Why was that, kids?

All the children   **Because God wants us just as we are.**

Script 51 Being First

Proper 17, Ordinary Time 22
(Sunday between 28 August and 3 September)

St Luke 14.7–11

THEME

We all scramble for places – a seat on the Tube, a seat next to our best friend, a good seat in the cinema. Jesus tells us to calm down. He doesn't like Christians pushing and shoving and, anyway, there's going to be some big surprises in Heaven. People who pushed to the front of the queue may well find themselves at the back.

SET UP

- The liturgical colour is Green.
- Masking tape.
- An audio player.
- A line of chairs.
- Two chocolate gold coins.

WELCOME *the children and lead them in* **The Sign of the Cross** ✠ **(p. xxxvi).**

THE KYRIE	Lord, you always forgive those who say they are sorry, Lord, have mercy **Lord, have mercy**
	Jesus, we are sorry for the times we have been unkind, Christ, have mercy **Christ, have mercy**
	Lord, we thank you for always loving and forgiving us, Lord, have mercy **Lord, have mercy**

Ask the children to repeat **The Prayer for Forgiveness** *after you* **(p. xxxvi).**

OPENING PRAYER	Lord God You sent your Son into the world To lead us back to Heaven. Help us to hear His word today And start on our homeward journey. We ask this through Jesus the Lord. **Amen**

BEFORE THE GOSPEL

Trains

Leader   Right, I want to think about train journeys.
Anyone been on one? *(React to the show of hands)*
Good! Let's make a train …

Line up a row of chairs, considerably less than the number of kids present

Excellent, now we need a platform.

Make a line with the masking tape, a good 10 feet away from the train

Right, everyone get behind the line …

Line up the kids – make sure that little children are in the care of the other Leaders

I think I can hear the train in the distance.
Does anyone know what a train sounds like?

Co-ordinate some train noises, getting louder, slower, and stopping

Right, you can't go across that line yet.
Sure you're behind it? Any toe poking over and you're out!
The train's stopped.
Wait …
They're opening the doors.
Go!

Inspect the result

OK, the ones sitting down are lucky, the rest of us will have to stand.
Off goes the train again – do what I do –

Join the standees, sway gently

This isn't too bad – uh oh, here comes a bend.
Bend one way   And another …
Bend the other   We're coming to a station …
Lurch   Fantastic – and two people get off.

Leader 2 taps two of the sitting passengers

Did anyone manage to sit down?

Great, just another three hours to go ...
Let's all get off the train.

Everybody gets off the chairs and sits on the floor

I liked that, but I suppose it wouldn't be much fun if you were very old. Does anyone know what you do if an old person gets on a crowded train? (**You give them your seat**)
Now Jesus was watching some people turn up for a dinner one day, and they were all pushing and shoving, and He didn't like it.
Partly because it was rude – and partly for another reason.
We're going to play a game to discover what that reason was.

Musical Chairs

Set up a line of chairs for Musical Chairs: *the limit is about 20 players, if you've got more kids than that, you may have to play in two shifts.*
The players circle the chairs as you play music, and rush to a chair the moment the music stops. Anyone left standing is out.
Set up enough chairs for everyone first time round (so they all have a chance of sitting down), then remove the chairs one by one. If there're lots of kids playing, keep the first rounds very short.
Make sure you remember who the first victim was.
At the end say:

Leader   Right we're going to give a medal to the person who came first.
Who was that? *(Name!)*
Well, *Name* did jolly well – well done, *Name*!

Shake him/her by the hand

But actually he's not the first – it's the kid who was out first – *Name*!
Come forward – here's your medal. *(Hand over the chocolate gold coin)*
Don't eat it yet ...
Let's give her a clap!
Now why did I do that?
The answer is in the Gospel.

THE GOSPEL PROCESSION

THE GOSPEL   *St Luke 14.7–11*

AFTER THE GOSPEL

Run through the Gospel – establish that:

Leader   Jesus said, if you go to an important party, go and sit somewhere
                really unimportant – like out on the stairs …
                And, if you've got a decent host, he'll find you and get you a better
                seat. 'Because,' said Jesus, 'everyone who pushes in will be put to the
                back, but the person who humbles himself will be honoured.'
                Now, when we played *Musical Chairs*, nobody was being rude – we
                were just playing. I'm sure Jesus wouldn't have minded *Name (the
                actual winner)* getting a medal – let's give him one now.

Do so – make sure he gets clapped

                But grown-ups aren't playing when they push and shove, and Jesus
                was very anxious that His followers weren't the sort of people who
                elbowed other people out of the way.
                In fact, in Heaven, Jesus said there's going to be a lot of surprises.
                The quiet people will end up at the front, and the pushy ones may
                well be at the back.

REHEARSAL

Practise your presentation for when you go back into church (see below).
(Make sure your two medal holders haven't eaten their medals …)

BEFORE THE FINAL PRAYER

Leader   *Put a prayer candle in the middle of the room*
                We'll gather round the candle in a circle.
                The nice thing about a circle is there's room for everyone.
                OK, we've done lots of things …
                Running for a train.
                Playing musical chairs.
                Listening to the Gospel.
                Now we're going to be still.

Play some quiet music on the audio player, a Taizé chant for example – 'Stay with me'
has a good tune, as does 'Laudate omnes gentes, laudate dominum' (Praise the Lord
everyone, praise the Lord). Fade it out gently in a couple of minutes

                We're going to say part of a Psalm together. *(From Psalm 46)*

Ask the children to say after you

God is with us
God is with us

Be still and know that I am God
God is with us

God is our hope and our strength
God is with us

Be still and know that I am God
God is with us

Finish with a **Glory Be** *... (see p. xxxvii).*

BACK IN CHURCH

Line up the kids down the front, with the two medal winners in the middle

Child 1	We played *Musical Chairs* today.
Child 2	And the winner was *Name. (This is the actual winner)*
Child 3	But we gave the prize to the first person who was out.
Child 4	That was *Name. (The first out)*

He/she holds up the medal

Leader	Why did we do that?
All the kids	Because Jesus said, 'The first shall be last!'
Leader	So He did.
	But we thought Jesus wouldn't mind if we gave *Name (the actual winner)* a prize too.

He/she holds up the medal

Script 52   Counting the Cost

Proper 18, Ordinary Time 23
(Sunday between 4 and 10 September)

St Luke 14.25a, 27–30, 33

THEME

Jesus warns his adult followers to count the cost before following Him. Children can't be expected to shoulder this burden, but they can see the good sense of working out whether they've got the resources to finish something before they start it – even if it's only a newspaper tower...

SET UP

- The liturgical colour is Green.
- Leader 2 starts the session with a pocketful of small change.
- Lots of newspapers – at least one whole paper between three children.
- Sellotape.
- Fake money – like *Monopoly* money, or the pirate coins you get in party shops. Don't use chocolate coins or real pennies; the children need to 'spend' their money without a qualm.
- An alarm clock with an old-fashioned ring.

WELCOME *the children and lead them in* **The Sign of the Cross ✠ (p. xxxvi).**

THE KYRIE	Lord, for the times we have forgotten to love you,
	Lord have mercy
	Lord have mercy
	Jesus, for the times we have forgotten to love others
	Christ have mercy
	Christ have mercy
	Lord, we thank you for never forgetting to love us
	Lord, have mercy
	Lord, have mercy

Ask the children to repeat **The Prayer for Forgiveness** *after you* (**p. xxxvi**).

OPENING PRAYER

Leader	Almighty God,
	Your Son Jesus called us to follow Him.
	Help us to hear that call
	And become His true and sensible followers. **Amen**

Counting

Leader 2 unostentatiously puts some money in his/her palm to count during the following greeting

Leader 1	Good morning, everyone!
	Good morning, *Name (Leader 2)*
Leader 2	*(Looking up)* Oh hallo …
Leader 1	What are you doing?
Leader 2	I'm just counting my money. I'm wondering if I've got enough.
Leader 1	Enough for what?
Leader 2	Well, I'm saving up to buy a car.
Leader 1	How much have you got? Let's count it together …

*Leader 2 tips the money into the midst of the children and everyone begins to count
Leader 2 produces cash from all sorts of pockets – but eventually it's all neatly piled in 10p amounts*

Leader 2	Wow! Five quid! *(Or whatever)*
	I should get a nice car with that.
Leader 1	What do you think, kids – is that enough?

Unless your children are very tiny, they'll say (**No**)

Leader 2	Oh, how about a bike? (**No**)
Leader 1	I think you've got just enough for a couple of bus rides …
Leader 2	*(Putting the money away)* I think that's really disappointing –
	I suppose I'd better go on saving.
Leader 1	*(To the children)* Have any of you ever saved up for something?

Take what comes – establish that it's a good idea to work out exactly how much something costs beforehand, so you don't get fed up

We're going to play a game now. It's called Newspaper Towers. I'm going to ask you to build the biggest tower you can out of newspaper – but you'll have to work out whether you've got enough money to pay for all the newspaper and Sellotape you need.

Newspaper Towers

*Split the children into twos and threes and give
each group about six sheets of newspaper, ten
coins of fake money and five strips of Sellotape.
The idea is that the kids make a building out of
newspaper – the tallest tower being the winner.
They can buy extra newspaper and Sellotape at
one coin per double sheet or strip of tape.*

*Give the children a moment to work out the best
way to tackle the problem: some hints on rolling
the paper up diagonally and thinking Eiffel
Tower may help. Send Leaders to help any group
that hasn't got a clue – and create a separate
grown-up/toddler group to construct their own
tower if necessary.*

*Keep the game brisk. Tell the children they've
only got ten minutes, set the clock to go off then,
wait for the wail when it happens, and allow
another few minutes. Play it by ear; the moment there is a feasible collection of
wobbly skyscrapers, stop the game.*

Admire the results and settle the kids for the Gospel.

BEFORE THE GOSPEL

Right, I don't think Jesus knew about newspaper towers, but He knew what it was
like to build a real one. Let's hear what He said about it.

THE GOSPEL PROCESSION

THE GOSPEL   *St Luke 14.25a, 27–30, 33*

Optional Paraphrase

Crowds of people were following Jesus, and He turned and said to them,
'Listen, nobody can be a disciple of mine unless he's prepared to take up his cross
and follow me.
'It's like building a tower. Supposing you decide to build a tower, you have to sit
down and work out how much it will cost. Because, if you don't, you might find you
could only build *half* a tower – and then people would make fun of you!

---

* It might seem a good idea to use Leader 2's pennies to dish out to the kids for paper and Sellotape
money – unfortunately it isn't. Some kids don't mind losing the game as long as they leave the session 5p
richer and we'd rather they used their ingenuity on the game.

'In the same way, a disciple of mine has to work out how much it will cost to follow me, he might have to give up everything he has.'

AFTER THE GOSPEL

Go through the Gospel and sum up along the following lines:

Leader	People loved following Jesus, but they were treating it rather like a picnic.
	So Jesus said, 'Get real! You're very sensible before you put up a building, be just as sensible when you decide to follow me; it could be tough.'
	Now, at this moment in England, it's not particularly tough to be a Christian. But in some parts of the world it's very dangerous indeed, and people have to think carefully before they follow Christ. We're going to remember them in our prayers.
FINAL PRAYER	Lord Jesus
	You warned us that to follow you would sometimes be hard.
	Bless all persecuted Christians:
	Those in prison
	Those who are bullied
	Those who are afraid.
	Help them in all their sufferings,
	And bring them safely home to Heaven
	Where you live with the Father and the Holy Spirit. **Amen**

REHEARSAL

Practise your presentation for when you go back into church (see below).

MUSIC

You could finish with 'He who would valiant be' or 'O Jesus, I have promised' (verses 1, 3, 4).

BACK IN CHURCH

The children bring forward the best of the paper towers

Child 1	Today we discovered that it took *Number* sheets of newspaper …
Child 2	… and *Number* strips of Sellotape to make a really tall tower.
Child 3	In the Gospel Jesus told us to work out the cost of following Him.
Leader 1	It will be much more difficult than building a tower – but we know it will be worth it.

Script 53   The Lost Coin

Proper 19, Ordinary Time 24
(Sunday between 11 and 17 September)

St Luke 15.8–10

THEME

The Gospel this morning has three really good stories – the Lost Sheep, The Lost Coin and the Prodigal Son. The Lost Sheep turns up in year B (*Script 46*). The Prodigal Son was the hero of Lent 4 (*Script 18*) so it's the turn of The Lost Coin. The story is unique in having a heroine, a Jewish housewife, but the moral is the same as in the other two stories – God loves all His children, the bad ones as much as the good.

SET UP
- Pictures from the CD-Rom.
- **CD53.4–13** should be as printed as large as you can make them.
- The sheet of saints and sinners **(CD53.14)** should be printed about five times. You'll need at least 50 of these little images.
- You needn't enlarge them, but you will have to cut them up and hide them round the room – Blu-Tacking them under chairs and so on – for a game of *Hunt the Sinner* (see below).
- You will be splitting the children into teams (anything from three to six kids).
- Estimate how many teams you're likely to have and bring along a shoe box for each of them.
- Make sure that another Leader is ready to suggest a game of *Hide and Seek* at the right moment (see below).

WELCOME *the children and lead them in* The Sign of the Cross ✠ (p. xxxvi).

THE KYRIE   Lord, you always forgive those who say they are sorry,
                     Lord, have mercy
                     Lord, have mercy

                     Jesus, we are sorry for the times we have been unkind,
                     Christ, have mercy
                     Christ, have mercy

Lord, we thank you for always loving and forgiving us,
Lord, have mercy
Lord, have mercy

Ask the children to repeat **The Prayer for Forgiveness** *after you* (**p. xxxvi**).

OPENING	Lord God, our Creator
PRAYER	You have given us sharp eyes
	And keen minds.
	Help us to use them to seek out
	Everything you want us to find.
	Help us to seek for
	Love, when we feel unhappy,
	Hope, when we feel alone,
	Faith, when we are tempted to forget you,
	And, most of all, help us to seek your Son, Jesus Christ. **Amen**

BEFORE THE GOSPEL

GAME

Hide and Seek

Leader	Well, I don't know about you, but I feel like a game today.
	What shall we play?

Take a couple of replies only to breezily dismiss them. Football? Nope not enough room, Piggy in the Middle? I forgot the ball. One of the Leaders could suggest Murder in the Dark? Gosh yes – well perhaps not on a Sunday
If you're lucky, a kid may come up with Hide and Seek, *otherwise make sure a grown-up suggests it*

Great idea!
I'll shut my eyes and count to – oh, 50, while one of you hides.

While you count out loud, the other Leaders choose a kid and help him/her find a good hiding place

... 50!
OK, who's missing? *(Name!)*
Right off I go – tell me if I'm getting warm ...

Look in ridiculous places – is she in your pocket? Are you sure? What about under that pot? etc. Do your absolute best not to see the obvious and only when you get warm the second or third time, begin to home in relentlessly on the hidden child

Gotcha!

That was a brilliant place to hide.

Has anyone played this game before?

It's got an odd name hasn't it?

'Hide' – well that's easy – 'and Seek'.

What does 'seek' mean?

See what they say – establish it means 'look for'

'Seek' doesn't mean that you look vaguely around and hope you'll find someone; it means you're going to take a lot of trouble to find them. You *seek* them out.

Jesus thought God spent a lot of time seeking. Let's hear one of His stories now.

THE GOSPEL PROCESSION

THE GOSPEL   *St Luke 15.8–10*

Optional Paraphrase

As Jesus was talking, all sorts of bad characters, tax collectors and sinners, came flocking to hear Him. And the good people, the ones who obeyed all God's rules, got fed up. 'What's going on?' they said. 'Jesus gets on with all these ghastly sinners, He even goes home and has supper with them!'

Jesus overheard what they were saying and told them this story …

Once upon a time there was a woman who had 10 silver pieces.

Like many Jewish ladies she kept them safe by stringing them on a

CD53.1   chain and wearing them across her forehead.

One day she was putting on her chain, when she noticed something odd about her coins.

CD53.2   She counted them.

How many were there? *(Get the kids to count)* (**Nine!**)

She'd lost a coin …

Well her house was an ordinary Jewish house. It had tiny windows and there wasn't much light, but she lit a lamp, and got a broom out and swept and swept until …

CD53.3   She found the coin she had lost. Can anyone see it?

They usually spot it at once

When she found it, she called all her friends and neighbours round and said, 'Rejoice with me! I've found the coin I'd lost. Let's have a party!'

'God is rather like that woman,' said Jesus. 'He loves it when one of His lost children turns up. In fact there is more rejoicing in Heaven over one sinner who says sorry than over 99 good people, who've never had to say sorry at all.'

AFTER THE GOSPEL

Leader   Look, here are the lady's ten coins.

CD53.4–13 *Put up coin shapes and stick them up with their backs facing the children*

She liked every single one of them, and the moment she lost one she swept her house until she found it.
Now, supposing these coins were some of God's children …

Turn **CD53.4–13** *over, counting as you go*

Leader   1, 2, 3, 4, 5, 6, 7, 8, 9 …
Heavens, they're all Saints!
God loves every one of them very much – but what about number 13? *(Slide it away from the others)*
God loves this person just as much – let's see what he looks like …

Turn him over   Oh dear – what do you think he is? *(Obviously … **a robber**)*
Yup, a robber …
Well, God watches him anxiously, and does His best to seek him out and if *Number 10* joins the others *(Make sure he does)*
God is so pleased that He and the angels have a party.
God our Father loves all His children, saints and sinners – which is a bit of luck for us …

GAME

Hunt the Sinner

Split the children into teams; place the shoe boxes down the front for each team to deposit saints and sinners in. Make sure each team knows which box is theirs.

CD53.14   OK, there are saints and sinners hidden all round this room.
I want you to seek them out. Put them in your box when you find them – you get 1 point for a saint, and 10 for a sinner.

If there are too many kids to play this comfortably, split the room into two teams and let two representatives hunt, simultaneously, for 30 seconds. Then choose another two. The rest of the team have to sit still, but nothing of course will stop them giving advice.

Leader	*Tot up the boxes and declare the winners*
	OK, let's clap the winners. *(Everyone claps)*
	And, as Jesus is deeply uninterested in who wins or who loses, a clap for everyone else. *(Another round of applause)*

REHEARSAL

Practise your presentation for when you go back into church (see below).

FINAL PRAYER

Ask the children to repeat this prayer after you

Leader	**Lord Jesus,**
	Friend of sinners,
	We thank you for seeking us when we are lost,
	And bringing us safely home. Amen

BACK IN CHURCH

All the children go down the front, ten of them bring in the large coin-shaped saints and sinners. (If you haven't got ten kids, rope in some grown-up help)

Child 1	Today we heard about a lady who had ten coins.

The kids hold up the coin shapes with only the backs showing

Child 2	She lost one –

The child holding number 10 moves away from the others

Child 3	And looked everywhere for it.
	When she found it –

Number 10 rejoins the others

Child 4	she had a party.
Leader	Jesus said that in the same way there was more rejoicing in Heaven over one repentant sinner –

The child holding number 10 turns it round – it's the robber

	than over 99 good people –

The other children turn their pictures round

	who'd never been bad to start with.
	And, as these guys really *are* good – they're very pleased to welcome the sinner too!

All the children circle number 10

Script 54   God vs Mammon

Proper 20, Ordinary Time 25
(Sunday between 18 and 24 September)

St Luke 16.13

THEME

It is almost impossible to make the Dishonest Steward's chicanery (a) compre-
hensible or (b) interesting to children: it goes straight over their heads. They are,
however, very good at understanding that you can't serve two masters. Conse-
quently we've cut today's Gospel down to its punch line and gone for that.

SET UP

- The liturgical colour is Green.
- Any headphones you possess and a mock radio mike – see template on CD-Rom
  (CD54.1).
- Frying pan.
- Fish slice and a piece of pitta bread.
- Pictures from the CD-Rom. Print up several copies of **CD54.4**.
- St Polycarp template.

WELCOME *the children and lead them in* **The Sign of the Cross** ✠ (p. xxxvi).

THE KYRIE	Lord Jesus, forgive us for not listening to you,
	Lord have mercy
	Lord have mercy
	Lord Jesus, forgive us for being unkind,
	Christ have mercy
	Christ have mercy
	Lord Jesus, we thank you for always hearing and forgiving us,
	Lord have mercy
	Lord have mercy

Ask the children to repeat **The Prayer for Forgiveness** *after you* (p. xxxvi).

OPENING PRAYER

Ask the children to repeat this after you

> Go before us Lord
> In everything we do.
> So that our work and play
> may be to your glory,
> now and for ever. Amen

BEFORE THE GOSPEL

Leader   This morning we're going to think about doing two things at once.
Hands up anyone who is learning the piano (or guitar).

If no child responds, make sure a grown-up puts up their hand

Can you play with both hands?

If they say 'no' – agree that it's difficult
If they say 'yes' – express admiration

Leader   So, when you sit down at the piano, your hands can do two different things at the same time! Amazing.
In that case you might find it easy to do this – I'm going to ask you to rub your tummy with your left hand and pat your head with your right hand, at the same time. Actually I'm going to ask everyone to do it.
Stand up everyone – let's see what happens …

There should be a certain amount of confusion. If they find it too easy, shout 'Faster!'

OK, with a bit of practice anyone can do that. What about this?

Bring two chairs forward and ask Leader 2 and one of the bigger children to sit down

Right, lift your right foot off the floor and make clockwise circles with it. Brilliant …
Now, while you're doing that, draw the number '6' in the air with your right hand.
There, I thought so – your feet have changed direction.
Anyone else like to try?

Run this a couple of times

Weird isn't it. Nobody knows why it happens.
And it's not just hands and feet that find it difficult to do two things at once.

Thinking Two Things at Once

Leader   Can anyone here text their friends, and play a computer game and
                do their homework all at the same time?

Kids always think they can do that

                Well, I expect you're better at it than me – but actually you don't
                learn so fast if you're using your brain for two things at once.
                Look at this bloke …

Leader 2 comes forward with the frying pan and the pitta bread

                He's cooking pancakes for his kids' supper – but he's also listening
                to the tennis commentary from Wimbledon.

*Another grown-up or a big kid dons the headphones, gets behind the radio mike, and
does a commentary on Wimbledon*

Commentator   So the Champion is getting ready to serve – she bounces the ball four
                times …

*Leader 2 bounces the pitta in the pan four times – realizes what he's doing and prods
it with the fish slice*

                She swings her racket …

Leader 2 just stops himself swinging the frying pan

                She's looking across the court – where is she going to place the ball?
                She raises the racket and *pow!* A brilliant serve right down the line!

At pow! Leader 2 brings the frying pan up and whams the pitta across the room

Leader 1   Yup, you really can't think of two things at once.
                And there's something else you can't do.
                Let's hear what that is in the Gospel.

THE GOSPEL PROCESSION

THE GOSPEL   *St Luke 16.13*

(Most modern translations use the word 'money' instead of 'Mammon'; go for money)

AFTER THE GOSPEL

Leader   That was very short, wasn't it? Let's hear it again …

Repeat the Gospel

There's a famous play, *The Servant with Two Masters*. The servant gets into terrible trouble as he tries to serve two masters. Jesus could have written that play …

You see, you might be able to *do* two things at once with your hands – if you practise. You may be able to *think* two things at once with your brain – though you won't do it very well.

But you can't *serve* two people at once. You've got to make a choice. Jesus is saying, you have to work out who comes first – is it God or money? God or TV? God or football? As soon as you hear the question, you know what the right answer is. God has to come first.

St Polycarp

Leader	There was a great saint who really understood about serving God.
CD54.2	His name was Polycarp *(picture of a very ancient bishop)* and he was born in the first century. He was a kind and gentle bishop and was taught the Christian faith by St John – Jesus' best friend. Unfortunately that didn't stop him having enemies. It was illegal to be a Christian in the first century and one of Polycarp's enemies betrayed him to the Romans.
CD54.3	The old man was brought before the Governor who said, 'Polycarp, the law says you must serve the Emperor and curse Christ!' Polycarp said, 'I have served Christ for 86 years and He has done me no wrong. How can I curse my King?'
CD54.4	So they killed him. And Polycarp went to Heaven, where he still serves God – and prays for us.*

ACTIVITY

This session has been heavy on thinking, so it's time for something gentle. Ask the children to colour in picture 3, of St Polycarp. Bits of it are left incomplete for them to fill in.

REHEARSAL

Practise your presentation for when you go back into church (see below).

---

* The Early Church greatly revered St Polycarp, and his church in Smyrna wrote a long letter to the church in Psidia, containing a detailed account of his martyrdom.

FINAL PRAYER

Gather the children round one of the Polycarp pictures

> St Polycarp knew that you couldn't serve two masters. The Romans wanted him to serve the Emperor, but Polycarp knew he had to serve God. Let's ask him for his prayers. The response is 'Pray for us'.
>
> Holy Polycarp, Servant of God
> **Pray for us**
>
> Holy Polycarp, Martyr of God
> **Pray for us**
>
> Holy Polycarp, Friend of Christ
> **Pray for us**
>
> Lord Jesus,
> We thank you for the example of Saint Polycarp.
> Help us to serve you as well as he did,
> And join him, to live with you in Heaven,
> For ever. **Amen**

BACK IN CHURCH

The children come back with their Polycarp pictures

Child 1	In today's Gospel Jesus said you couldn't serve two masters.
Child 2	We listened to the story of St Polycarp.
Child 3	The Romans told him to serve the Emperor and curse Jesus.
Child 4	But Polycarp said, 'I've served Christ for 86 years, I can't curse my King.'
Leader	So the children have drawn a picture of St Polycarp – with the two masters he was asked to choose between. The Emperor, and God – which one did he choose, children?
All the children	God!

Script 55   Dives and Lazarus

Proper 21, Ordinary Time 26
(Sunday between 25 September and 1 October)

St Luke 16.19–31

THEME

This morning we hear Jesus' parable of a Rich Man called Dives* and Lazarus, a beggar who sat at his gate. The story itself is very old (apparently it started in Ancient Egypt) but Jesus gave it a new ending. His original audience, who knew the Jewish version of the story, would have looked up in amazement when He added Dives' shouting match with Abraham across the abyss.

Seeing that 'Lazarus and Dives' *is* a folk tale, there's no need to worry the children with the details it gives of the afterlife. A discussion on Hell or hell-fire is not useful at their age.

SET UP

- The liturgical colour is Green.
- A Fairy Story book.
- Pictures from the CD-Rom.
- Lazarus and Dives puppets – template on CD-Rom.
  (There are five puppets: Lazarus 1 and Dives 2, alive; Lazarus 2 and Dives 2, as they appear once they are dead; and Abraham.)
- Ask Leader 2 and a couple of kids to handle the puppets during the Gospel: they should see the script before the session.
- Several inflated balloons, a packet's worth.
- A clock with a second hand.

WELCOME *the children and lead them in* **The Sign of the Cross** ✠ (p. xxxvi).

THE KYRIE   Lord Jesus, we are sorry for the times we have been unkind,
Lord have mercy
Lord have mercy

---

* The Rich Man does not have a name in the Gospel; 'Dives' is his traditional name. It's pronounced Die-vees, and is Latin for 'rich man'.

Lord Jesus, we are sorry for the times we have forgotten to pray
Christ have mercy
Christ have mercy

Lord Jesus, we thank you for never forgetting us
Lord, have mercy
Lord, have mercy

Ask the children to repeat **The Prayer for Forgiveness** *after you* (**p. xxxvi**).

OPENING   Lord Jesus,
PRAYER   You came to earth to find the poor
                 and bring them back to your Heavenly Kingdom.
                 Help us to be generous to the poor,
                 so we may all eventually be one family in Heaven,
                 with you and the Father and the Holy Spirit. **Amen**

BEFORE THE GOSPEL

Cinderella
Leader   *(Sitting down at the front with the Fairy Story book)*
                 Right, let's have a story.
                 It's all about a girl called Cinderella – anyone heard of her?

React to the show of hands

                 Gosh, all of you, OK I'll keep it short.

Refer back to the book

                 Anyway, Cinderella lived at home with her Father and two Ugly
                 Sisters. And one evening Dad and the sisters went off to a Ball – and
                 left Cinderella all alone.
                 What happened then?

*Let the children tell you about the Fairy Godmother and how Cinderella got to the
Ball*

                 You're absolutely right. Cinderella had a lovely time at the Ball;
                 she danced all evening and fell in love with a Prince and then, at
                 midnight, she rushed off, leaving something behind. What was it?
                 (**A glass slipper**)
                 Exactly. Well the Prince found the slipper, and went round trying
                 to find the girl whose foot it fitted. Eventually he turned up at
                 Cinderella's house. Cinderella and the Ugly Sisters lined up to try on
                 the slipper.

> The eldest Ugly Sister tried first, and the shoe fitted perfectly!
> So the Prince had to marry her – poor chap! – and they lived unhappily ever after.

Cries of outrage – let the children put you right

> Goodness, well this book must be wrong … *(Put it away)*
> It gives you a shock when a story doesn't end properly, doesn't it?

Pick up the Lazarus 1 and Dives 1 puppets **(CD55.1–2)**

Leader   There was a story going round the Holy Land when Jesus lived there.
           It was about a poor guy …

Hold up Lazarus 1

> And a rich guy …

Hold up Dives 1

> They both died – and the poor guy went up to Heaven,

Whoosh Lazarus 1 up

> While the rich guy went down to Hell.

Dive Dives 1 down

> And that's the story. Short, isn't it?
> But Jesus seems to have thought, 'I wonder what the rich man thought when he landed up in Hell?'

Bring up the Dives 1 puppet and address it

> What *did* you think?

The puppet just looks back at you

> Well, he's not saying – let's find out in the Gospel.

THE GOSPEL PROCESSION

THE GOSPEL   *St Luke 16.19–31*

Use the version of the Gospel below, with Leader 2 and two children moving the puppets (cues in text)

Narrator   Jesus said,
           There was once a rich man, Dives, who had wonderful clothes and feasted every day.
           Enter Dives 1

And, at his gate, lay a poor man named Lazarus, who would have been pleased to eat the stuff that fell off the rich man's table.

Enter Lazarus 1

Well, Lazarus died, and was carried by the angels to be with Abraham in Heaven.

*The Lazarus puppeteer swaps Lazarus 1 for Lazarus 2 (**CD55.3**). Somebody else holds up the Abraham puppet (**CD55.4**). Lazarus 2 flies up to meet Abraham*

Dives also died and was buried.

*The Dives 1 puppet is swapped for Dives 2 (**CD55.5**)*

He landed up in Hell.

Dives goes down to Hell – not too low, you've still got to see him

And Dives looked up and saw Abraham far away, with Lazarus by his side.

'*Oi!*' said Dives.

Lazarus 2 and Abraham both jump with surprise

'Did someone say something?' said Abraham.

'Father Abraham!' shouted Dives. 'Send Lazarus down to give me a drink of water!'

Abraham couldn't believe he was hearing this – it wasn't in the story. However, he looked down out of Heaven …

The Abraham puppet comes slightly nearer Dives

… and saw Dives down in Hell. 'Listen, son,' he said, 'it's impossible. No one can cross from Heaven into Hell.'

'Oh,' said Dives, and then he said, 'well could you send Lazarus back to Earth and warn my five brothers about this place?'

Abraham replied, 'Your brothers have the Bible to listen to.'

'Yeah …' said Dives, 'but they don't read it. Now if someone was to come back from the dead …'

'No,' said Abraham. 'If they don't take any notice of the Bible, *nothing* will convince them – not even if someone came back from the dead.'

AFTER THE GOSPEL

Leader   *Pick up the Lazarus 2 and Dives 2 puppets*

So, though that story usually ended up with Lazarus going up …

Hold Lazarus up

And Dives going down …

Swoosh Dives down

> Jesus got Dives talking.

Jerk Dives up again

> Dives had a lot to say.
> He yelled at Abraham, and gave orders to Lazarus, and was worried about his brothers.
> And Abraham … *(look round)* … where's Abraham?

A child holds up Abraham

> Abraham had to tell him it was too late.
> Why do you think Dives went to Hell in the first place?

Take all answers – establish that it was probably not because he was rich, but because he ignored Lazarus when he was a poor beggar

> Look, kids, this is just a story. It didn't happen. I don't know whether guys like Dives really go to Hell.
> But Jesus wanted us to think about this chap –
> *Waggle Dives*
> Dives ignored Lazarus while he was alive, and then tried to boss him about when he was dead.
> Jesus is saying, 'Don't end up like him!'
> Notice other people – be generous, and kind.

GAME

Stay in Heaven

Pick up two balloons

Leader	OK, everybody wants to get to Heaven. These balloons for example …
Bat them up	Can you keep two balloons in Heaven for one minute? It's not as easy as it looks …

Make sure one of your balloons hits the ground

> Rats! I'm out!

Give each kid two inflated balloons (you might have to work this in shifts with larger groups) and start the timer. If anyone finds it too easy, give them three balloons

REHEARSAL

Practise your presentation for when you go back into church (see below).

FINAL PRAYER

Ask the children to stand in a circle

> Before Jesus went back to Heaven, He said to His friends,
> 'Stay together and pray.'
> He loves seeing Christians gathered together, like a family.
> Let's say the Family Prayer of the Church.

Our Father ... (see p. xxxvi).

MUSIC

The modern hymn 'Brother, sister, let me serve you' *goes well here.*

BACK IN CHURCH

Go in with the puppets

Leader   Today we heard one of Jesus' stories.
                It was about a poor man, called Lazarus.

A child holds up Lazarus 1

                And a rich man, called Dives.

A child holds up Dives 1

                They both died.

The children lower Lazarus 1 and Dives 1

                And Lazarus went up to Heaven ...

A child swoops Lazarus 2 up

                to be with Abraham.

Another child holds up the Abraham puppet to be with Lazarus 2

                While Dives went down to Hell.

Another child holds up Dives 2, then swoops him down

                And Dives looked up into Heaven and saw Lazarus and Abraham ...

Dives 2 jerks up a bit

                And he started shouting and giving orders.

The child waggles Dives 2 around

                Abraham had to tell him:
All the children It's too late!
Leader   We think Jesus told this story to warn us not to end up like Dives.

Everyone bows and exits

Script 56   Faith

Proper 22, Ordinary Time 27
(Sunday between 2 and 8 October)

St Luke 17.5–6

THEME

The Gospel today is a vivid little illustration of the power of faith – the mulberry tree which, if we had but the faith, would uproot itself and land in the middle of the sea. Children need to be warned not to take the passage literally. (If only to stop them getting discouraged when they rush out and start ordering mulberry trees about.) Faith is quite exciting enough without trees uprooting themselves, as this session seeks to show.

SET UP

- The liturgical colour is Green.
- Large soft ball.
- A large person to act as Goalie – he/she should look at the script beforehand.
- Props for a re-enactment of Abraham and Isaac:
  - bundle of sticks,
  - matches,
  - walking stick,
  - sun hat (baseball cap is fine),
  - two rucksacks and stuff to put in them. Anything you think appropriate, for example:
    - socks
    - sun cream
    - toothbrush
    - bottle of water
    - food – e.g. pitta bread, biscuits, apple.
- A toy lamb (essential).
- Make a checklist of everything you have gathered (bar the lamb, the thicket and the angel wings – see below) and give it to the person playing Abraham.
- He also needs a pencil and a toy dagger.

Optional extras

- A 'thicket' – i.e. a tangle of branches. Place the lamb in the thicket.
- Any angel gear you may have left over from a Nativity play.

Scatter the contents of Abraham's list round the hall, including the stuff that will ultimately go in the rucksacks. (The children are going to help Abraham prepare for his journey by finding the things he needs.)

Cast Leader 2 as Abraham, and two children as the Angel and Isaac. Run through the script beforehand with them.

WELCOME *the children and lead them in* **The Sign of the Cross** ✠ (**p. xxxvi**).

KYRIE	Heavenly Father,
	For the times we have forgotten you,
	Lord have mercy
	Lord have mercy
	Lord Jesus
	For the times we have forgotten to trust you,
	Christ have mercy
	Christ have mercy
	Holy Spirit
	For the times we have forgotten to listen to you
	Lord have mercy
	Lord have mercy

Ask the children to repeat **The Prayer for Forgiveness** *after you* (**p. xxxvi**).

OPENING	Lord God,
PRAYER	**Help us to know that,**
	However often we forget you,
	You never forget us.
	We thank you for your constant love,
	Through Jesus Christ our Lord. Amen

BEFORE THE GOSPEL

Faith

Leader	Today we're going to think about Faith.
	What does 'Faith' mean?

Take all answers – they may be quite wide ranging – end by establishing that …

> Faith means believing in things:
> believing in God, in other people, in the Bible, in the Church – and in ourselves.
> Let's start with ourselves.

GAME

Faith Football

Set up a goal with two chairs, and put the biggest person you can find between them as the Goalie

Leader   OK, there's the goal – there's the Goalie – and here's me …
Bounce the ball Do you think I can score a goal? (**Yes!**)
> I don't know, he/she looks very big …

The Goalie lunges over to intimidate you

> and scary.
> Oh well, here goes …

Get ready to kick the ball, the Goalie roars – lose your nerve and do a mis-kick

> Rats! I just didn't believe I could do it …
> Could any of you do any better?

Let the children have a go. The Goalie develops butter fingers when it's the turn of the small children. He/she can catch some of the older children's shots, but make sure they win on the second attempt

Leader   Yes, I can see you have faith in yourselves.
> Sometimes you have to have faith in other people.

Give any example from sport or adventure that comes to mind. I use the following example …

> A friend of mine told me that, on the island of Madeira, kids are taught to swim by being chucked into the sea from a boat. The grown-ups in the boat say they won't drown – and they simply have to believe them!
> But what about faith in God, and the Church, and the Bible?
> That can be difficult, God has to help you with that …
> We're going to tell a story together about a man who had great faith in God.

Abraham

Leader   His name was Abraham and he lived about 4,000 years ago. That was so long ago that people didn't know very much about God. They thought He wanted them to sacrifice sheep and goats to Him – sometimes they thought He even wanted children sacrificed to Him. Well God didn't mind sheep and stuff – but He had to teach Abraham that He never, *ever*, wanted a child sacrificed.
And He did this by testing Abraham's faith.

The Story of Abraham and Isaac

Narrator   Right, *Name (Leader 2)* is going to be Abraham – and *Name* is going to be Abraham's son, Isaac – and *Name* is going to be an Angel.
But I need two people to carry rucksacks, and somebody who can be the Voice of God.

Cast these; the Voice of God will need a script

The rest of you are Abraham's servants and are going to help him pack. I'll tell you when.
Once upon a time there was a man called Abraham.

Abraham comes forward

He had a son called Isaac.

Isaac comes forward

And both of them were greatly loved by God.
One day, while Abraham was praying ...

Abraham kneels

he heard God say to him,
Voice of God   'Abraham! I want you to take your son Isaac to a high mountain, and there I want you to sacrifice him to me.'
Narrator   Abraham got up and thought, Well, I've got to do it.
So he told his son Isaac that they were going on a journey to make a sacrifice to God, and got out a checklist ...

Abraham pulls out his list

And he asked his servants to find all the things he needed for the journey.

Abraham reads out the items on his checklist and the children scatter to find them. Abraham ticks the items off with his pencil and picks up the walking stick, while Isaac gets a sun hat. (Abraham already has the toy dagger on him)
Meanwhile the Angel puts on any angel gear you have – and gets a script – and a grown-up quietly appropriates the lamb (and thicket) that will be caught in the thicket

Narrator	And when everything was ready, Isaac said,
Isaac	'Dad, we've got everything for the journey except the lamb we're supposed to sacrifice.'
Narrator	And Abraham said,
Abraham	'God will provide the lamb, my son.'
Narrator	So Isaac put his sun hat on, and Abraham looked at him and felt very unhappy – but he had faith in God, so he said to his servants,
Abraham	'Pack those rucksacks!'

The children do this – make sure the wood and the matches are on the top

Narrator	Then two of Abraham's servants shouldered the rucksacks *(they do)* and off they went.
	The journey took for ever.

Abraham, Isaac and the servants lap the hall a couple of times

And all the time, Abraham got more and more worried – but he had faith in God, and trudged on.
Finally they got to the mountain. Abraham told his servants to stop at the bottom *(they sit down)* and he pulled the wood and matches out of the luggage, and gave the wood to Isaac to carry *(do all this)* and they went on alone.

If you've got a platform, Abraham and Isaac climb on to it – if not, they just move away from the servants

Narrator	Then Abraham made an altar *(bring forward a table)* and put the wood on the top and got the matches ready. And Isaac said,
Isaac	'Dad! Where's the lamb for the sacrifice?'
Narrator	And Abraham said,
Abraham	'God will provide the lamb, my son.'
Narrator	Then Abraham held Isaac, and pulled out his knife ...

Raise the knife – no acting from Isaac please! We don't want graphic terror

And an Angel rushed up ...

Make sure he/she does

	and said,
Angel	'STOP!

Don't touch the boy ...
Look! There is a lamb
caught in a thicket ...

Slide the lamb (and thicket) under the table – Isaac picks it up

sacrifice the lamb
instead!'

Narrator   So Abraham sacrificed
the lamb to God.

Place it on top of the bundle of wood

He and Isaac thanked
God for sending a lamb
(they kneel) and then got
up and went home.
And Abraham never
forgot that God *did*
provide him with a
lamb – *and* that God
never wanted anybody to
sacrifice a human being to Him, ever.

After the Story

Leader   That was a scary lesson for Abraham, wasn't it?
And I don't suppose Isaac liked it very much.
But it wasn't until Abraham thought he might have to kill his son
that he realized how important faith was.
He went on that journey, trusting God would provide – and God
did, He sent Abraham a lamb.

REHEARSAL

Practise your presentation for when you go back into church (see below).

BEFORE THE GOSPEL

Leader   Jesus talks about Faith in the Gospel today. Let's hear what He says.

THE GOSPEL PROCESSION

THE GOSPEL   *St Luke 17.5–6*

AFTER THE GOSPEL

Leader
The disciples asked Jesus to increase their faith and He replied,
'If your faith was *that* big *(pinch your fingers)* you could get a mulberry tree to throw itself into the sea!'
Jesus was joking of course – Christians aren't supposed to go round throwing trees about.
But He was serious about Faith. It really is very powerful.
With faith we can do amazing things – learn to swim, shoot goals, stand up to people, and **believe in God.**
God will give us the gift of Faith, if we ask Him. Let's do that now.

FINAL PRAYER

Ask the children to repeat this after you

> **Loving Father,**
> **Grant me the gift of Faith,**
> **That I may believe and trust in you**
> **My whole life long.**
> **Through Jesus our Lord. Amen**

BACK IN CHURCH

Child 1
Today we heard the story of Abraham and how God tested his faith.

Child 2
God asked Abraham to sacrifice his son Isaac.

Child 3
So Abraham took Isaac away to sacrifice him.

Child 4
It was a scary story, but all the way through Abraham had faith in God.

Child 5
And every time Abraham was frightened he said,
'The Lord will provide.'

Leader
And God did provide. He sent Abraham a lamb to sacrifice instead of his son.
The story helped us realize that, any time we needed it, God would provide. But we had to have faith.
So we prayed for – What did we pray for kids?

All the children   **The gift of Faith!**

Script 57 The Ten Lepers

Proper 23, Ordinary Time 28
(Sunday between 9 and 15 October)

St Luke 17.11–19

THEME

The ten lepers: on the one hand this is an introduction to the non-PC world of the first century and, on the other, it's about something that never changes – the importance of saying 'thank you'.

SET UP

- The liturgical colour is Green.
- A globe or a map of the world.
- Stick-on spots for the lepers.
- Ten handbells (or as many as you can muster).

Cast Leader 2 as Jesus in the drama, and see if you can get a grown-up or a teenager to be down the bottom of the room to send the Grateful Leper back.

Optional

- Stiff paper folded over to look like a card and colouring pens for the kids.

WELCOME *the children and lead them in* **The Sign of the Cross** ✠ **(p. xxxvi).**

THE KYRIE	Jesus, friend of sinners, have mercy on us, **Lord have Mercy**
	Jesus, healer of the sick, have mercy on us, **Christ have mercy**
	Jesus, help of Christians, have mercy on us, **Lord have mercy**

Ask the children to repeat **The Prayer for Forgiveness** *after you* (**p. xxxvi**).

OPENING PRAYER	Let's pray the Family Prayer of the Church. **Our Father … (see p. xxxvi).**

BEFORE THE GOSPEL

God's Family

Leader   *Produce the globe or the map*
                  OK, we're going to start off by looking at the world …
                  What can you tell me about it?
                  Can anyone tell me where Africa is?

Ask a kid to come and point it out

                  How about Italy?

Same business

                  Does anyone know what this country is? *(Point to Australia)*
                  And this one? *(Point to the USA)*
                  You're good at this!
                  Where do we live?

This is so easy that you can ask any child who hasn't shone so far to come and show you

Foreigners

Adapt as necessary …

                  OK, we live in England and we're called 'English'.
                  And anyone who doesn't live in England …

Wave your hand over the whole globe

                  is a foreigner.
                  But supposing you don't live in England, supposing you lived in
                  France …
                  Anyone know where France is?

Establish the location of France

                  Right, that's France.
                  What do we call the people who live in France? (**Frenchmen, the
                  French**) *(If someone says 'Frogs' clock up the comment but don't
                  riposte just yet)*
                  So if you lived in France, all these people are foreigners …

Indicate the rest of the globe

                  Including us.
                  Everyone in the whole world is surrounded by foreigners. People
                  who look different to us and speak different languages. Sometimes
                  they're so different that it gets on our nerves, and we call them names.

This is the moment to clock up any 'Frog' remark; if nobody said it, leave this out

(People only call the French names when they've beaten us at rugby or something.)

Actually it's better not to call foreigners names at all, because it makes us forget we're related.

You see, we've just called God, Our Father. And God is the Father of everyone on this planet.

God is the Father of the French, and the Indians, and the Germans, and the Americans, and the New Zealanders, and the Chinese *(point out all these nations as you mention them)* and He expects us to love one another and get on.

Being rude to the other guys really doesn't help.

Well, back in Jesus' time, nobody minded being rude to foreigners. The Jews were rude to the Romans, the Romans were rude to the Jews, and *everyone* was rude to unlucky people – like lepers.*

Lepers were people who had leprosy, their hands and feet got scrunched up, and their skin looked awful, *and* it was catching – so people kept away from them.

One day Jesus met 10 lepers – we're going to hear about that now.

Ten Lepers

Leader   First I need ten lepers.

If you haven't got ten kids, just make sure that the three or four you have got keep joining the queue to see Jesus so they make up ten

OK, well to show you're lepers, you need some spots ...

Put a few stick-on spots on each kid

And because leprosy is catching you can't sit near the others.
Over here you lepers!

Isolate the kids

If anyone comes near you'll have to ring a bell, to warn them you're a leper.

Hand out the bells

OK, now we're all set up.
Well one day, the ten lepers saw Jesus walking towards them.

Leader 2 (Jesus) approaches

They rang their bells ... *(They do)*
But Jesus didn't run away.

---

* Articulate this word very clearly; children have been known to come away from this session with the idea that the story is about ten leopards.

So the lepers came up to Jesus, knelt down, and asked Him to make them well …

The children kneel

And Jesus healed them all.

Count off the lepers one by one as Leader 2 removes the spots
Leader 1 impounds the bells
Clear a space down the hall

Leader 1   They were so happy to be cured that all ten rushed off home.

The children run to the other end of the hall

Except one. He stopped …

The grown-up (or teenager) at the other end stops one of the children

and came back.

The child does so

Why did he do that? Let's find out in today's Gospel.

THE GOSPEL PROCESSION

THE GOSPEL   *St Luke 17.11–19*

AFTER THE GOSPEL

Leader   Why did the leper come back? (**To say 'thank you'**)

The child who came back shakes hands with Leader 2 ('Jesus')

Did you notice something else? He wasn't just a leper, he was…

Look in the Bible again

A foreigner.
Jesus wasn't surprised because He liked everyone, but His disciples were amazed: fancy a foreigner saying 'thank you'!
I think that's a great Gospel. It's telling us that foreigners are fine, just like us – nicer than us sometimes – and that all of us ought to say …?
(**'Thank you'**)

BEFORE THE ACTIVITY

Leader   Actually we all say 'thank you' a lot, especially when we get presents and things, but sometimes we forget to say 'thank you' to God.
You know what it's like: we ask Him to help us out, and He does and – just like the lepers – we say, 'Wow! Great!' and whizz off – and forget to thank Him.

Let's put that right now.

ACTIVITY

Leader   What sort of things shall we thank God for?

See what they come up with – it's usually their family, sometimes their pets, open it up – what's the weather like? Thank God for the sun

> Oh is it raining? – Well, let's thank God for the rain – and for puddles – and for being able to splash about.
> How about our legs and our arms?
> Let's thank God for being able to run and play games. *(And so on)*

Select three of the ideas and ask the kids, if you've got time, to make a 'thank you' card illustrating one of them.
Dish out the paper and pens, and encourage the children to draw quite bold images, so they can be seen in church.
Or move straight on to constructing a Thanksgiving Prayer.
Establish three things you'd like to thank Jesus for (above) and insert them into the script you'll use Back in Church.

REHEARSAL

Practise your presentation for when you go back into church (see below).

FINAL PRAYER

Finish with a **Glory Be … (p. xxxvii).**

MUSIC

The classic 'All things bright and beautiful', *or the more grown-up* 'Now thank we all our God', *work well here.*

BACK IN CHURCH

Line up the children at the front of the church

Leader   Today we learnt how one leper came back to thank Jesus for healing him – and *we'd* like to thank Jesus too.

If the children have had time to make pictures, they hold them up at the appropriate petition

Child 1   Lord Jesus, we thank you for …
Child 2   Lord Jesus, we thank you for …
Child 3   Lord Jesus, we thank you for …
Everyone   **Amen**

Script 58   The Unjust Judge

Proper 24, Ordinary Time 29
(Sunday between 16 and 22 October)

St Luke 18.1–8

THEME

This can be a worrying parable for the literal minded – who is the Unjust Judge? God? No, it's a rattling good story. Children like the widow's persistence and have no trouble with the moral, which is, if a wicked Judge can hear the prayers of the poor, you can be quite sure that God hears them too. Of course there *is* the problem that God doesn't always answer our prayers in the way we'd like; that's an aspect of prayer we think about in this session.

SET UP

- The liturgical colour is Green.
- Pictures from the CD-Rom.
- Widow's letter for the Judge.
- Pack of cards and/or toy bricks.
- Make a Prayer Letter Box – an ordinary box, covered with coloured paper with a slit in the top and a label ('Prayers') on the front.
- Pen and plenty of small sheets of paper for you to write some prayers on.
- Ask the priest if it will be OK for you to hand this over when you come back into church.

WELCOME *the children and lead them in* **The Sign of the Cross** ✠ (p. xxxvi).

THE KYRIE   God our Father,
you hear the prayers of everyone who says they are sorry,
Lord have mercy
Lord have mercy

Lord Jesus, you came to Earth to teach us to pray to the Father,
Christ have mercy
Christ have mercy

Holy Spirit, you fill our hearts with the Father's love
Lord have mercy
Lord have mercy

Ask the children to repeat **The Prayer for Forgiveness** *after you* **(p. xxxvi).**

OPENING PRAYER	We're going to pray some of Psalm 120 together. The response is: God is our help **God is our help**

I lift up my eyes to the hills,
From whence shall come my help?
God is our help

My help shall come from the Lord
Who made Heaven and Earth
God is our help

The Lord is my guard and my shade
At my right hand He stands
God is our help

The Lord will guard us from all evil
Both now and for ever
God is our help

PRAYER

Leader   We've done a lot of praying this morning.
Can you guess how many prayers God gets every day?

Take anything that comes

Does He listen to them all? (**He certainly does**)
Does He answer them all? (**Yes**)
And does he always say 'yes'? (**No**)
How true, you get lots of answers from God – sometimes He says 'yes', or 'no', or 'wait' or – and this is the answer we're going to think about today – 'try again'.
Trying again is a good idea sometimes.
Has anyone here tried hard at something?

You may have to start the ball rolling; tell them about something you find difficult – riding a bike, working out your mobile phone ...
Make sure you or someone else mentions piano practice, or anything likely to raise a groan

Yup, I never liked it either – but I think it's worth it.
Let's practise something, how about building towers …?

Building Practice

Show the kids how to build a tower out of cards and/or bricks. Dish out building materials – bricks for the little ones as they'll find them easier. Encourage them to build high and, if they find it too easy, impose a time limit – 30 seconds should induce a sense of panic. Sympathize when a tower falls over and encourage them to try again. Admire the result, clear the cards and bricks away, and ask the kids to sit down.

Persistence

Leader	OK, I thought you did that really well, even when your tower fell down, you had another go.
	I think you're good at practising – tell me, how many of you dressed yourselves this morning?

Just take a show of hands

Wow, impressive.
And how many of you can do up your shoes?
Pretty good.
I bet you couldn't do that when you were a baby, you must have been practising …
God loves to see us practise: doing up shoelaces, playing the piano, even praying. He likes us to have a go and never give up.
He calls that 'persistence'.
Jesus told a story about persistence, we're going to hear it now.

THE GOSPEL PROCESSION

THE GOSPEL   *St Luke 18.1–8*

Use this version of the story; there are several sentences that come straight from the Bible

Leader	'The Unjust Judge'.
	Jesus told His disciples this story.
	Once upon a time there was a Judge.
CD58.1	Here he is – what do you think? Does he look a nice chap?
	No, you're right, he was horrible.
	He was called the Unjust Judge.
CD58.2	What he liked doing best was saying …
	NO! to people.
CD58.3	*This is a blank speech bubble. Leader 2 sticks it up and writes 'No!' in it*

Back in Jesus' time, Judges were the people that helped you with your business. If you needed to get a paper signed or something like that, you went to a Judge. That was the bit of the job this Judge hated.

CD58.2   If a rich man wanted some help buying a house, the Judge would say, *(point to speech bubble with 'no' in it)* 'NO!'

If a poor man needed help getting someone to pay back the money he was owed, the Judge would say – ?

CD58.4   *(Put up speech bubble, with 'Go away!' in it; get the children to call it out)*

If a priest asked for help, the Judge would say –

CD58.5   *(Speech bubble, same business)* 'GET LOST!'

In fact the people in his town said, 'That Judge cares for neither God nor man ...'

CD58.6   One day a poor widow asked for some help. *(Picture of the widow)* She needed to sort out her husband's will. As soon as the Judge saw her he shouted –

CD58.7   *(Speech bubble, same business)* 'CLEAR OFF!'

The widow said,

'Please help me', and the Judge said 'NO!'

He stamped off home, but the widow followed. She tried to talk to him – but he slammed the door.

CD58.8   Eventually the Judge went to bed *(picture)*; he was just falling asleep when he heard somebody outside calling up to him, 'Please help me.'

It was the widow again. What do you think he shouted down to her?

CD58.2   *(Speech bubble, same business)* (**NO!**) Quite right.

Next morning the Judge came down to breakfast feeling very grumpy.

Pick up prop letter; make sure the letter is folded

There was a letter by his breakfast – it was from the widow and it said ...

Get the children to tell you; open it up

('**Please help me**') You're right.

For the rest of that day, the widow followed the Judge about – beseeching him to help her and eventually the Judge couldn't

CD58.9   stand it any longer – 'AAAUGHH!!' he said.

'Even though I fear neither God nor anyone else yet because of all the trouble this widow is giving me I will see to it that she gets her rights; or else she will wear me out!'

CD58.10   And he called the widow over and said,

CD58.11	'OK, tell me what you want.' 'At last!' thought the widow – but out loud she said,
CD58.12	*(Last speech bubble)* 'Thank you very much!' Jesus told us that story to show how important it is never to give up. Even that awful Judge heard the widow eventually. Well of course God's not like the Judge, He loves helping people. But He does like you to be persistent and practise praying. Let's have a go.

Posting Prayers

Produce the Prayer Letter Box

Leader	We'll make some prayers together, post them in this, and ask the priest to offer them to God.

ACTIVITY

Write some prayers to the kids' dictation.
Talk it through. Don't discourage them from asking for things but extend the petitions to include other people's wants. Suggest other things they can talk to God about. He'd like to hear our news, good and bad, and we can thank Him for His gifts. Ask the children to fold the prayers up for you and post them in the box.

REHEARSAL

Practise your presentation for when you go back into church (see below).

FINAL PRAYER

The children have done a lot of praying, keep this short and
finish with a **Glory Be ... (p. xxxvii)**.

BACK IN CHURCH

The children go back into church with the Prayer Letter Box; three children and the Leader address the congregation

Child 1	Today we heard Jesus' story of the widow who made an Unjust Judge listen to her.
Child 2	We think Jesus liked the way she kept on praying and never gave up.
Child 3	So we thought we'd practise praying ourselves.
Leader	We've put our prayers in this box and we'd like *Name of Priest* to offer them to God on our behalf.

A child hands over the box to the priest

Script 59   The Pharisee and the Tax Collector

Proper 25, Ordinary Time 30
(Sunday between 23 and 29 October)

St Luke 18.9–14a

THEME

Jesus makes the difference between praying badly and praying well painfully clear in His parable of the Pharisee and the Tax Collector. Children, who are not afflicted with the sin of hypocrisy, usually find the story very funny. We use the Gospel as a springboard to think about some of the difficulties of praying.

SET UP

- The liturgical colour is Green.
- One large soft ball.
- Cast Leader 2 as the Pharisee and another grown-up, or older child, to be the Tax Collector. They should see the script beforehand.

WELCOME *the children and lead them in* **The Sign of the Cross** ✠ **(p. xxxvi).**

BEFORE THE KYRIE

A re-run of the liturgical action of knocking your chest (Script 35)

Leader   Before we say the Kyrie, I'd like us to look back over the week.
                Was there anything that went wrong?
                And, this is the important bit, was it your fault it went wrong?
                Let's think about that for a moment.

Pause, think about it yourself

                OK, we're going to confess our sins by saying, three times, that our
                sins are all our fault. And, as we say 'through my fault' we're going
                to thump our chest like this …

Clench your fist and knock your chest – enough to make a 'thump' noise

                That's to show we know whose fault it is.

Can you do that?
Let's try – repeat this prayer after me.

CONFESSION

Merciful God
Last week I sinned against you
Through my fault *(thump)*
Through my fault   *(thump)*
Through my own deliberate fault   *(thump)*
I am very sorry for all my sins
And ask you to forgive me
Through Jesus our Lord. Amen

THE KYRIE   Lord, have mercy
Lord, have mercy

Christ, have mercy
Christ, have mercy

Lord, have mercy
Lord, have mercy

Ask the children to repeat **The Prayer for Forgiveness** *after you* (**p. xxxvi**).

OPENING   We thank you Father
PRAYER   For blotting out our sins
          As though we'd never done them.
          Help us to do better in the coming week.
          For Jesus' sake. **Amen**

BEFORE THE GOSPEL

PRAYER

Leader 1   Today we've already prayed in two ways.
           We've *said* our prayers *(point to your mouth)* and we've *acted*
           our prayers. *(Thump your chest)*
           Sometimes of course we *think* our prayers *(point to your head)* – it's
           all going on in there.
           When we go to church we often see people praying by themselves.
           How do you know if somebody is praying?

See what the children suggest – some signs are the person is kneeling, or has his/her head bowed, hands together, eyes shut, or he/she may be lighting a candle or saying the rosary

> Can you hear what they are saying? (**Not usually**)
> Well, just for a moment we are going to hear two people praying.
> Have a listen and see what you think of their prayers.

Leader 2 and whoever is going to play the Tax Collector come forward

Leader 2   *Standing straight and looking up to Heaven*
Dear God, thank you for making me good.
Thank you for making me so much better than all the ghastly people round me …

Survey the kids for a moment and look up again

> … especially the people in this room.
> I am really glad I am such a nice person.
> Thanks again. Amen.

Second Person   *Bowing his head*
Lord, have mercy on me. Amen.

Leader 1   Which one do you think is praying properly?

Take all answers, but don't comment

> Well we're going to hear what Jesus thought.
> In His time people used to pray out loud, so you *could* hear what they were saying – and Jesus told a story about two men who went to pray.
> One of them was a Pharisee …

Leader 2 looks up

> That's me!

Leader 1   A Pharisee was somebody who obeyed all the Jewish rules.

To Leader 2 aka the Pharisee

> Do you keep all the rules?

Pharisee   Yup!
Leader 1   How many are there?
Pharisee   Six hundred and thirteen.
Leader 1   Blimey! And do you keep all 613?
Pharisee   Yes, every one – I'm really good at it.
Leader 1   *(Dubiously)* OK …
Well the other person in Jesus' story was this chap.

Bring forward the Tax Collector

Leader 1	Hi, what's your job?
Tax Collector	I'm a tax collector.
Leader 1	You mean you go round getting money out of people?
Tax Collector	That's right.
Leader 1	Do they like you?
Tax Collector	Not very much …
Leader 1	I bet they don't.

To the children Let's hear the story Jesus told about these people.

THE GOSPEL PROCESSION

THE GOSPEL   *St Luke 18.9–14a*

The Pharisee and the Tax Collector flank Leader 1

Leader 1	One day Jesus told a story to some people who thought they were better than everybody else. 'Once,' Jesus said, 'two men went into the Temple to pray.' One was a Pharisee and the other was a Tax Collector. The Pharisee stood down the front, looked up to Heaven, and prayed …
Pharisee	I thank you, God, that I am not like other people. I thank you I am not greedy or dishonest – and I'm really pleased that I'm not like this Tax Collector here. As you know, I am always praying to you and keeping your rules. Amen.
Leader 1	But the Tax Collector stood at the back. He didn't think he was good enough to look up to Heaven, so he kept his head down and just stood there, pounding his chest, and saying,
Tax Collector	*(Pounding his chest)* Lord, have mercy on me!
Leader 1	Then Jesus said, 'And, when the two men went home, it was the *Tax Collector*, not the Pharisee, who was pleasing to God.'

AFTER THE GOSPEL

| Leader 1 | So which of the two men was praying properly? (**The tax collector**) You're right. I don't think the Pharisee had got the hang of praying. What was he doing wrong? |

Take all answers, and sum up

It's not a good idea to boast when you pray – or be horrible about other people. Still, at least the Pharisee was having a go at prayer – even if he got it wrong.

After all, praying can be difficult. Jesus' friends thought it was.

He was always telling them to keep trying.

I think one of the problems is you say a prayer, and it sort of disappears.

Look up, as if you've just said a prayer

Where did it go? Is it real? Well, actually, prayer is as real as ...

Produce the ball

this football ...

Bounce it   You just can't see it so well.

Prayer Football

Leader   Let's play prayer football.
Think about praying; sometimes it feels as difficult as football.
You want to pray – and something gets in the way. It might be laziness, or the TV or a bad mood. Something stops you.
Look, here's Heaven.

Set up two chairs as goalposts

And here's our prayer.

Bounce the ball

And here's whatever it is that's trying to stop our prayer.

Get a large grown-up or teenager to act like a panto villain, and put him or her in front of the goal

And here's you trying to get a prayer through.

Ask a child to wham that ball in – the goalie misses it completely

Fantastic, that prayer got through!

Let all the children have a go. Block a few prayers (ensure they get in on a subsequent attempt) and make sure the little ones score a goal, however weedy the shot ...

REHEARSAL

Practise your presentation for when you go back into church (see below).

FINAL PRAYER

Gather the children round you

Leader   Can anyone remember the prayer Jesus gave to the Tax
Collector? (**Lord, have mercy on me, a sinner**)
We say that prayer every Mass, it's the Kyrie. We'll say it now as the response to Psalm 33.

Lord have mercy
Lord have mercy

I will bless the Lord at all times
The humble shall hear me, and be glad.
Lord have mercy

The Lord is close to the broken-hearted
Those who are unhappy, He will save.
Lord have mercy

The Lord saves the souls of His servants
Those who hide in Him will be safe.
Lord have mercy

Finish with a **Glory Be ... (p. xxxvii)**.

BACK IN CHURCH

Go back in with the Pharisee and the Tax Collector

Child 1	In the Gospel today Jesus told a story about a Pharisee.

The Pharisee steps forward

Child 2	And a Tax Collector.

The Tax Collector steps forward

Child 3	They both went to the Temple to pray – and the Pharisee prayed like this.
Pharisee	*(Looking straight up to Heaven)* I thank you, God, that I am not like other men. I thank you I am not greedy or dishonest – and I'm really pleased that I'm not like this Tax Collector here. As you know, I am always praying to you and keeping your rules. Amen.
Child 4	But the Tax Collector kept his head down. He just stood there, pounding his chest, and saying,
Tax Collector	*(Pounding his chest)* Lord, have mercy on me!
Leader	Jesus said that only one of those chaps was pleasing to God.
To the children	Which one was it?
All the children	**The Tax Collector!**

Script 60   The Man in the Tree

4 before Advent, Ordinary Time 31
(Sunday between 30 October and 5 November if not kept as All Saints Sunday)

St Luke 19.1–10

THEME

Zacchaeus is another story we only find in St Luke's Gospel. Children sympathize with Zacchaeus and should have no difficulty in telling you, at length, how annoying it is to be small. The most interesting thing about Zacchaeus, however, is not his size, or his tree climbing, but his sturdy determination to be good. St Luke says he 'stood his ground' when his neighbours complained about him, and promised to amend his ways.

SET UP

- The liturgical colour is Green.
- Three shiny wrapped sweets.
- Blu Tack (or similar).
- A small step-ladder or chair strong enough for a child to stand on.
- Pictures from the CD-Rom (when copying up the 'Cross Faces' **(CD60.7)** make enough for every child to have one for the presentation at the end).
- A grown-up (preferably a tall one) to help you in the session before the Gospel by falling down when you ask. Find out, before the children appear, how high you can stick the sweets on the wall (see below).
- Something to play music on (if you opt for 'Musical Statues', see below).

WELCOME *the children and lead them in* **The Sign of the Cross** ✠ **(p. xxxvi).**

BEFORE THE KYRIE

Gather the room together, grown-ups and children, and ask them to think back over the week. Think about the people we know – our family, other children at school, people at work

Leader	How have we got on with them? Were there any times we were unkind? Or rude? Let's get rid of that now by telling God we are sorry.

THE KYRIE   Lord Jesus, we are sorry for the times we have been unkind
Lord have mercy
Lord have mercy

Lord Jesus, we are sorry for the times we have forgotten you
Christ have mercy
Christ have mercy

Lord Jesus, we thank you for always listening to us, and forgiving us, when we do wrong
Lord have mercy
Lord have mercy

Ask the children to repeat **The Prayer for Forgiveness** *after you* (**p. xxxvi**).

OPENING
PRAYER
The Opening Prayer is taken from Psalm 144
Ask the children to stand as we say it together
The response is:

I will bless your name for ever
I will bless your name for ever

I will give you glory O God
I will bless your name for ever.
I will bless you day after day
I will bless your name for ever

The Lord is kind and full of compassion,
Slow to anger and abounding in love.
How good the Lord is to all His creatures
I will bless your name for ever

The Lord supports all who fall
And raises all who are bowed down
I will bless your name for ever

BEFORE THE GOSPEL

Leader   I like that psalm – especially the last bit, when it says
God helps people who have fallen down.

Can you fall down? Let's see ...
1, 2, 3 FALL!

Everyone, including the grown-up you've chosen, falls to the ground

Brilliant.
Can you jump up again? WAIT –
Let's see ...
1, 2, 3 UP!

The kids jump up – the grown-up doesn't

Fantastic! – Oh, no, I can see *Name* is having difficulty.
Let's give him a hand ...

Pull him or her up

	Why couldn't you get up, *Name*?
Grown-up	Well, the trouble with being big is you often get stiff as well ...
Leader	You think little people can bounce up and down?
Grown-up	They certainly can – watch ...
	OK kids, down! *(They all crash down again)*
	UP! *(And leap up)*
	Down! *(And so on ...)*
	You see it's easy for them.
Leader	OK, being small has its advantages, but it's not always fun being little. Watch this ...

Take a sweet, put some Blu Tack on it, and stick it well above kids' height. Ask the children to reach for it; they can go on tiptoe but no jumping. This is all about being little, so bar any lanky teenagers. After a frustrating couple of minutes, ask:

Do you think you could get it if you jumped? (**Yes!**)
OK –

Place the sweet higher, even more out of reach. Choose some kids to jump for it – make sure you ask the small ones, this has to be a no-win exercise

	How about you, *Name*?
Grown-up	Easy!

Grabs the sweet (disappointed howl from the kids)

Leader	It's really tough being little sometimes.
	Tell me, is there anything else you can't do when you're small?

Throw it open – you can't reach books on shelves or things in the supermarket, door handles are too high, you can't see when a grown-up sits in front of you, you get squashed in crowds, you can't ride motorbikes, you can't sit at the front of a car ... The list is endless

Yes I can see it's tough.
Still being little must make you smart.
Look, I'll put up another sweet.

Do so, on a level with the last one

Can anyone think of a way they *could* reach it?
Hands up only …

The children will almost certainly say 'stand on something', but lean on the chair or the step-ladder if they hesitate

All right, have a go …

Some lucky child now gets the sweet

So, though it's tough being small, you can often get round it. Jesus once met a very small man – we're going to hear about him now.

THE GOSPEL PROCESSION

THE GOSPEL *St Luke 19.1–10*

Tell the story using the pictures on the CD-Rom – you could ask a child to place Zacchaeus in his tree.

Optional Paraphrase

Leader	One day, Jesus decided to visit Jericho.
	In that town lived a greedy Tax Collector whose name was Zacchaeus. He took more money in taxes than he was supposed to
CD60.1	– and kept it for himself.
	Nobody liked him very much.
	Zacchaeus was very small so, when Jesus walked through his town
CD60.2	he couldn't see Him: there was always somebody in the way.
	So Zacchaeus ran ahead of the crowd, and climbed a sycamore tree.
CD60.3	'This is great,' he thought. 'When Jesus comes down this street,
	I'll be able to see Him as He walks underneath.'
	And sure enough he could see Jesus perfectly as He came down the road. But, when Jesus got to the tree, He stopped, looked up …
CD60.4	and saw Zacchaeus.
	'Hey Zacchaeus!' He said. 'Get out of that tree and run home – I want to have a meal with you today!'
	The crowd couldn't believe their ears, but Zacchaeus jumped out of the tree and ran home as fast as possible. And when Jesus arrived, the meal was ready and so was Zacchaeus. He welcomed Jesus into his

CD60.5

home and they sat down to eat. But all the neighbours complained: 'Fancy Jesus going to the house of a sinner like him!' they said. Zacchaeus didn't care what they said. He stood his ground and said, 'Jesus, you know how rich I am, well, I am going to give half my money to the poor. And if I have cheated anybody, I'm going to pay him back four times what I owe him.'

CD60.6

And Jesus said, 'Zacchaeus, from today you and your family will be blessed. I was sent by God to look for people like you – and I'm very glad I found you!'

AFTER THE GOSPEL

Leader

Run through the Gospel
Sort out Zacchaeus' job and what he was doing wrong.

He overcharged people on their tax bills and hung on to the extra money*

Zacchaeus was a thief and a cheat, no wonder nobody liked him. He must have been amazed when Jesus invited Himself round to supper.
Do you think Jesus liked Zacchaeus?

Take all answers – I think He did – He probably loved seeing Zacchaeus up his tree

Jesus knew Zacchaeus was a cheat, but that didn't stop Him loving him.
What did Zacchaeus promise? (**To give half his money away to the poor and repay four times anything he owed**)
Yes, everyone was yelling at him, nobody believed him, but the Gospel says Zacchaeus 'stood his ground' and made his promise to Jesus.
No wonder Jesus blessed him.
I wonder if we could stand as firm as Zacchaeus?

GAMES

If you've got the time, play any game that involves standing still. In small rooms this could be Musical Statues; *larger rooms can accommodate* Stuck in the Mud.

---

* In Zacchaeus' defence, one may point out to older children that Tax Collectors didn't get a wage; they were expected to overcharge and live off the surplus. The point was that Zacchaeus overcharged far too much. He was a wealthy man.

Musical Statues

Play some music and either let the children run round or get them to dance on the spot. When the music stops they have to freeze. One wobble and they're out. The winner is the most rock solid.

Stuck in the Mud

One kid is 'It'. The other children run round and, if caught, have to stand stock still, legs apart, hands stretched out. They can only be released if someone crawls between their legs. If they are caught more than once, they are out. The game finishes when the whole room (which means whoever is left) is standing still.

BEFORE THE FINAL PRAYER

Dish out the cross faces from the CD-Rom to the other grown-ups (**CD60.7**), *big kids, anyone around: they hold them behind their backs. One Leader has the Jesus face* (**CD60.8**). *Ask the children to sit down*

Leader   Let's imagine what it was like to be Zacchaeus.
There he was, very small, looking up at huge people like *Name*, and *Name* and *Name* …

The grown-ups come up as you name them

And when he looked round all he saw were these sorts of faces.

The grown-ups hold up the cross faces – don't use them like masks, it unnerves sensitive kids. Do some patter as the faces go up

Leader   Gosh, look at him, he's not happy … Nor is she, Zacchaeus must have really cheated her. Look at her, she doesn't like him either …
And the more people didn't like him, the more Zacchaeus didn't like them. But one day he saw a face that was quite different.

Hold up the Jesus face

Who was that? (**Jesus**)
Exactly. And as soon as Zacchaeus saw Jesus' face he knew that Jesus loved him. So he thought he'd have a go at loving other people too. Let's think about that as we pray.

FINAL   Lord Jesus,
PRAYER   Thank you for loving Zacchaeus.
Help us this week to try and be like you
Help us to be kind to people
To smile at them,

Play with them,
And make them feel we like them,
For your Name's sake. **Amen**

Dish out the faces to the children and run through the presentation to take back to church (below).

BACK IN CHURCH

The children line up down the front with the faces held behind their backs; the child with the Jesus face stands in the middle

Leader   Today we heard about Zacchaeus the Tax Collector.
            He was a thief and a cheat and, everywhere he went, people looked at him with this sort of expression on their faces.

The children hold up the cross faces

They didn't like him.
And Zacchaeus didn't like them either.
But one day he met Jesus. And Jesus looked at him like this.

A child holds up the Jesus face

Zacchaeus could see Jesus loved him – so he thought he'd have a go at loving other people as well.

The cross faces go back behind the kids' backs

So we thought *we'd* have a go at loving people this week.

Hello Zacchaeus!

(CD60.4)   (CD60.8)

Sample cartoons for this script

Script 61 The God of Abraham

3 before Advent, Ordinary Time 32
(Sunday between 6 and 12 November)

St Luke 20.37–38

THEME

Today Jesus discusses the Resurrection of the Dead with a Jewish group, the
Sadducees, who don't believe in the idea. The main story – the one about the
widow who married seven times – rarely catches the children's interest. However,
the status of the dead, where they are – from God's point of view – does intrigue
them, so this session uses the last two verses of the Gospel to explore this idea.

SET UP

- The liturgical colour is Green.
- Pictures from the CD-Rom.
- Black and red marker pens.
- A long strip of card or paper on which to construct a time line. Draw a line along
  its base and mark it up in centuries from 0 BC to 2013. (Template on CD-Rom.)
- Pens and paper for the children.
- Scissors, glue or Sellotape.
- A long washing line.
- A large candle.

Warn the clergy that you'll be coming in with a time line; one of them might like to
comment on the pictures.

WELCOME *the children and lead them in* **The Sign of the Cross** ✠ (p. xxxvi).

THE KYRIE   Lord Jesus, for the times we have been unkind,
Lord have mercy
Lord have mercy

Lord Jesus, for the times we have forgotten you,
Christ have mercy
Christ have mercy

Lord Jesus, thank you for listening to us, and forgiving us,
Lord have mercy
Lord have mercy

Ask the children to repeat **The Prayer for Forgiveness** *after you* (**p. xxxvi**).

OPENING PRAYER

Leader   This morning we're going to say part of Psalm 27;
                the response is:
                The Lord is my light
                The Lord is my light

                The Lord is my light, whom then shall I fear?
                The Lord is my light

                The Lord is my strength, of whom shall I be afraid?
                The Lord is my light

                In the time of trouble, He shall hide me in His tent
                The Lord is my light

                I believe I shall see the goodness of the Lord in the land of the living.
                The Lord is my light

BEFORE THE GOSPEL

Dates

Leader   Today we're going to talk about time.
                We all live in time: if you haven't lived for very long, you're quite
                small like *Name (choose a baby or the youngest child present)*, and
                if you've been alive for ages, you're unbelievably old and venerable
                like *Name.*

Any grown-up will do; they don't have to be very old

                Most of us have been alive for years and years – who's been alive for
                ten years? *(Register the show of hands)*
                It's a long time, isn't it?
                Actually five years is pretty good – anyone been alive five years?
                That's impressive.

*Respond to any kids in the room who are dying to tell you how old they are. You may
have to resort to 'Hands up anyone who's four' and go through every number from
one to twelve*

OK, let's have some birthdays – *Name (any child under twelve)*, can you tell me when your birthday is? *(Write it up)*
Do you know what year you were born?

The kid may or may not know; work it out and write that up. Run this with a couple of other under-twelves. Look at the dates

Goodness, everyone so far has been born in the 21st century. Is there anyone here who was born in the 20th century?

Choose kids in preference to adults, but adults will naturally put up their hands
Write up the year of their birth – and then choose a willing adult to amaze us with the information that they were born in the 1970s (or whenever)

OK, does anyone remember a relation born back in the 19th century?

Adults can usually dredge up a great grandma or great great grandma – write that date down

Look at the dates

Leader   So we've already got back to the 19th century – I think what we need is a time line!

ACTIVITY

Time Line

Unroll the large paper strip across two or three tables – and produce the CD-Rom pictures (**CD61.1**); *they are of various historical personages (Nebuchadnezzar, Queen Elizabeth I, Abraham, William the Conqueror, etc.) spanning the centuries. Ask the kids to stick them on the line. There are a few gaps. Look at them …*

Leader   We need Romans, and cavemen, Ancient Egyptians, knights in armour, people from the Bible, and us (that's very important) and, goodness, look at 0 AD, we need Jesus!

Share out these jobs among the kids; cut out their pictures and stick them on. Encourage the children to add people in the gaps – pop groups are fine, so are footballers. No dinosaurs – or you'll run into trouble as you discuss the dead (below)
Guidance on dates is provided on the CD-Rom template. Keep the picture of the present-day child back
Add a few specific dates, if anyone knows them: the classic 1066 for William the Conqueror for example. If the children are interested, show how year numbers decrease as we go back towards the time of Jesus' birth (AD) and increase again in the centuries before He arrived (BC). Admire the result

Leader   Where are we on this line?

Indicate the year in which you find yourself doing this session and stick on the picture of a present-day child

Leader	So, all this *(sweep your hand along the time line)* is the past? (**Yes**) That's amazing, how many people do you think are now alive on this line? *(20th and 21st century people – more or less)* So all these people *(sweep your hand along from the 19th century)* are dead? (**Yes**) Does God know about them? (**Yes**)

Extend the line from 2013 and mark in 2014, 2050, 2100

Leader	I'm putting in years that haven't happened yet. There will be loads of people alive here *(indicate 2100)* but we can't draw them; we don't know who they are. Does God know about them? (**Yes**) How?

Various answers – He knows everything, some children know God lives outside time

Leader	Let's think about that.

Extend a washing line along the room

OK, here's another time line.
Name, (any child) you stand here *(near the end of the line)* that's now. *Name*, you be Queen Victoria – round about there.
Name, you be Shakespeare, round about there,
and *Name*, you can be Jesus in the middle …

Carry on until you get to the caveman

Leader	OK, I'm going to be with *Name* at 2013 *(or whenever)*, let's turn round – how many people can we see? (**Hardly anyone – just the person beside us**) If we bend *(do so)* we can just see the caveman at the end – goodness, it's Fred Flintstone – and if we turn *(do so)* we can't see anyone in the future at all. But God – *Name, (Leader 2)* could you be God for a moment?

Leader 2 steps very deliberately away from the line

Leader 1	But God can see the whole line. He can even – *Name*, jump into the future for me, will you? – see the future. That's because God is outside time. And watch this, God can walk up and down the line …

Leader 2 does this

Leader 1	to be close to His people whenever He wants to.

You see, from God's point of view, Adam and Moses and William the Conqueror aren't people who lived centuries ago, lost in time; they are as near to Him as you and me – and that kid who hasn't been born yet.

Jesus talked about time and the dead in the Gospel today. Let's hear it.

THE GOSPEL PROCESSION

THE GOSPEL   *St Luke 20.37–38*

Optional Paraphrase

Jesus was talking to people about the dead. He said, 'Moses showed that the dead are raised to life when he wrote down the story of the Burning Bush. In that story, God spoke to Moses from the bush and said, "I am the God of Abraham, the God of Isaac and the God of Jacob." All those men were dead when Moses heard God – but God is the God of the living, not the dead, as far as God is concerned, Abraham, Isaac and Jacob are alive. For God all people are alive.'

AFTER THE GOSPEL

Leader   So Jesus said, although we put Abraham way back on our time line, from God's point of view he's as close to God as me or you – and he's still alive.

Where do you think Abraham lives now? (**Heaven**)

Exactly.

For the moment we can't see those who have died but we trust that God looks after them and we can remember them in our prayers.

REHEARSAL

Practise your presentation for when you go back into church (see below).

FINAL PRAYER

Ask the children to sit down as you get out the large candle and a red and black marker pen

Leader   God is the Lord of time.

Every Easter we remember that when we mark up the Paschal candle – that's the big candle that stands by the font.

That's done by the priest who says a very ancient prayer and marks the candle with a cross, some letters and the year as he does so.

Watch me as I do it ...

The Paschal Candle

Pick up the red marker pen

Christ yesterday and today, the beginning and the end.

Mark the cross in red on the candle; take up the black pen

'A' and 'Z'.*

Mark A and Z at the top and bottom of the cross
Follow the text illustration to get the numbers right

All time belongs to Him.

Mark the first number of the year

And all ages.

Mark the second number of the year

To Him be glory and power.

Mark the third number of the year

Through every age and for ever.

Mark the fourth number of the year

Amen.

Leader   Let's finish by saying that prayer together.

Ask the children to repeat this after you

Christ yesterday and today,
the beginning and the end
A and Z
The beginning and the end
All time belongs to Him
And all ages
To Him be glory and power
Through every age and for ever. Amen

---

* This should of course be Alpha and Omega (the A and Z of the Greek alphabet). Since the children are in danger of suffering from information overload, the English letters have been used. However, if your kids know about Alpha and Omega, put them in. The Greek A is the same as ours, Omega looks like this: Ω.

BACK IN CHURCH

The children come in with their time line rolled up

Leader	Today we thought about time – the present, the past and the future. And we made a time line …

The children unroll their time line; go (briefly) through some of the highlights with the kids – or encourage your priest to do so

Leader	Kids – does God know about all these people?
Children	**Yes!**
Leader	Even the dead ones?
Children	**Yes!**
Leader	What about the ones we can't see? The ones in the future? Does He know about them too?
Children	**Yes!**
Leader	Why?
Child 1	Because God is outside time.
Child 2	He is the God of the Living, and to Him everyone is alive.

Sample Time Line

(CD61.1)

Script 62 Troubled Times

2 before Advent, Ordinary Time 33
(Sunday between 13 and 20 November)

St Luke 21.5, 12–19

THEME

As we near the end of St Luke's Gospel, Jesus speaks about the grim times ahead:
the fall of Jerusalem, the persecution of the Early Church, and (finally) the End of
the World. Even so, the Gospel (naturally) ends on an upbeat note and reminds us
of another of Jesus' sayings, 'In this world you will have trouble, but take heart,
I have overcome the world!'

SET UP

- The liturgical colour is Green.
- Tape a line along the floor.
- Copy *'Temple in Jerusalem in Jesus' time'* into an internet search engine for an
  image of the Temple that Jesus knew. Then type in *'Wailing Wall'* to bring up an
  image of all that is left of the 1st century Temple. Print both images – or bring them
  along on your laptop.
- Several small holy objects: little crosses, crosses on chains, pocket-sized Bibles,
  prayer cards, holy medals, icons, rosaries – anything that can fit into a pocket.
- Ask three or four older kids to stow these objects away in their pockets, or round
  their necks. Tell them they'll be searched by Customs later on and you'd like them
  to look brave if they're arrested. Show them how to do it. Feet apart, arms folded.

WELCOME *the children and lead them in* **The Sign of the Cross** ✠ **(p. xxxvi).**

KYRIE	Heavenly Father,
	For the times we have forgotten you
	Lord have mercy
	Lord have mercy

Lord Jesus
For the times we have been unloving
Christ have mercy
Christ have mercy

Holy Spirit
For the times we have forgotten to listen to you
Lord have mercy
Lord have mercy

Ask the children to repeat **The Prayer for Forgiveness** *after you* (**p. xxxvi**).

OPENING	Lord Jesus
PRAYER	Help of Christians
	Keep us faithful to you,
	And the Church,
	And bring us safely to your Heavenly Kingdom
	To live with you for ever. **Amen**

Standing Firm

Leader   Right, in the Gospel today Jesus tells His friends to 'stand firm'. Let's have a go …

Epic Push

Range a couple of older kids, of about the same weight and height, each side of the taped line. Their right foot should touch the line and the other kid's foot. The left foot can be placed as they wish – but must remain stationary. The kids put their hands together and try, by pushing or pulling, to get the other child's foot to move. Limit the game to 30 seconds a go, even if there's no clear winner. Congratulate the children however they did

Leader   OK, I can see most of you are rock solid. Let's move on and look at this …

The Temple

Gather the children round your laptop or show them a picture of the Temple

Leader   This is a building Jesus knew very well – the Temple in Jerusalem. It was like a huge church, and Jesus loved it.
He and His friends went round it one day and His disciples were amazed at the beauty of the building. But Jesus, as He looked at the stones, felt sad. We'll hear why in today's Gospel.

THE GOSPEL PROCESSION

GOSPEL *St Luke 21.5, 12–19*

Optional Paraphrase

Jesus was in the Temple with His disciples. They were admiring the building and pointing out the beautiful stonework and the gifts people had left there. But Jesus said, 'Do you see these stones? There will come a time when not a stone will be left on top of another – they will all be knocked down.'

Then He said, 'Before that happens, you will be in trouble. You will be arrested and put in prison. Kings and rulers will judge you and you will be betrayed by your own families. But do not be afraid. I will give you the wisdom to know what to say and not a hair on your head will be lost. Stand firm and you will be saved.'

AFTER THE GOSPEL

Leader	What did Jesus say would happen to the Temple? (**It would be destroyed**)
	What Jesus said came true. Forty years later,* in AD 70 the Romans destroyed the whole building. This is all that is left of the Temple today.

Show them a picture of the Wailing Wall

This is just one of the outer walls of the Temple, not the building itself. It's all gone.

Do you think that could ever happen to our church?

See what they think

Well, I don't suppose the Romans will knock down St *Name*, but even so, it won't last for ever – because nothing does.

God likes to give us things, but He makes some of them breakable. The breakable things are the things around us.

Rap the table, hold up a book, or a toy – anything that comes to hand

Books, toys, buildings, even the world itself, will come to an end one day.

Fortunately we don't really need the breakable things. It's the unbreakable stuff we've got to hang on to.

Let's see if we can sort out what we need and what we don't.

Pick up the Gospel

---

* The Temple, and most of Jerusalem, was destroyed in AD 70.

After Jesus foretold the destruction of the Temple, He said, 'You too will be arrested and put in prison.'

That's what happened to His friends. Peter and James were arrested – and probably most of the others.

Well, Christians are quite safe in England, but in some countries they're persecuted. Let's get on a plane and see where we land up.

A Trip Abroad

Form the kids up to Follow my Leader. Put a teenager or bright kid at the front, arms out, and take them on an exciting flight round the room. Don't forget to turn some sharp corners, and go through a spot of turbulence. Make an emergency landing and hit the ground with a bump

Leader   Oh dear, this is a country that doesn't like Christians. We're in for it. Let's line up at Customs and, remember, stand firm!

Put the kids with rosaries etc. at the front of the queue

Customs

Enter Leader 2 – the Customs Officer

Leader 1   Rats, this is the meanest Customs Officer in the world.

Leader 2 aka the Customs Officer

Make this a comic act, you don't want to frighten the little kids. The Officer can't believe his/her bad luck as more Christians turn up

Hallo, what's your name?

Where do you come from? *Chiswick! (Insert your home town)*

Oh no, not that awful place. Are you a Christian? (**Yes!**)

I thought as much …

Frisks the kid – just a pat on the pockets

What have we got here? A cross! Right, I'll have that!

Puts it on a nearby table

And a Bible!

OK, mate, you're under arrest – stand over there.

Next kid comes forward

Where do *you* come from? Not *Chiswick* as well!

I'll never get home for tea … *etc.*

Once the kids who've got Christian contraband have been arrested, Leader 2 waves an exhausted hand at the others and lets them through

Ask the other children to sit down, and bring the detainees forward

Leader   These chaps are in big trouble. But look at them,
                standing upright and looking brave.
                They've lost their Bibles and crosses ...

Pass your hand through the pile on the table

                but they've got something we can't see.
                Has anyone ever seen a Baptism?
                The priest makes a mark on the baby's forehead – like this.

Inscribe a cross on a child's forehead with your thumb

                Did you see what that was? (**A cross**)
                Yes and, though you can't see it, that cross stays on your forehead
                for the rest of your life. It's the badge of a Christian.
                And, even more wonderful, all Christians have the Holy Spirit in
                their hearts. *(Touch your chest)* So these kids have got Jesus' cross
                on their heads, and God Himself in their hearts. Nobody can take
                that away from them.
                It doesn't matter if our crosses are taken away from us, or our
                churches fall down, because we have the cross on our heads and
                God in our hearts.
                God is unbreakable, nothing can destroy Him.
To the detainees I think you'll be OK, guys, come and sit with us.

FINAL PRAYER

Ask the children to sit in a prayer circle

Leader   We don't need to put anything in the middle of the circle this week.
                We'll make the Sign of the Cross instead and – though we can't see
                it – Jesus' cross will stay in front of us as we pray.

Lead the children in the Sign of the Cross

                ✠ **In the Name of the Father, and of the Son
                and of the Holy Spirit. Amen**

                Lord Jesus
                You said that,
                'In this world you will find trouble.'
                But then you said,
                'Take heart, I have overcome the world.'
                Help us never to be afraid, but to stand firm
                And trust in you, now and always. **Amen**

REHEARSAL

Practise your presentation for when you go back into church (see below).

BACK IN CHURCH

The children stand in a line down the front

Leader   In the Gospel today we heard Jesus warn us that, one day, buildings
                would fall down, cities collapse and the world itself would end.

Child 1   Jesus told us to stand firm.

The children stand with their feet apart and their arms folded

Child 2   And He said, 'In this world you will find trouble.'

Child 3   But then He said, 'Take heart …

All the children   … I have overcome the world.'

Script 63   Christ the King

Last Sunday before Advent, Last Sunday of the Year
(Sunday between 20 and 26 November)

St Luke 23.35–43

THEME

The Christian year finishes with the glorious feast of Christ the King. This session uses the traditional story of the Harrowing of Hell to discover what sort of king Jesus is.

SET UP

- The liturgical colour is White or Gold.
- Pictures from the CD-Rom.
- Access some pictures of the Crucifixion and the harrowing of Hell (sometimes called Jesus' Descent to Limbo).

  In the Crucifixion you will be looking for the two thieves and the inscription over Jesus' head. Normally the inscription just says INRI (which is shorthand for the Latin phrase 'Iesus Nazarenus Rex Iudaeorum' – Jesus of Nazareth the King of the Jews). But the *Crucifixion* by Velasquez has the inscription written out in full and it is worth trying to find a copy of this painting in an artbook to show the children.

  The National Gallery in London also has a picture which shows part of the full inscription. It's called the *Deposition* and it's by the Master of St Bartholomew.

  Also at the National Gallery there is a *Crucifixion* by the Master of Delft which shows the two thieves on either side of Jesus.

  The best two pictures of Jesus' descent to Hell are by Jacopo Bellini and Duccio, though there is an interesting *Descent to Limbo* in the National Gallery by Giovanni dal Ponte. It's at the top of a picture, in the round bit, and shows Jesus is in the centre, welcoming people out of Hell – who are coming up from the right – while, on the left, the devil has collapsed beneath the broken gates of Hell. It's very easy to find.

  If you access these pictures on the Internet, follow the guidelines on page xiv.
- A Bible, bookmarked at St John 19.
- Paper, pens, scissors and glue for the children to make their Christ the King triptych.

- Three large pieces of card, cut out in the triptych shape – see the template on the CD-Rom.
- Tell your priests that the children are coming in with a major work of art.

WELCOME *the children and lead them in* **The Sign of the Cross** ✠ **(p. xxxvi).**

BEFORE THE KYRIE

Show the children a painting of Jesus on the Cross. Talk them through it

Leader   It's a very simple picture – Jesus alone on the cross – but look at the inscription above His head.

Show them the inscription **(CD63.10)**

What does it say?

Go down the lines one by one – Hebrew at the top, then Greek, then Latin

Well, I don't know any of those languages *(adapt as necessary)* but I know what this means, because it's in the Bible …

Open your Bible at St John 19

Pilate wrote a notice and put it on the cross. The notice was written in Hebrew, Greek and Latin and said, 'Jesus of Nazareth, King of the Jews'.

Today is the feast of Christ the King. Let's remember that even though He was a King, He died for us on the cross.

THE KYRIE   King Jesus, you died because you loved us,
Lord have mercy
Lord have mercy

King Jesus, you died to save us,
Christ have mercy
Christ have mercy

King Jesus, you died so that we may be forgiven,
Lord have mercy
Lord have mercy

Ask the children to repeat **The Prayer for Forgiveness** *after you* (p. xxxvi).

OPENING PRAYER

Leader   *(This is taken from Psalm 93)*
Say the response to the psalm after me:

The Lord is King
The Lord is King

The Lord is King
He is robed in majesty
The Lord is King

He has made the world so firm
It cannot be moved
The Lord is King

His throne has stood firm
From all eternity
The Lord is King

BEFORE THE GOSPEL

Leader   Before we hear the Gospel, I'd like us to look at another picture of Jesus on the cross.

Show the children a painting showing the three crosses and people watching

There are three people on crosses here – which one is Jesus? (**The one in the middle**)
Who are the other two? (**The two thieves**)
Yes, we usually call the thieves the Good Thief and the Bad Thief. Does anyone know why?

Clock up any hands that go up, but don't comment

I can see some of you do – let's find out in the Gospel.

THE GOSPEL PROCESSION

THE GOSPEL   *St Luke 23.35–43*

AFTER THE GOSPEL

Look at the picture again

Leader   Well, I can see the people who shouted at Jesus – can you? (**They are on the right of the picture**)
Can anyone see Mary? (**She's on the left in dark blue**)
Yes, there she is, looking up at her Son.
Now, which do you suppose was the thief who yelled at Jesus?

It doesn't matter if they get it right or wrong – he's on the right of the picture

He's called the Bad Thief.

So this man must be the Good Thief. *(Indicate the Thief on the left of the picture)*

He's the one who said, 'Jesus, remember me when you come into your kingdom.' How do you suppose he knew Jesus' name?

I think he read the inscription – 'Jesus, the King of the Jews'. Can you remember what Jesus said to him? (**'Today you will be with me in Paradise'**)

Well, Jesus died and He went down to the Kingdom of the Dead and, as the Good Thief was going to end up in Paradise with Jesus, we think he must have gone down with them. But what was Jesus doing, going down to the Dead?

Settle into story-telling mode while Leader 2 puts up the pictures from the CD-Rom

The Harrowing of Hell

Show the children a painting showing the harrowing of hell

Leader	Now listen, guys, this is a story – it's not in the Bible.
CD63.1	We know from the Creed* that Jesus descended to the dead, but what happened when He got there is just a story. It goes like this …
	Jesus went down to a place called Hades.
	That's where all the dead had been bottled for centuries.
CD63.2	And He knocked at the door. Some ghastly person inside – a devil probably – said,
CD63.3	'Go away! You can't come in!'
CD63.4	So Jesus knocked the door down.
CD63.5	And inside He found all the dead – His father Joseph, and His cousin John the Baptist, and famous people from the Bible – like Abraham and Moses. And right at the front were the first people who had ever died – Adam and Eve.
	Jesus looked at Adam and Eve, and pulled them out, then He pulled out Abraham, then all the other dead people – and all the while the
CD63.6	Good Thief was standing there, he couldn't believe his luck.
	Then Jesus saw someone, right at the back, who had died beside
CD63.7	Him – the Bad Thief.
	What do you think He did?
	Well, I think He pulled him out too – Jesus died for everyone.

---

* The Apostles' Creed affirms that: 'He descended to the dead' or, in the traditional translation, 'He descended into Hell'.

Then all the dead winged their way to Paradise, but Jesus went back to Earth for a while.

CD63.8   He had to see His friends and show them He had conquered death. Now we don't know whether Jesus really knocked down the gates of Hades – but we *do* know that He conquered Death, because He rose from the dead.

And we know the Good Thief landed up in Paradise, because Jesus said he would.

CD63.9   So, if we look at this inscription I think we need to add something to it, because Jesus isn't just the King of the Jews – he's the King of the Living, King of the Dead, King of Heaven and King of the Universe.

ACTIVITY

The children make a Christ the King triptych. You will see from the template on the CD-Rom **(CD63.11)** *that all the Harrowing of Hell pictures fit into the triptych shape. The children colour them in, and stick them on.*

FINAL PRAYER

You will probably only have time for a short prayer at the end. Admire the triptych and say together the prayer of the Good Thief

Leader   Let us say together
**Jesus
remember me,
when you come into your Kingdom.
Amen**

MUSIC

Supposing you have time to sing, the Taizé chant 'Jesus remember me' has an easy tune and would finish the session perfectly.

BACK IN CHURCH

Close the triptych and lead the children back to church

Leader   Today is the Feast of Christ the King, and we've made a triptych of one of the first people to call Him 'King' – the Good Thief.

The children open the triptych and the Leaders, or better still the clergy, admire it and go through the pictures with them

Script 64   Saint Spotting

Any Saint's Day

Revelation 7.9–12

THEME

This is an extra session, in case you find your church is celebrating a major saint and has, for once, ditched the Gospel of the Day.

As you'll see, the script accommodates any saint and – if your one isn't mentioned – just look him or her up and put them in. Wikipedia has a good section on saints under 'saint symbolism'. What you want to know is the attribute of the saint, the thing he/she holds in pictures. (St Peter, for example, always holds keys.) This session is about recognizing saints by their attributes (their props), most of which you'll find you can replicate. (Though you'll have trouble with St Agatha, her attribute is two breasts on a plate.)

However we're not just into Spot a Saint, we want the children to realize that there are millions of unknown saints and that they themselves are saints in training.

SET UP

- Pictures from the CD-Rom.
- There is a list of saints and their attributes at the end of the script, choose the ones you can do (adding to their number as you see fit).
- Stick the attributes in a large container, like a wastepaper basket.
- Create an 'L-plate', put it on some string so a child could wear it round its neck.

WELCOME *the children and lead them in* **The Sign of the Cross** ✠ (p. xxxvi).

Leader	Today is St *Name's* day, so we are going to think about all the saints in Heaven as we pray.
OPENING PRAYER	God our Father, Today we thank you for the holy men and women who are your saints.

> May they pray for us as we try to follow their example,
> We ask this through Jesus Our Lord. **Amen**

Leader   When the saints lived on Earth they were just like us.
They behaved badly, just like us, and they asked God to forgive them.
Let's follow their example,

THE KYRIE   Lord Jesus, we are sorry for the things we have done wrong,
Lord have mercy
Lord have mercy

Lord Jesus, we are sorry for forgetting to listen to you
Christ have mercy
Christ have mercy

Lord Jesus, thank you for your promise to love and forgive us
Lord have mercy
Lord have mercy

Ask the children to repeat **The Prayer for Forgiveness** *after you* (**p. xxxvi**).

Prop Show

Pull out the prop basket, it should be bristling with interesting things like large rulers and plastic axes
Talk through how many saints there are, and how difficult it is to remember their names

Leader   It is even more difficult if you want to make pictures of them.
How do you know if a painting is of St Peter?
You could put his name underneath of course, but the painting would look like a cartoon.
So painters have come up with a cunning wheeze – they give the saint a 'prop'.
Something to do with the sort of person they were.
So when you see the prop you know the saint.
Can anybody remember what St Peter's prop is? (**Keys**)

If the children can't remember, just put up the picture

CD64.1   What's Peter holding? (**Keys!**)
CD64.2   OK, let's think of another saint. St Agnes.

'Agnes' means lamb – what do you think her prop is? (**Lamb**)

Put up the picture (**CD64.3**)

> Quite right.
> Now, we've got a basket of props here, all belonging to various saints.
> Let's get the saint attached to his or her prop.

Start pulling out props, get kids down the front to hold them

> Ah, this scythe is for St Isidore *(swish it)*. He is the patron saint of farm workers …

Put Isidore's name up on the whiteboard

> This chalice is for St John.
> Have we got a John or a Joanna here? …
> Great hold that – ugh, what's inside? *(A plastic snake)*
> John always holds a chalice with a snake in it because somebody tried to poison him once …

Write John's name up

> And this ruler is for St Thomas …

And so on, you've got a list of saints and props at the end of this script
At the end you should have an impressive line up of saints

GAME

Put all the props back and invite the kids up to take a prop – but only if they can remember the saint to whom it belongs. (Give some outrageous hints.)

FINISH

Leader   How many saints do you think there are? Nobody knows, not even the Bible. There are **millions** of saints – and there'll be even more when we get to Heaven …
Let's hear about them in the Bible

BIBLE READING   *Revelation 7.9–12*

AFTER THE READING

Leader   There are lots of odd things in that bit of the Bible – but you get the picture, there are loads of saints, round the throne of God.
But if we were there we'd know who they were immediately.

If we saw a saint with eyeballs, for example, we'd know it was ....?
(**St Lucy**) *(They always remember her)*
Now here's a saint you probably haven't heard of ...

Call a victim to the front

This is Saint *Name*.
Do you think she's a saint? (**No!**)
Well, what does saint mean? (**Holy**)
And what are Christians called? *(A rhetorical question)*
'The Holy People of God'.
Well if Christians are holy, young *Name* here must be holy, she's got
to be a saint. What attribute do you think St *Name* should have?
I know what I think ... *(give them the L-plate)*
She's a learner saint
And so are we.

FINAL   Learners need lots of help so let's ask the saints to pray for
PRAYER   us ...

*Get a line of kids down the front, holding the saint props, and construct the litany
round their names*

Litany   Holy Peter
               Pray for us
               Holy Helena
               Pray for us

And so on. Finish with

God our Father,
We thank you for the saints
May their prayers help us,
And may we join them one day,
to live with you for ever in Heaven. **Amen**

MUSIC

*There's a fine crop of modern and traditional hymns for this day. 'For all the saints'
is the classic, but 'Be thou my vision' and 'He who would valiant be' are stirring calls
to service. If you have focused on the children's capacity for sainthood, 'I the Lord of
sea and sky' fits in well.*

BACK IN CHURCH

Line up the kids and props – as you point to them, each child calls out the name of his or her saint

'I'm St Isidore, and I've got a scythe.'

Even so you might have to go along the line and gently extract the information
End with the learner saint

Saints and their attributes

St Peter	Keys (of Heaven and Purgatory)
St John	Chalice (borrow a spare one from the Sacristan) with rubber snake: John was offered a poisoned chalice once, and survived
St Isidore	Plastic scythe (he is the patron saint of farm workers)
St Joseph	Toy hammer or saw
St Olaf	Toy axe (Olaf used an axe as a unique method of converting the heathen)
St Paul	Toy sword
St Gabriel	A lily (actually the lily belongs to our Lady, he must have plucked it in one crucial picture and has been stuck with it ever since)
St Lawrence	Gridiron, grill, grill tray from oven (he was grilled)
St Roche	Toy dog (who used to beg for him – St Roche had plague and couldn't approach people, so his dog got bread for him instead)
St James	A shell: the badge of the pilgrims who go to St James's shrine in Spain
St Andrew	A (chocolate) fish: he was a fisherman
Sts Cosmas & Damian	Toy stethoscope: they were brothers and doctors
St Stephen	Stones (get some from the Lent desert): he was stoned to death
St Thomas	Long ruler or T Square, he was an architect
St Leonard	Chains, he is the patron of prisoners
St George	Toy dragon or an England flag, he's the patron saint of England
St Patrick	Shamrock or clover leaf – a large cardboard version – or a plastic snake (he ejected all the snakes from Ireland)

St David	A dove, rather a difficult prop to find, you might have to make do with a leek. Annoyingly neither prop has a satisfying explanation. He is however the patron saint of Wales
St Lucy	Eyeballs, you can actually find these among the children's section in various tourist shops, or joke shops. Making a couple out of a pair of ping pong balls is just as good. St Lucy was blinded.

St Agnes	A woolly lamb (a pun on her name)
Our Lady	Baby Jesus, borrow the Infant Jesus from the Crib set
St Mary Magdalene	A jar of oil: make it see-through so the kids can see the oil; it's the oil she brought to the Tomb
St Clare	A lamp – another pun, she shines as clear (Clara) as light.
St Helen	Either a wooden cross, or some nails: she found the True Cross.
St Mary of Egypt	Plastic Skull: she meditated on skulls and death as a hermit in the desert
St Catherine	A wheel – they tried to kill her on a wheel, it didn't work, the wheel went out of control and killed 50 heathen philosophers. I suppose a Catherine wheel firework would just pass muster

You don't have to do all these saints, pace the session and do as many as keeps it zingy. Balance out the male and female saints – but don't be gender specific with the kids. If a boy wants to hold a lamb, fine.

Index of Biblical References